# LAW AND EVIDENCE

## A Primer for Criminal Justice, Criminology, Law, and Legal Studies

Charles P. Nemeth J.D., Ph.D., LL.M.

California University of Pennsylvania
Professor and Director of Criminal Justice
Member of the North Carolina, Pennsylvania,
and New York Bars

Prentice
Hall

Upper Saddle River, New Jersey 07458

**Library of Congress Cataloging-in-Publication Data**

Nemeth, Charles P., 1951–
    Law and evidence : a primer for criminal justice, criminology, law, and legal studies /
Charles P. Nemeth.
      p. cm.
    Includes bibliographical references and index.
    ISBN 0-13-030811-0 (case)
     1. Evidence, Criminal—United States. 2. Evidence (Law)—United States. I. Title.

KF9660 .N46 2001
345.73′06—dc21

00-058868

**Publisher:** Dave Garza
**Senior Acquisitions Editor:** Kim Davies
**Managing Editor:** Mary Carnis
**Production Editor:** Gail Gavin
**Interior Design:** Clarinda Publication Services
**Production Liaison:** Adele M. Kupchik
**Director of Manufacturing and Production:** Bruce Johnson
**Manufacturing Buyer:** Ed O'Dougherty/Cathleen Petersen
**Creative Director:** Marianne Frasco
**Cover Design Coordinator:** Miguel Ortiz
**Editorial Assistant:** Lisa Schwartz/Liberty Price
**Marketing Manager:** Chris Ruel
**Marketing Assistant:** Joe Toohey
**Marketing Coordinator:** Adam Kloza
**Printer/Binder:** R.R. Donnelley and Sons, Inc.
**Cover Printer:** Phoenix Color

Prentice-Hall International (UK) Limited, *London*
Prentice-Hall of Australia Pty. Limited, *Sydney*
Prentice-Hall Canada Inc., *Toronto*
Prentice-Hall Hispanoamericana, S.A., *Mexico*
Prentice-Hall of India Private Limited, *New Delhi*
Prentice-Hall of Japan, Inc., *Tokyo*
Prentice-Hall Singapore Pte. Ltd.
Editora Prentice-Hall do Brasil, Ltda., *Rio de Janeiro*

10  9  8  7  6  5  4  3  2
**ISBN 0-13-030811-0**

# LAW AND EVIDENCE

*To Eleanor, my oldest daughter—*
*musical and wise in the arts and soon to commence*
*her journey beyond the nest*

———•◦•———

*and to St. Thomas Aquinas, who said:*

*To give evidence is necessary for salvation, provided the*
*witness be competent, and the order of justice observed.*

*Quod testificari est de necessitate salutis, supposita*
*testis idoneitate et ordine juris.*

# Contents

# *Preface*

The study of evidence is often a forgotten component in justice studies. For some, evidence law is the province of lawyers and judges alone. For others, its technical and statutory nature makes it too complex for the average undergraduate. There are even those who fail to appreciate the relevance of evidence analysis. These perceptions are flawed for a host of good reasons.

In evidence law, the justice system reaches its fruition, its ending point, and its ultimate aim. Evidence is the stuff of conviction and judgment. Without it, the functions and roles of criminal justice are meaningless. Evidence is what drives the machinery of the justice system. Evidence convicts people. Evidence leads to verifiable damage claims in civil actions. Evidence provides the basis for the injunction, the protective order, or the restraining order. Evidence serves as the underpinning in judicial case law and analysis. Evidence is what guides jurors as they carry out their profound responsibilities. Evidence opens up improper convictions, serves as the basis for appeals, and triggers judicial intervention. In short, why students and practitioners should be shortchanged in evidentiary analysis is a mysterious phenomenon in justice education.

It is my hope that this text will change some of these erroneous preconceptions. It is an overview of evidence law, not a compendium or treatise. Readers will soon discover that its overall approach is primarily litigation driven. Why? Because evidence law lives, for the most part, in the environs of courthouses, not the theoretical think-tanks of justice policy-makers. Evidence law commences its life on the street, as police and investigators toil in the collection. It then leaps to those entrusted with its evaluation and advocacy, whether it be private lawyers, prosecutors, public defenders, or judges and magistrates. Put another way, this text hopes to take you on a trip filled not only with concepts, but also with action—the action of litigation. This is the best place for evidence law to come to life. For more than two decades, I have instructed hundreds of students in evidence analysis, and it is clear that theoretical evidence alone cannot convey the richness of these principles.

Within this text, I have attempted to infuse energy, to vivify often very dull concepts, and to show how the lawyer, the investigator, and the judge contend with evidence principles. In addition, I have made a concerted effort to portray evidence law in a realistic light, not as detached principles left to the intelligentsia to determine. How evidence is argued, how it is evaluated, how it is included or excluded, and how trials depend on its content are a few of the many topics this work covers. In this way, it is very different from its competition. I want you to finish this journey with a feel for how evidence law works in the place it lives—the courthouse.

Chapter 1 commences the journey with definitional parameters. Excactly what is evidence, and how many types are there? Where does evidence law come from? How can we find the basis for an evidentiary principle? Is it custom, habit, common law, or statute, or has a court defined it? How much weight is given particular types of evidence? Are some things presumed to be true? Who has the evidentiary burden to prove or disprove a case? Other introductory questions are sprinkled throughout this first chapter.

Chapter 2 zeroes in on the most fundamental evidence form—*real evidence.* If it is real, what is not? What types of evidence are real—guns, blood, fingerprints, paint chips, physical injuries, and the like? Is real evidence the best type of evidence? When is it relevant and irrelevant? How does one ensure its reliability and integrity? How can an advocate challenge it? When will police be on the defensive about its content? Who is responsible for its preservation?

The illustration of *demonstrative evidence* occurs in Chapter 3. Demonstrative evidence portrays or manifests the real form. Our litigation system heavily depends on its usage. How do police rely on the demonstrative form? Why is it an essential part of the investigator's arsenal? Why are cases more understandable with demonstrative evidence? How do lawyers employ the demonstrative means? What types of demonstrative evidence are there—photographs, charts, diagrams, molds, casts, animations? What evidentiary rules guide the use of demonstrative means? What legal challenges are successfully employed to deny admissibility?

Chapter 4 focuses on *documentary evidence.* Documents are the most relevant form of evidence in many types of criminal and civil cases, such as fraud and forgery, official tampering, kidnaping, and commercial crimes. Documents instruct investigators on criminal profiles and identity. The chapter deals with traditional and expanding evidentiary principles applicable to documents. What is the *best evidence rule?* What is an original? What is a copy? Who can attest to the authenticity of a document? What types of documents are automatically admissible? What documents are helpful during the investigative process?

Witnesses are not often termed evidentiary, but, in fact, they are. Chapter 5 covers the testimony of *lay witnesses.* Whether law enforcement officers or security specialists, witnesses are evidentiary sources during the investigation of cases. Lawyers utilize witnesses in and out of the courtroom. Cases are built or deconstructed using witnesses. Exactly what the admissibility requirements for lay witness testimony are is the central theme of this chapter. What makes a lay witness competent to testify? How can a lay witness be challenged before giving testimony? How is a lay witness prepared? What role does cross-examination play in the tug and pull of advocacy? Even though lay witnesses lack scientific or specialized expertise, their testimony is just as probative as that of their expert counterparts.

Chapter 6 dwells in the land of *expert evidence.* An explosion of expert evidence has occurred in all American jurisdictions over the last 30 years. Experts, those holding themselves out as having specialized knowledge that is beneficial to the trier of fact, communicate their expertise in a host of ways, including pretrial assessment, evaluation of damages, determination of the viability of defenses, and mental and physical competency reviews. During trial, experts often dominate the proceedings. Whether the expert testifies on mental health or ballistics, the judicial system increasingly looks to specialized evidentiary presentations before issuing judgments. What qualifies experts? Where do they come from? How are they to be utilized and prepared? How can they be challenged or puffed up? What are the pitfalls of expert usage in the trial environs? How much power do experts have in the adjudication of cases? How have our courts attempted to define or redefine their role?

Chapter 7's content is rather provincial—that of *admissions and stipulations.* Evidence that can be agreed on is evidence without dispute. The identification of evidence that both parties agree not to challenge fosters efficiency in the courtroom environment and reduces the trifles and turmoil of objection and appeal. In this short review, readers will see how effective these two tools of the justice system are in ferreting out evidence that should not be subject to challenge and in identifying those forms of evidence that are surely subject to disagreement. Admissions and stipulations eliminate contentiousness in the legal arena.

The world of *motions* and its intimate relationship with evidence law are the subject matter of Chapter 8. Evidence motions encompass a vast array of legal strategies. For example, defendants may wish evidence excluded or suppressed, or they may wish even more fervently for the admission of some avant garde evidence form that will buttress their defense (e.g., the PMS or the Twinkie defense). Motions address matters of dispute or controversy. When police acquire evidence in violation of a constituional principle, a motion to exclude or suppress will be likely. When a defendant claims he or she is insane, the motion for a physical or mental examination, if granted, verifies or refutes the claim. When physical evidence has been tainted or corrupted, a challenge by motion makes perfect sense. Motions in limine are appropriate when new and controversial evidence will be introduced. Motions are as varied as the evidentiary subject matter. It seems ludicrous not to cover such essential concepts when motions often make or break the state's or the defense's case and support or refute the claims in a civil action.

Chapter 9 ends this long journey through evidence law by gazing deeply into the final resting place of evidence—the courtroom. Exactly how is evidence employed in the trial setting? What form and format are required? How is evidence packaged? What is an exhibit? What rules govern the usage of evidence in the trial environment? How will the proponent of the evidence use witnesses to confirm or corroborate content? How does a litigation team prepare for trial? What skills of administration and organization are essential to courtroom success?

To be sure, the study of evidence law is a lifelong journey. Even experienced litigators and investigators are stumped by the natural problems that emerge in the acquisition and advocacy of evidence. It is a highly technical enterprise. From documents to witness recollection, from serological specimens to photographic displays, from psychological profiles to forensic innovaton, evidence law covers broad territory. It takes a person with an eclectic mind to master it all.

This text begins that challenging and sometimes cumbersome excursion. One hopes that upon reaching the end of the book, readers will tangibly appreciate how evidence is used in the justice system and how heavily our justice operations depend upon it. Evidence, in its many forms, is what we need to see and discern to carry out justice. Hunches and surmises will not suffice. The beauty of evidence law lies in its rigor and complexity; even after a lifetime of working with it, one never tires of it. Good luck as your adventure unfolds.

# Acknowledgments

This project would not have reached completion without the assistance of so many individuals. None was more central to success than Hope Haywood, whose editorial work continues to be remarkable. I am forever impressed by her ability to corral details, to administratively center the production, and to be steadfast in keeping me on the straight and narrow. A person of extraordinary talent, Hope has a very bright future.

To Kim Davies of Prentice Hall, I deliver gratitude for the opportunity to publish with this major player in the collegiate marketplace. Her quick and efficient negotiations are unrivaled in the rough and tumble world of publishing.

At the State University of New York at Brockport, the climate is favorable to scholarship. President Pau Yu, Academic Vice President Timothy Flanagan, and Dean Joseph Mason appreciate the quality and significance of these types of activities, while balancing them with the university's ultimate end—the education of students. I was also fortunate to have the assistance of Linda Ferguson, whose service is sterling by any measure. Students aided and abetted as well. In particular, my thanks go to Pamela Chimino, whose contributions were regular during this production. Her editorial skills are impressive for an undergraduate. On the final revisions, student Christopher Rice was most helpful. As I embark on a new appointment at California University of Pennsylvania, I am already indebted to President Angelo Armenti, Vice President/Provost Curtis Smith, and Dr. Ronald Michael, who chaired the search committee.

Many of the photographs, artwork, tables, charts, proprietary material, and commercial input come from an eclectic source base. Some need mentioning. Lieutenant Charles Loray and Sergeant Richard Gosnell of the Central Investigations Unit at the Rochester Police Department, New York, were exceptionally generous in making dead case files available. These representations and graphics give life to often dull concepts. Many other service providers graciously lent their materials to complement the text. They include Concord Press; Legal Graphic Communicators;

Anatomical Chart Company; Bionet, Inc.; Wesley Neville, Forensic Artist; Forensic Imaging Systems; TASA; Medical Legal Art; Wolf Technical Service; and Suplee Envelope Co., Inc. Thanks are also extended to Lawyers-Cooperative Publishing and West Group; The American Bar Association; Aspen Publishers, Inc.; North Carolina Bar Foundation; and George T. Bisel Co.

Finally, there is little I can accomplish without the loyalty, fidelity, and, most important, generosity of my family. To Jean Marie, partner of 29 years, and my wonderful children, Eleanor, Stephen, Anne Marie, John, Joseph, Mary Claire, and Michael Augustine, my perpetual love and affection for making these projects come to life.

Charles P. Nemeth JD, Ph.D., LL.M.
*Gazing at the Floating Ice of Ontario*
February 10, 2000

# LAW AND EVIDENCE

CHAPTER 1

# Overview of Evidence

## § 1.1 INTRODUCTION: THE NATURE OF EVIDENCE

Most evidentiary experiences are only partially theoretical, normally being planted in the context of trial and litigation. Evidence is the stuff of proof — manifesting truth about particular facts or circumstances. From the Latin *video,* "to see," and its prepositional qualifier, *e,* "out of" or "from," evidence law is the demonstration of reality.

Without evidence, there is no proof. Without proof, burdens are not met, and convictions, verdicts, or judgments are an impossibility. Evidence directs the tribunal, the jury, and the practitioners advocating its content toward actions to be taken. Evidence is that which leads us to the truth; it is a piece of life, a fact, a real or tangible thing that elucidates a proposition. Evidence is the key to things as they are. Evidence is that which we see, touch, feel, conjecture, and imagine. Evidence is derived from deductive reasoning, logical inference, and supposition. Evidence law is the law's substantive and procedural instruction for the use of evidence.

This text's direct aim is to arm practicing and aspiring justice professionals with information about evidence; suggestions about how evidence affects investigation and litigation, whether civil or criminal; and an understanding of the integral purpose evidence plays in the evaluation of cases.[1]

Evidentiary analysis is primarily a product of the mind and the manner in which it relates to the physical world. Evidence analysis deals with possibilities, probabilities, and predictable events and circumstances.[2]

Since evidence is viewed in such a dynamic and behavioral light, it is not a drudging undertaking, even though guided by technical rules of application. Evidence collection, analysis, organization, and delivery comprise an intellectual activity directed toward a specific goal or end, namely, the truth of the matter. [In general, evidence is anything to be submitted to the trier of fact, the court and to the judge for review, inspection and possible ruling."[3] The term *evidence* has many definitions, including *testimony* of a witness; *real, tangible, physical* and *documentary* evidence; *chattel; microscopic* fibers; *biological* material and open *forensic* matter; *character evidence; intellectual* copyrights, trademarks, and patents; *habits* and *customs; conviction* records; *public* records; *recordings, motion pictures, photographs,* and *videotapes; vital statistics; confessions; reputation* evidence; *mental state* or condition; and *judicially noticed* findings. The evidentiary array is limited only by reality and legality.

Evidence, however, is not always an accurate reflection of reality. Its representation may be tainted or biased by the person inspecting it. Professor Edmund Morgan, an acclaimed academician on evidentiary matters, portrays evidence in its rational context:

> [T]here must be a recognition at the outset that nicely accurate results cannot be expected; that society and litigants must be content with rather rough approximations of what a scientist might demand. And it must never be forgotten that in a settlement of disputes in a court room, as in all other experiences of individuals in our society, the emotions of the persons involved—litigants, counsel, witnesses, judges, and jurors—will play a part. A trial cannot be a purely intellectual performance.[4]

## § 1.2 JUSTICE PRACTITIONERS AND EVIDENCE LAW

For those assigned to investigation, evidence collection and analysis, pretrial preparation, and trial usage of evidence, a rudimentary understanding of evidentiary principles is imperative. Evidence is what gives meaning to individual cases and serves as a benchmark for the entire justice system. Police and law enforcement officers need a fundamental understanding of evidence, its quality and content, and the rules governing its admissibility. The functions of policing are intricately tied to evidence analysis. Law enforcement first collects, preserves, and packages evidence and then amasses and coordinates this evidence for prosecutorial staff. Law enforcement conducts field interviews and other investigative surveillance, and locates and prepares witnesses for questioning. See Figures 1.1 and 1.2.

Law enforcement's basic tasks are guided by constitutional prescriptions that defense counsel know only too well. In litigation, prosecution and defense counsel, with staffs of investigators and legal assistants, evaluate the quality and content of evidence; file pleadings in the form of complaints, motions, admissions, and stipulations; and monitor the status of admissibility.

Litigation teams are in dire need of evidence understanding. In civil and criminal cases, evidence analysis and trial tactics are closely intertwined. If they are doing their jobs, lawyers and litigation specialists will evaluate evidence by placing themselves in the shoes of the jury. Without evidence, a jury cannot "decide how an

**FIGURE 1.1**   Murder scene.

**FIGURE 1.2**   For police, the tragedy of murder drives evidentiary collection.

event occurred. Time is irreversible, events unique, and any reconstruction of the past, at best, an approximation. As a result of this lack of certainty about what happened, it is inescapable that the trier's conclusions must be rooted in evidentiary ground."[5]

Understanding not only the various areas of evidence law, but also its actual application, assures a more competent justice professional. One who understands evidence will "perform investigative functions more intelligently, converse with witnesses more effectively as well as prepare them for examination and to see flaws in an opponent's case."[6]

## § 1.3 SUGGESTED READINGS ON EVIDENCE LAW

Treatises, hornbooks, and other scholarly materials are plentiful and signify the centrality of evidence analysis in the justice system. The classic treatise on evidence by Dean John H. Wigmore, *Wigmore on Evidence: Chadbourne Edition* (1972, 1975), is the best investment possible in this area. Despite its scholarly approach, it is replete with real-life examples and applied problems. Another publication of significant interest to the justice professional is the Model Code of Evidence, an evidentiary synthesis produced by the American Law Institute, a legal think tank. While the provisions of the Model Code of Evidence are nonbinding and merely suggestive, the influence of the model recommendations is obvious during legislative hearings, advisory input, and other preliminary inquiries when evidence statutes are under construction. The Model Code of Evidence's hypothetical fact patterns educate readers on complicated evidentiary principles.

Another sound investment is the abridged one-volume edition of Charles T. McCormick's *The Handbook on the Law of Evidence*. Other evidentiary treatises with enviable reputations are:

Edmund Morris Morgan, *Basic Problems of Evidence* (1961)

James Bradley Thayer, *Preliminary Treatise on Evidence* (1898)

Edward W. Cleary, *McCormick on Evidence* (3rd ed. 1984)

John MacArthur Maguire, *Evidence: Common Sense and Common Law* (1947)

Jack B. Weinstein, *Weinstein on Evidence* (1981)

For those interested in the more investigatory end of evidence law, see

John Klotter, *Criminal Evidence* (1993)

Richard H. Fox and Carl L. Cunningham, *Crime Scene Search and Physical Evidence Handbook* (1987)

Gilbert B. Stuckey, *Evidence for the Law Enforcement Officer* (1978)

Mark R. Hawthorne, *First Unit Responder: A Guide to Physical Evidence Collection for Patrol Officers* (1998)

Robert R. Ogle, *Physical Evidence Manual* (1995)

Claude W. Cook, *A Practical Guide to the Basics of Physical Evidence: A Reference Text for Criminalist, Investigator, Student and Attorney* (1984)

On the commercial level, practitioners may subscribe to various statutory services that annotate the state and federal rules of evidence. Publications are available from local bar associations, local and national professional groups, and various agencies providing continuing education in both the for-profit and the nonprofit sectors. For example, within Pennsylvania, the Pennsylvania Bar Foundation conducts an annual evidence institute, where practitioners are apprised of recent changes in evidence law.

## § 1.4 SOURCES OF EVIDENCE LAW

Until very recently, most evidentiary determinations were the product of common law tradition. Common law principles such as *competency, relevancy, attorney-client* and *priest-penitent privilege,* and *hearsay* are well established in Western jurisprudence. Case law analysis of these common law principles adds to or detracts from the developing law of evidence. Surprisingly, prior to the twentieth century, the majority of interpretations regarding evidence were nonstatutory. In the American tradition, statutory analysis is a recent phenomenon in the law of evidence. Dean Guido Calabrese proclaims the present era as the "age of statutes," in which much of American law has undergone, using the Dean's phrase, "statutorification."[7]

For veterans in the law, this statutory tendency is a trend not fully understood. Legislatively, the Federal Rules of Evidence were not adopted until 1975. Presently, however, practitioners tend to view statutory constructions as the only means to interpret evidence law. To the amazement of some, this statutory dominance is yet to be realized in the law school curriculum and educational philosophy.[8]

While justice professionals should never neglect the common law heritage, it is mandatory that their approach cling to the design of and be aggressively dependent on the "words" of any controlling statute relating to evidence law. Overreliance on the language of a statute or rule does have a downside. The "textualist," ever faithful to words, will allow justice to be relegated to secondary status. However, no code, including evidentiary promulgations, was ever intended to be so rigid that it would have complete inflexibility, regardless of the circumstances.[9] Evidential reasoning is therefore more textual than traditional. While lawyers are free to ponder novel evidence schemes, they must do so within the confines of the courthouse and rules. For example, whether evidence is relevant or not is largely a question of statute, not attorney wisdom.

Within this reality, justice practitioners soon discover that statutes control the ebb and flow of evidence in a typical court case. A majority of American states have adopted either almost identical or modified versions of the widely respected Federal Rules of Evidence. Adoption at every federal venue is mandatory.

The Federal Rules of Evidence, promulgated by the U.S. Congress, serve within this text as a guidepost. But please keep in mind that state differences do exist. At face value, the Federal Rules of Evidence provide about as good an evidentiary scheme as can be expected, and their ample description and corresponding analysis are easy to digest and apply.

The content of the Federal Rules of Evidence is outlined at Figure 1.3.[10]

## § 1.5 THE CONTENT AND QUALITY OF GOOD EVIDENCE

Discussed throughout this text will be diverse approaches to the use of evidence during trial. Before going to court, evidence to be submitted to the trier of fact must be "good"—meaning that it has substance, relevance, and purpose and can pass the substantive and procedural barriers to admissibility. Also to be considered is whether or not the evidence is material—that is, tends to a central force or issue in the underlying litigation—and is so prejudicial it ruins its power of proof. Therefore, evidence that is "good" accomplishes two major ends: (1) It can scale any barrier to admissibility, and (2) it is relevant and material without being too inflammatory.

### The Nature of Relevancy

Relevant evidence is evidence that tends to prove any matter provable in a civil or criminal action. The Model Code of Evidence at Rule 1 defines "relevant" evidence as evidence "having any tendency in reason to prove any material matter and includes opinion evidence and hearsay evidence."[11] FRE Rule 401 portrays a similar picture:

> "Relevant evidence" means evidence having any tendency to make the existence of any fact that is of consequence to the determination of the action more probable or less probable than it would be without the evidence.[12]

To merit its qualification, relevant evidence must have a logical nexus or connection between its inherent value and a proposition it seeks to prove. "In other words, legal relevancy denotes, first of all, something more than a minimum of probative value. Each single piece of evidence must have a plus value."[13]

FRE Rule 402 provides that irrelevant evidence is not admissible:

> All relevant evidence is admissible, except as otherwise provided by the Constitution of the United States, by Act of Congress, by these rules, or by other rules prescribed by the Supreme Court pursuant to statutory authority. Evidence which is not relevant is not admissible.[14]

# FEDERAL RULES OF EVIDENCE

## TABLE OF CONTENTS

### ARTICLE I. GENERAL PROVISIONS

101. Scope
102. Purpose and Construction
103. Rulings on Evidence
104. Preliminary Questions
105. Limited Admissibility
106. Remainder of or Related Writings or Recorded Statements

### ARTICLE II. JUDICIAL NOTICE

201. Judicial Notice of Adjudicative Facts

### ARTICLE III. PRESUMPTIONS IN CIVIL ACTIONS AND PROCEEDINGS

301. Presumptions in General in Civil Actions and Proceedings
302. Applicability of State Law in Civil Actions and Proceedings

### ARTICLE IV. RELEVANCY AND ITS LIMITS

401. Definition of "Relevant Evidence"
402. Relevant Evidence Generally Admissible; Irrelevant Evidence Inadmissible
403. Exclusion of Relevant Evidence on Grounds of Prejudice, Confusion, or Waste of Time
404. Character Evidence Not Admissible to Prove Conduct; Exceptions; Other Crimes
405. Methods of Proving Character
406. Habit; Routine Practice
407. Subsequent Remedial Measures
408. Compromise and Offers to Compromise
409. Payment of Medical and Similar Expenses
410. Inadmissibility of Pleas, Plea Discussions, and Related Statements
411. Liability Insurance
412. Sex Offense Cases; Relevance of Victim's Past Behavior

### ARTICLE V. PRIVILEGES

501. General Rule

### ARTICLE VI. WITNESSES

601. General Rule of Competency
602. Lack of Personal Knowledge
603. Oath or Affirmation
604. Interpreters
605. Competency of Judge as Witness
606. Competency of Juror as Witness
607. Who May Impeach

**FIGURE 1.3** Federal Rules of Evidence.

608. Evidence of Character and Conduct of Witness
609. Impeachment by Evidence of Conviction of Crime
610. Religious Beliefs or Opinions
611. Mode and Order of Interrogation and Presentation
612. Writing Used to Refresh Memory
613. Prior Statements of Witnesses
614. Calling and Interrogation of Witnesses by Court
615. Exclusion of Witnesses

ARTICLE VII. OPINIONS AND EXPERT TESTIMONY

701. Opinion Testimony by Lay Witnesses
702. Testimony by Experts
703. Bases of Opinion Testimony by Experts
704. Opinion on Ultimate Issue
705. Disclosure of Facts or Data Underlying Expert Opinion
706. Court Appointed Experts

ARTICLE VIII. HEARSAY

801. Definitions
802. Hearsay Rule
803. Hearsay Exceptions; Availability of Declarant Immaterial
804. Hearsay Exceptions; Declarant Unavailable
805. Hearsay Within Hearsay
806. Attacking and Supporting Credibility of Declarant

ARTICLE IX. AUTHENTICATION AND IDENTIFICATION

901. Requirement of Authentication or Identification
902. Self-authentication
903. Subscribing Witness' Testimony Unnecessary

ARTICLE X. CONTENTS OF WRITINGS, RECORDINGS, AND PHOTOGRAPHS

1001. Definitions
1002. Requirement of Original
1003. Admissibility of Duplicates
1004. Admissibility of Other Evidence of Contents
1005. Public Records
1006. Summaries
1007. Testimony or Written Admission of Party
1008. Functions of Court and Jury

ARTICLE XI. MISCELLANEOUS RULES

1101. Applicability of Rules
1102. Amendments
1103. Title

**FIGURE 1.3** *Continued*

But even irrelevant and minimally probative evidence has a place in the fact finder's menu, according to some legal scholarship.[15]

## The Nature of Materiality

Material evidence is that evidence that addresses a matter, the existence or nonexistence of which is provable in an action. FRE Rule 401 states that evidence that has a "tendency to make the existence of any fact that is of consequence to the determination of the action more or less probable"[16] is material (if a fact or consequence). At common law, the terms *material* and *relevant* are often used interchangeably in conjunction, with a party objecting to evidence as "irrelevant and immaterial." "Clarity in this area is, however, fostered by distinguishing between the propriety of the proof offered to establish it."[17]

In the criminal realm, any physical evidence aids in the solution of the case because it can

1. Develop M.O.s or show similar M.O.s,
2. Develop or identify suspects,
3. Prove or disprove an alibi,
4. Connect or eliminate suspects,
5. Identify loot or contraband, or
6. Provide leads.

Physical evidence proves an element of the offense; for example:

1. Safe insulation, glass, or building materials on a suspect's clothing may prove entry;
2. Stomach contents, bullets, residue at the scene of a fire, semen, blood, or tool marks may prove elements of certain offenses; and
3. Safe insulation on tools may be sufficient to prove violation of a possession of burglary tools statute.

It proves the theory of the case; for example:

1. Footprints may show how many were at a scene, or
2. Auto paint on clothing may show that a person was hit by car instead of otherwise injured.[18]

See Figure 1.4.

## Relevant and Material, Yet Inadmissible Evidence

*Relevant* and *material* evidence may never see the inside of a courtroom. If the evidence is relevant to a particular fact, but is highly prejudicial and inflammatory, its admission will be denied. FRE Rule 403 sets out the standard dilemma:

**FIGURE 1.4**  Multiple shots fired from a house are traced from inside to the projectiles' resting places.

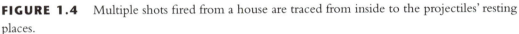

> Although relevant, evidence may be excluded if its probative value is substantially outweighed by the danger of unfair prejudice, confusion of the issues, or misleading the jury, or by considerations of undue delay, waste of time, or needless presentation of cumulative evidence.[19]

There is no shortage of examples that typify the prejudicial potency of evidence: *gruesome photographs, biased witnesses, expert witnesses on a fee,* and *witnesses granted total immunity,* to name a few. As for confusion, various forms of novel scientific evidence can often confuse the court and jury more than aid in their deliberation. Evidence based on a scientific discipline that has scant academic support or is too avant garde, is unlikely to be admitted despite its inherent relevance.[20] The traditional understanding of what probativeness means is certainly under fire by those propounding novel scientific theories.[21] While some evidence is universally indisputable, at least in a scientific sense, some of it seems to unfold over time. If Galileo was condemned at one point in history, his views now appear self-evident. "Much of what is universally accepted as science today was once considered to be outside of the scientific mainstream. And they suggest that judges and juries are fully capable of making the distinction between a legitimate scientific claim and an unfounded one."[22]

Finally, repetitious, duplicative presentations of the same evidentiary content, whether through documentation, testimonial witnesses, experts, or other duplicative efforts, are frowned upon by most courts. To be sure, duplicative evidence may be relevant, but its admission is so cumulative that it harms a case more than assists it.

In general, relevancy is a troublesome inquiry. Even evidence that was once relevant can change to an inadmissable form. As a rule, be able to address these queries:

1. For what purpose is the testimony being offered?
2. To what purpose or point will these photographs be directed?
3. For what reason would the cross-examiner desire an examination of a victim's character?
4. What purpose does an examination of a party's reputation in the community have?
5. What influence, either direct or circumstantial, will a forensic test result have in a criminal case?
6. How influential, or for that matter, prejudicial would the admission of a previous criminal record be?[23]

More on these issues will be discussed as the text develops.

## § 1.6 TYPES AND FORMS OF EVIDENCE

Under the broad rubric of "evidence" exist many types and forms. A summary review follows.

### Judicially Noticed Evidence

Most jurisdictions automatically admit judicially noticed facts or conditions without advocacy of foundational requirements, formal identification, or authentication. The court is so confident in the evidence that it recognizes it without the typical procedural requirements. The evidence is deemed so reliable that the court will declare it "judicially noticed." Judicially noticed evidence is that information "generally known by the community at large or . . . so scientifically acceptable and reliable that it is given to be true and accurate."[24] Under FRE Rule 201, the idea of judicial notice is defined:

(b) Kinds of facts. A judicially noticed fact must be one not subject to reasonable dispute in that it is either (1) generally known within the territorial jurisdiction of the trial court or (2) capable of accurate and ready determination by resort to sources whose accuracy cannot reasonably be questioned.

(c) When discretionary. A court may take judicial notice, whether requested or not.[25]

Generally, judicially noticed evidence is a straightforward fact, an indisputable issue, or a bit of common knowledge. That the sun rises and sets is a fact that would be judicially noticed. For residents of Pennsylvania, the name of the governor is a well-accepted, judicially noticed fact. These are facts so universally known that their existence is not arguable. A court can judicially notice that there are 24 hours in a day or that a person is composed of certain chemical elements, such as carbon. However, the issue of whether or not blood plasma was infected with a virus is a matter not commonly known and therefore laden with actual or potential dispute. The Advisory Committee note to FRE Rule 201 states that judicially noticed evidence is to be distinguished from the other forms of evidence:

> The usual method of establishing adjudicative facts is through the introduction of evidence, ordinarily consisting of the testimony of witnesses. If particular facts are outside the area of reasonable controversy, this process is dispensed with as unnecessary. A high degree of indisputability is the essential prerequisite.[26]

The typical categories of judicially noticed evidence are

- Adjudicative findings of other courts,
- Laws of science,
- Natural principles widely accepted by the community,
- Official records,
- Government publications,
- Legislative facts,
- A judge's personal knowledge,
- Public statutes,
- Natural scientific forces, and
- Qualities and properties of matter.

A court may judicially notice evidence under either a discretionary or a mandatory scheme.[27] A party is entitled, upon timely request, to be heard regarding the propriety of taking judicial notice.[28] A request for evidence to be judicially noticed may be taken at any stage of the proceedings.[29] Jury instructions should contain a commentary about what evidence has been judicially noticed.[30]

Legal implications of the doctrine are obvious, in that the proponent of the evidence need not prove relevance or meet other admissibility standards. In a sense, the doctrine of judicial notice promotes efficiency in the analysis of evidence. "The primary purpose of judicial notice is to achieve the maximum of convenience that is consistent with procedural fairness. In doing so, expert testimony with respect to statistics, scientific facts, and other natural phenomena may be avoided."[31]

Form 1.1[32] is a Notice that a party intends to request that the court judicially notice certain evidence. Form 1.2[33] is a Motion for Judicial Notice.

To: _____ [each party] and to the
_____ [the attorney of record for each party in
the action].

Notice is hereby given that on _____,
[20]_____ at _____, _____.m., or as soon thereafter as the matter can be heard _____ [at the
courtroom of _____ (presiding judge), or in
_____ (specify department or division or as the
case may be)] of the above-entitled court at _____
_____ [address], in the City of _____, the
County of _____, State of _____
_____, _____ [moving party] will re-
quest the court to make judicial notice of _____
[describe matter to be judicially noticed].

Notice is further given that at the above-mentioned time and place
_____ [moving party] will submit to the court in-
formation to enable the court to take judicial notice of this matter, as follows: _____[set forth information relied on to
support the request].

_____ [If applicable, add: This request will
be based on this notice of request, the attached information to enable the
court to grant the request, the attached memorandum of points and authorities, such supplemental memoranda of points and authorities as may
be filed subsequently herein, and oral and documentary evidence that
may be presented on the hearing of the request.]

Dated _____, [20]_____.


_____
[Signature]

**FORM 1.1**  Notice—request that judicial notice be taken. (Reprinted by permission of
West Group.)

Plaintiff, _____, hereby respectfully moves this court, under the provisions of _____ [cite statute or rule] to take judicial notice of _____ [legislative act of sister state] of the State of _____ _____, _____ [Section _____ Chapter _____ of that act, passed on 19_____ and amended in 19_____, is entitled "_____," and reads as follows: "_____."

By a copy hereof the attorneys of record for the defendant are being advised of this request of the plaintiff for this court to take judicial notice of this _____ [designate sister state] statute, notice of plaintiff's intention to invoke such statute having been given in his complaint.

Wherefore, plaintiff requests that the court take judicial notice of _____ [legislative act of sister state] of the State of _____.

Dated _____, 20_____.


_____

[Signature]

**FORM 1.2**  Motion—For judicial notice of statute of sister state. (Reprinted by permission of West Group.)

## Direct Evidence

Direct evidence is evidence that proves a fact or proposition directly, rather than by secondary deduction or inference. Examples of direct evidence include eyewitness testimony, an oral confession of a defendant, and the victim's firsthand account of a criminal assault. Direct evidence is the foundational support for many cases. The eyewitness's testimony regarding an accident scene or a victim's testimony regarding his or her injuries is direct evidence. As a general rule, the more direct evidence amassed, the better the advocate's case.

## Circumstantial Evidence

Indirect or circumstantial evidence, the bulk of proof in most civil and criminal litigation, never speaks directly to innocence or guilt or liability or harm. A bullet in a murder case is only circumstantial evidence, since it does not signify direct agency. See Figures 1.5 and 1.6. The bullet is not judicially noticed, but it is a secondary form of evidence, generating inferences about criminal activity. A case involving Thomas Capone, the former Delaware Assistant D.A., who was found to have killed the Governor of Delaware's secretary, Anne Marie Fahey, is an instructive example of a conviction based solely on circumstantial evidence. No body was ever discovered. But motive, opportunity, blood, fibers, and a diary, all of which are circumstantial evidence, were convincing enough for a jury to not only find guilt, but also impose the death penalty.

In a typical charge of homicide, evidentiary sources potentially include blood, fingerprints on a weapon, a ballistics report, bodily fluids, motive, agency, past relationship, an expert's report, and hairs and fibers located at the crime scene—all of which are circumstantial.

## Testimonial Evidence

Evidence solicited or provided through oral or written testimony, whether by oath or by affirmation and whether at trial or in the discovery process, is testimonial.

**FIGURE 1.5**

Cartridge case from suspected weapon tells only a circumstantial tale.

**FIGURE 1.6**    Blood on a lamp shade in a murder case.

FRE Rule 601 outlines the a priori conditions precedent to the legal admissibility of testimonial evidence: *competency* and *personal knowledge*. There is a presumption that all witnesses about to testify are competent.

> Every person is competent to be a witness except as otherwise provided in these rules. However, in civil actions and proceedings, with respect to an element of a claim or defense as to which State law supplies the rule of decision, the competency of a witness shall be determined in accordance with State law.[34]

## Personal Knowledge

Another foundational element addressing the quality and integrity of testimonial evidence is whether or not the witness, either lay or expert, has some personal knowledge relevant to the case. FRE Rule 602 highlights the knowledge requirement:

> A witness may not testify to a matter unless evidence is introduced sufficient to support a finding that the witness has personal knowledge of the matter. Evidence to prove personal knowledge may, but need not, consist of the witness' own testimony. This rule is subject to the provisions of rule 703, relating to opinion testimony by expert witnesses.[35]

Procedurally, testimony under oath is construed as more reliable than other forms of testimony. An oath or affirmation forces the witness to consider the grave consequences of false testimony. FRE Rule 603 imparts the value of oath or affirmation:

> Before testifying, every witness shall be required to declare that the witness will testify truthfully, by oath or affirmation administered in a form calculated to awaken the witness' conscience and impress the witness' mind with the duty to do so.[36]

How will this rule's admonition on truthfulness be played out after its dilution in the President Clinton affair?

## Opinion Evidence

Opinion testimony by lay witnesses is possible only when personal knowledge of the events and conditions, the subject matter of testimony, exists. A more liberal attitude concerning opinion is accorded experts. Opinion testimony of lay witnesses is governed by FRE Rule 701:

> If the witness is not testifying as an expert, the witness' testimony in the form of opinions or inferences is limited to those opinions or inferences which are (a) rationally based on the perception of the witness and (b) helpful to a clear understanding of the witness' testimony or the determination of a fact in issue.[37]

As for expert opinions, FRE Rule 702 tells the judicial system to permit the testimony of experts "[i]f scientific, technical, or other specialized knowledge will assist the trier of fact to understand the evidence or to determine a fact in issue. . . ."[38] The opinion of an expert is not permissible unless it is based on facts or data perceived by that expert or made known to that expert before the hearing.[39] For expert opinion or evidence to be "good," it must meet these criteria:

1. The testimony will assist the trier of fact,
2. The scientific evidence is sufficiently reliable, and
3. The particular expert has sufficient specialized knowledge to assist jurors.[40]

The only current constraint on the testimony of opinion witnesses involves the ultimate issue doctrine, whereby expert testimony is improper on the matter of innocence or guilt in a criminal case (a subject of discussion within FRE Rule 704).[41]

## Character Evidence

When is evidence of a person's character, as a victim, defendant, party, or witness, relevant? Undermining character is a powerful litigation tactic, but the evidence used should be reputational. Character is not simply a personal observation, but a communitarian perspective.[42]

At no place is the character evidence issue more visible than in sexual offenses cases. To the chagrin of many, courts grapple "with the issue of a rape complainant's previous sexual partners, sexual acts, their style and duration, quantity and quality."[43] FRE Rule 412 attempts to structure the propriety of evidence dealing with sexual propensities or proclivities in crime victims:

> (a) Evidence generally inadmissible. The following evidence is not admissible in any civil or criminal proceeding involving alleged sexual misconduct except as provided in subdivisions (b) and (c):
> (1) Evidence offered to prove that any alleged victim engaged in other sexual behavior.
> (2) Evidence offered to prove any alleged victim's sexual predisposition.[44]

At subpart (b) of the same rule, an exception has been carved out:

> (1) In a criminal case, the following evidence is admissible, if otherwise admissible under these rules:
> (A) evidence of specific instances of sexual behavior by the alleged victim offered to prove that a person other than the accused was the source of semen, injury, or other physical evidence;
> (B) evidence of specific instances of sexual behavior by the alleged victim with respect to the person accused of the sexual misconduct offered by the accused to prove consent or by the prosecution, and
> (C) evidence the exclusion of which would violate the constitutional rights of the defendant.
> (2) In a civil case, evidence offered to prove the sexual behavior or sexual predisposition of any alleged victim is admissible if it is otherwise admissible under these rules and its probative value substantially outweighs the danger of harm to any victim and of unfair prejudice to any party. Evidence of an alleged victim's reputation is admissible only if it has been placed in controversy by the alleged victim.[45]

Using character evidence as a means of impeachment in rape litigation raises a volatile evidentiary issue. On the one hand, introducing such evidence implies that a woman's credibility is dubious. On the other, defendants, raising the due process banner and their right to a zealous defense, feel cheated when thwarted in using all avenues available.[46] Criminal defendants desiring to impeach the character of the rape complainant pose constitutional questions involving due process and confrontation rights. The U.S. Supreme Court, in an opinion crafted by Justice Sandra Day O'Connor, evaluated the Michigan rape-shield statute, which forbids victim impeachment unless the defendant provides ten days' notice of his intention to do so. In this case, the defendant disregarded the ten-day notice requirement and thus was precluded from introducing such evidence. Justice O'Connor appreciated this statute's constitutional dimension:

> In light of *Taylor* and *Nobles,* the Michigan Court of Appeals erred in adopting a *per se* rule that Michigan's notice-and-hearing requirement violates the Sixth Amendment in all cases where it is used to preclude evidence of past sexual conduct between a rape

victim and a defendant. The Sixth Amendment is not so rigid. The notice-and-hearing requirement serves legitimate state interests in protecting against surprise, harassment, and undue delay. Failure to comply with this requirement may in some cases justify even the severe sanction of preclusion.[47]

While the rape scenario is legally and socially turbulent, addressing character evidence as it relates to the credibility and truthfulness of any witness is an evidentiary necessity. FRE Rule 608 provides that opinion and reputation evidence of character is admissible under the following circumstances:

> The credibility of a witness may be attacked or supported by evidence in the form of opinion or reputation, but subject to these limitations: (1) the evidence may refer only to character for truthfulness or untruthfulness, and (2) evidence of truthful character is admissible only after the character of the witness for truthfulness has been attacked by opinion or reputation evidence or otherwise.[48]

Under subsection (b) of the same rule, for the purpose of attacking or supporting the witness's credibility, specific instances of conduct may, if "probative of truthfulness or untruthfulness, be inquired into on cross-examination of the witness (1) concerning the witness' character for truthfulness or untruthfulness, or (2) concerning the character for truthfulness or untruthfulness of another witness as to which character the witness being cross-examined has testified."[49]

As to specific criminal conviction records, the law is restrained, yet reasonable. FRE Rule 609 states that the credibility of any witness may be attacked if the witness has been convicted of a crime punishable by death or imprisonment in excess of one year and that prejudice does not outweigh probativeness.[50] Second, the witness may be attacked for crimes involving falsehood. Crimes qualifying under this definitional test would be *embezzlement, larceny, robbery, fraud, computer theft, theft of services, perjury, extortion,* and *organized crime activities.*[51]

Of pertinent interest is FRE Rule 404, which states that character evidence is not admissible to prove criminal propensity. This theme is relatively elementary: Think of a criminal with eight rape convictions during a rape trial for a ninth charge. Is it permissible for his character to be attacked by plastering his horrid past of previous convictions before a jury? Doesn't this record manifest a propensity or proclivity toward this form of criminal conduct? Under FRE Rule 404, "[e]vidence of a person's character or a trait of character is not admissible for the purpose of proving action in conformity therewith. . . ."[52] While this general standard is upheld with regularity, Rule 404(b), entitled *Other crimes, wrongs, or acts,* molds an exception. The rule states, in part, that crimes, criminality, or bad acts or wrongs may "be admissible for other purposes, such as proof of motive, opportunity, intent, preparation, plan, knowledge, identity, or absence of mistake or accident. . . ."[53]

Returning to our rapist charged for the ninth time, if the evidence is being offered to show a modus operandi, a plan of action that was regular and signatory, or to show that the act was hardly one of mere mistake or neglect, the criminal conviction record may be admitted. "Since rule 404(b) is a specialized rule of evidentiary relevance, the proper test is whether the charged misconduct is relevant, not whether it is similar."[54]

Of corollary interest is FRE Rule 405, relaying that any opinion of character is permissible if the result not of individualized opinion, but instead, of a community perception.[55] "Strictly speaking, a witness's personal opinion of someone's character is unacceptable. The character evidence adduced ought also be of the broad type impugned by the charges in the case. Negative character testimony of the type 'I have never heard anything ill of the defendant's character' will, however, be admitted."[56]

## Documentary Evidence

Documentary evidence consists of memorialized writings or other inscriptions, such as confessions, pleadings, contracts, memoranda, checks, or fraudulent bank notes. Documents are dealt with at every phase of the justice model from investigation to pretrial to actual trial to appeal. Soon to be covered in this text are rules pertinent to documentary forms, such as authentication and foundational requirements[57] and the best evidence rule and chain of custody doctrine. See Chapters 4 and 2, respectively.

In documentary evidence, preference should always be for the original. FRE Rule 1002 summarizes:

> To prove the content of a writing, recording, or photograph, the original writing, recording, or photograph is required, except as otherwise provided in these rules or by Act of Congress.[58]

See Figure 1.7.

Documentary matters involving *public records, summaries, interrogatories,* and *depositions* will also be covered in Chapter 4.

## Hearsay Evidence

Attorneys and legal scholars can spend a lifetime comprehending the hearsay doctrine. Seasoned practitioners know the *hearsay rule* as an overrated evidentiary restriction. At its heart, hearsay evidence is an out-of-court declaration or statement, with the person who uttered it, called the "declarant," unavailable to question. In addition, it is hearsay because the statement of the declarant is being offered to prove the truth of its content, although it is being testified to by a second or third party.

FRE Rule 801(c) defines hearsay as follows:

> "Hearsay" is a statement, other than one made by the declarant while testifying at the trial or hearing, offered in evidence to prove the truth of the matter asserted.[59]

**FIGURE 1.7**    Paper money can prove a drug trade by inference.

Therefore, a statement testified to at a trial or hearing by a declarant witness other than the original declarant is hearsay.

The purpose of the statement is a key factor in whether the rule applies or not. It may yet not be hearsay. For what purpose is the out-of-court assertion being offered to the court? Is it being offered to prove the truth of a statement or the truth of a writing or an act? If it is being offered for that specific purpose, it is hearsay. An out-of-court assertion that is offered for any purpose other than to prove its truth is not hearsay. An out-of-court assertion that has direct legal significance, regardless of it truth or falsity, is not hearsay. For example, "an out of court assertion that constitutes[ ] an offer or an acceptance, or a defamation, or a representation or a misrepresentation, or a guarantee or a notice, etc. is not hearsay."[60]

Why can't a witness testify to the statements of an out-of-court declarant when offered to prove the truth of the matter asserted? Foundationally, the exclusion rests on the opposing party's inability to cross-examine the content of the testimony being related. The out-of-court declarant is not available. James McCarthy, in his work *Making Trial Objections,* gives three principal reasons for the exclusion.

> First the declarant being quoted or relied on cannot be examined concerning his ability to perceive or retain the fact; thus, the right of cross-examination is denied. Second, no opportunity is given to the trier of fact to observe the demeanor of the defendant. Third, although the witness is under oath, the declarant is not.[61]

Evaluate the testimony of a witness who says that he heard his friend, on out-of-court declarant, say, "I did not poison my wife." Is the statement being offered to prove guilt? Does the hearsay rule prohibit the use of another person's narrative as an equivalent to the direct testimony of the declarant? Unless the party who made the declaration testifies in court, in a witness chair and under oath, where the party may be probed and cross-examined, the statement is hearsay.

Granting the rule's complexity, the rationale is one of evidentiary credibility. Firsthand witness testimony is more reliable than testimony further down the chain. Remember how rumors work and stories evolve. Convictions should not rest on what people hear others say when those who allegedly said it are not available. If the crux of the case is murder, it is a subversion of evidentiary integrity to allow a witness to testify, "I heard from a friend of mine that John heard from someone else that Bob committed the murder." This multiple hearsay, assuming it is being offered to prove that Bob committed the murder, is hapless, unreliable evidence.

## Exceptions to the Hearsay Rule

Some argue that the *hearsay rule* is much ado about nothing. After viewing the landscape of exceptions under FRE Rule 803, they are partially correct. In a long list of exceptions, the availability of the declarant becomes immaterial. Even when a clearly delineated exception is not mentioned, FRE Rule 807 leaves the door wide open for the discretionary admission of hearsay. Under the heading *Residual Exceptions,* the federal courts can admit hearsay under this elasticized provision:

> A statement not specifically covered by *Rule 803* or *804* but having equivalent circumstantial guarantees of trustworthiness, is not excluded by the hearsay rule, if the court determines that (A) the statement is offered as evidence of a material fact; (B) the statement is more probative on the point for which it is offered than any other evidence which the proponent can procure through reasonable efforts; and (C) the general purposes of these rules and the interests of justice will best be served by admission of the statement into evidence.[62]

The "interests of justice" standard has lots of room to grow and expand. To be certain, FRE Rule 807 takes the wind out of the hearsay threat. But even within the formal definition of hearsay at FRE Rule 801, certain statements are categorized as nonhearsay.

***Prior Statements Under Oath*** In analyzing whether or not hearsay evidence can be admitted, courts are looking for exceptional circumstances that justify abandonment of hearsay principles. A prior statement by a witness who has testified at trial, who has been subject to cross-examination, and whose statement is inconsistent or even consistent with the current testimony is viewed as nonhearsay. In the case of a prior statement by a witness, there is at least a feeling that when testimony is given under oath and is subject to the rigors of cross-examination, the evidence has credibility.

California recently adopted a specific exception to the hearsay rule for domestic violence cases. Similar exceptions already apply in a number of jurisdictions for out-of-court statements by child sexual abuse victims, but California is the first to apply this type of exception to adults. To qualify for admission, a statement must narrate, describe, or explain the infliction or threat of physical injury, and the declarant must be unavailable to testify. The statement also must have been made within at least five years of the infliction of the injury and must be written, electronically recorded, or provided to a law enforcement official.[63] Critics, while condemning the extraordinary pathology of spouse and child abuse, perceive such enactments as exacting too heavy a toll on the traditional hearsay model. Unfortunately, although the California exception seeks to provide the trier of fact with additional, relevant information about a defendant's abusive past, the exception allows potentially unreliable allegations of past physical abuse to be admitted into evidence against a defendant, thereby undermining important procedural safeguards that the hearsay rule provides by removing "safeguards that help to ensure that all defendants, regardless of the charge against them, receive a fair trial."[64]

***Admissions Against Interest***  Another express exemption from the exclusionary aspects of the hearsay rule is an admission by a party opponent. The definition of such an admission is as follows:

> The statement is offered against a party and is
>
> (A) the party's own statement, in either an individual or representative capacity or
>
> (B) a statement of which the party has manifested an adoption or belief in its truth, or
>
> (C) a statement by a person authorized by the party to make a statement concerning the subject, or
>
> (D) a statement by the party's agent. . . .[65]

The general principle behind the admission exception is that making statements against one's own interest is neither natural nor a willing falsification. If a person says, "I am responsible for what happened," the adverse comment is not a fabrication. People generally do not say negative things about themselves.

***Present Sense Impressions***  In civil actions, typically cases of medical malpractice or auto negligence, the present sense impression is a useful hearsay exception. A party who was an eyewitness to an accident or a doctor's medical negligence and who made the statement during the actual occurrence has little time for falsehood. The statement is considered genuine enough because of its spontaneity, there being no extrinsic opportunity to modify the truth. A party walking up to another who recites, "I'm crazy and I know it," is either doing it in jest or doing it because it is true.

Statements for purposes of medical diagnosis or treatment—written statements or communications with a medical professional that describe medical history, past or present symptoms, pain, and ongoing sensations—are considered hearsay, but reliable admissions and therefore admissible.

***Excited Utterances*** When individuals witness startling events, catastrophes, and circumstances whirling with tension and emotion, their declarations are deemed trustworthy. When a volcano erupts or an earthquake takes place, a human commentary is hardly the result of intentional lies and deceit. In spontaneous circumstances, people rarely utter untrue statements because they lack the time to engage in the sort of mental chicanery the rule seeks to avoid.[66]

An excited utterance is admissible if the following elements exist:

1. A startling occurrence sufficient to produce stress or excitement in persons of ordinary sensibilities took place;
2. The declarant was present at the occurrence, and the utterance came very soon thereafter;
3. The startling occurrence is the subject of the remark; and
4. The declarant may or may not be available to testify.[67]

In a prosecution for sexual assault arising out of the defendant's assault on a four-year-old boy, the court properly allowed the child's mother, physician, and responding police officer to testify to statements made to each by the child, pursuant to the excited utterance exception to the hearsay rule. These statements were allowed even though made on the morning after the alleged assault occurred because the fact that the statement was not made either contemporaneously with the event or immediately thereafter does not preclude its admissibility.[68]

***Dying Declarations*** Very few people wish to end their existence with an intentional falsehood. While certain individuals are chronic liars, the out-of-court declaration of the dying person is trustworthy enough to overcome the hearsay objection. The deathbed patient who implicates another by the utterance, "It was Sally who did it, not Steve!" is probably telling the truth. One who is soon to meet his or her ultimate destiny, especially in the spiritual sense, is not inclined to lie. Agreement on the rationale for the exception is far from uniform. Bryan A. Liang's study *Shortcuts to "Truth": The Legal Mythology of Dying Declarations* exhaustively attacks our historical willingness to tolerate the legal exception. Our justification, he claims, is formed "on the basis of unsubstantiated armchair psychology, religious notions, and a cynical perspective of necessity to emphasize the law's ability to convict."[69] His comprehensive review, while open to debate, quantitatively dissects and measures this particular rule—a jurisprudential trend known as "jurimetrics."

***Recorded Recollections*** Recorded recollections are letters, memoranda, or records that can be used by a witness testifying on the stand to refresh memory. Since the content of the recollection is formalized in a written document, the lack of alteration potential makes the hearsay doctrine less necessary. FRE Rule 803(6) and (7) deal with business records, medical and hospital records, and other documents that are so regularly and automatically kept that alteration or intentional falsehood is only remotely possible.[70] Laying a proper foundation for this hearsay exception is accomplished by the following type of witness inquiry:

1. Do you presently have any recall of these facts?
2. Did you have personal knowledge of the facts in the past?
3. Was that knowledge recorded contemporaneously in writing?
4. I show you exhibit X; do you recognize it?
5. What is exhibit X?
6. Who prepared exhibit X?
7. When did you first see exhibit X?
8. Is exhibit X the accurate recordation of your knowledge at the time?
9. Your Honor, I offer exhibit X as a past recollection recorded, and I ask leave to read it into the record.[71]

***Records/Government Documents/Vital Statistics*** Public records; vital statistics; marriage, baptismal, and similar certificates; and the vast array of government documents in existence are excepted under this hearsay exception. A baptismal certificate offered into evidence to prove the birth, time, date of baptism, name, and other personal particulars is clear-cut hearsay, since the out-of-court declarant, the author of the certificate, is not available to testify as to its contents. If the courts required that government agents, church authorities, and institutions provide an attestor before admission of their documents, the pace of litigation would come to a grinding halt. Since government officials who record and create such documents and reports generally have no bias or prejudicial interest, the courts classify these as hearsay, but reliable enough to be admissible.[72] It seems unlikely that religious organizations such as churches, nonprofit entities, or genealogical groups affiliated with churches or others would intentionally falsify records.

***Matters of Pedigree*** Even more fantastic would be the assertion that personal family histories inscribed within family Bibles, genealogical charts, ring engravings, or family portraits are subject to falsification. It is reasonable to assume that families will transcribe honest information regarding pedigree.

***Miscellaneous Exceptions*** Ancient documents, documents more than 20 years old, by their longevity are inherently reliable. Market reports and commercial publications, quotations, tabulations, lists, directories, and other published compilations available to the public are hearsay, but admitted, since their "rote" nature minimizes treachery.

In the case of a natural tool of the expert witness, the learned treatise, the court does not require its author to attest to the content. Until recently, the learned treatise exception was a distinct minority view in the United States. However, with the enactment of the Federal Rules and the adoption of evidence codes patterned after the Rules in most states, the exception has gained the status of a majority view. Nevertheless, it must be conceded that the scope of the exception is rather narrow.[73]

Other exceptions include statements and documents affecting an interest in property, statements on reputation as to character, and records of previous convictions.

As a policy matter, the hearsay rule's best intention is to force litigants to question the value and credibility of their evidence and to find and present the original declarant. Hearsay forces the practitioner to gauge the quality of not only the testimony, but also the witnesses themselves.

## § 1.7 THE WEIGHT OF EVIDENCE

How much weight we accord evidence at trial depends on the type of case or proposition being advocated. "Weight" is largely a term of art, with courts giving some evidence more respect than others. From one extreme of the evidentiary spectrum, where no weight is attached to evidence and the evidence is stricken or excluded from trial, to the other, where evidence is judicially noticed, weight is basically how much something is worth. In the general scheme of things, only "competent" evidence is entitled to weight. Judges instruct juries that only competent evidence is worthy of their evaluation. The jury instruction at Form 1.3[74] assesses the distinction properly.

Another view on the weight of evidence would be whether the evidence is direct or circumstantial. For example, is the weight of the evidence sufficient in a charge of murder when the evidence relied upon is strictly circumstantial? Is a finding of homicide possible when the corpus delicti is unavailable, as in the Capano case? Would blood spatters alone prove a victim's homicide? See Figure 1.8. Is a fingerprint alone sufficient circumstantial evidence in a charge of homicide? In some respects, the weight of any evidence is its sufficiency, whether its proof convinces or produces a conclusion that is acceptable.[75]

Form 1.4[76] contains jury instructions on the calculation of evidential weight of circumstantial evidence.

At the center of evidentiary analysis, courts and juries weigh positively or negatively the quality of evidence, accepting or rejecting it either totally or partially, despite its competency and relevance. To prove this point, examine the influence of testimonial evidence. The impression left by a witness may be one of truthfulness or trickery. When the witness is done, the testimony may fail in the jurors' eyes because

As the sole judges of the facts, you must determine which of the witnesses you believe, what portion of their testimony you accept and what weight you attach to it. At times during the trial I shall sustain objections to questions asked without permitting the witness to answer or, where an answer has been made, shall instruct that it be stricken from the record and that you disregard it and dismiss it from your minds. You may not draw any inference from the unanswered question nor may you consider testimony which has been stricken in reaching your decision. The law requires that your decision be made solely upon the competent evidence before you. Such items as I exclude from your considerations will be excluded because they are not legally admissible.

**FORM 1.3** Instruction to jury—consideration of competent evidence only. (Reprinted by permission of West Group.)

the witness exudes falsehood or because the testimony manifests a lack of personal knowledge. Or the opposite result may occur. The trier is so impressed that the witness can do no wrong. Therefore, while evidence may be admitted, relevant, and competent, its quality and the method of presentation either increase or dilute its force and effect. Dilution diminishes weight; when a witness is commendable, the reverse happens.

## Presumptions

Evidentially, presumptions exist as rules and as litigation controls. While presumptions are not strictly evidentiary, they are positions or findings on particular questions.

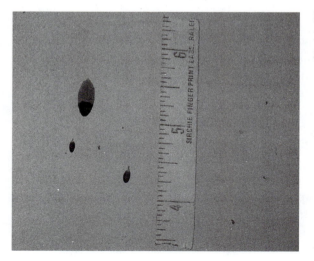

**FIGURE 1.8**
Blood prints/spatters in murder investigation.

Some evidence has been introduced in this case which in its nature is circumstantial evidence. You are instructed that circumstantial evidence is proof of certain facts from which you may infer other and connected facts which usually and reasonably follow according to the common experience of mankind. Circumstantial evidence is legal evidence and is not to be disregarded merely because it is circumstantial. Circumstantial evidence may be quite as conclusive in its convincing power as direct and positive evidence of eyewitnesses. When it is strong and satisfactory you will so consider it, neither enlarging nor belittling its force. A fact sought to be proved cannot be said to be established by circumstantial evidence alone unless circumstantially relied on and proved, and are of such a nature and are so related to each other that it is the only conclusion that can reasonably be drawn from them. It is not sufficient that they are merely consistent with the facts sought to be proved. However, circumstantial evidence should have its just and fair weight with you, and if, when it is taken as a whole and fairly and candidly weighted, it convinces the guarded judgment, you should give such circumstantial evidence its just and proper weight. You are not to imagine situations and circumstances which do not appear in the evidence, but you are to make those just and reasonable inferences from the circumstances proved which the guarded judgment of a reasonable person would ordinarily make under like circumstances, and you will consider such evidence in connection with all the other evidence, facts and circumstances proved on the trial.

**FORM 1.4** Instruction to jury—circumstantial evidence to be considered in connection with other evidence. (Reprinted by permission of West Group.)

"Presumptions have been used to accomplish four distinct ends. They have been used to construct rules of decision to avoid factual impasse at trial; to allocate burdens of persuasion; to instruct the jury on the relationship between facts; and to allocate burdens of production."[77] A presumption is a condition, a status that exists without the slightest ounce of argument. It is a fact without proof or rebuttal. Examples of presumptions are that the law presumes innocence, that the law presumes sanity rather than insanity; that the law presumes volitional acts rather than acts of coercion, that the law presumes that a certain spouse died first in a multivictim collision, that a burden of persuasion rests upon a defendant pleading affirmative defenses, and that the law presumes a spouse is permanently absent after a specific time frame. Again, presumptions are not evidence in a conceptual sense because they may or may not be true.[78] A presumption is not evidence; "it is merely a label that has been applied to a perceived relationship between facts."[79]

But presumptions have a powerful impact on the advocacy of cases. If the presumption, the assumed condition or fact, is not rebutted or attacked, that status or condition remains inviolate. In the case of criminal insanity, the defendant must raise the question of insanity. The defense must overcome the presumptuous burden that all people are basically sane. In this context, presumptions force the litigants to either persuade or attack, to reaffirm or rebut the presumption. In a way, presumptions are baggage that can be attached or thrown away. In the end, the confusion and ambiguity that characterize presumptions are largely the result of a failure to recognize that presumptions are labels applied to the resolution of standard evidentiary problems.[80]

Presumptions tend to be fluid concepts, since they shift.[81] Initially, a presumed fact rests comfortably in a party's camp. In response, the opposing party produces evidence that rebuts or undermines the integrity of the presumed fact. If successful in rebuttal, the presumption's influence dissipates. In the alternative, the burden of proving a once-established presumption has shifted to its original owner. The Model Code of Evidence defines a presumption synonymously with a presumed fact:

> Presumption means that when a basic fact exists the existence of another fact must be assumed, whether or not the other fact may be rationally found from the basic fact. Presumed fact means the fact which must be assumed.[82]

Child custody cases have long been influenced by the law of presumption. The tender years doctrine presumed that child placement with the maternal party made better sense. A variety of states have enacted a presumption against the award of child custody to a spouse abuser. "The theory behind this type of statute is that the batterer should not be rewarded for his cruelty. The presumption statutes also differ greatly from state to state, and the presumption against awarding custody to a spousal abuser may be addressed in either a joint or sole custody statute, or a best interests of the child statute. In some states, the presumption may be rebutted by such evidence as successful completion of a batterer treatment program, or extraordinary circumstances which show there is no risk of continuing violence."[83]

That presumptions influence the tenor of litigation is well documented. The existence of the presumed fact or conduct is taken as truth until it is attacked or rebutted. At Rule 704 of the Model Code of Evidence, the effect is addressed:

> Subject to Rule 703, when the basic fact of a presumption has been established in an action, the existence of the presumed fact must be assumed unless and until evidence has been introduced which would support a finding of its non-existence or the basic fact of an inconsistent presumption which has been established[84]

At FRE Rule 301, presumptions are summarily dealt with:

> In all civil actions and proceedings not otherwise provided for by Act of Congress or by these rules, a presumption imposes on the party against whom it is directed the burden of going forward with evidence to rebut or meet the presumption, but does not shift to such party the burden of proof in the sense of the risk of nonpersuasion, which remains throughout the trial upon the party on whom it was originally cast.[85]

Once the presumption has been factually and legally established, its existence is assured unless the opposing party attacks and rebuts its integrity. If successful, the original presumption evaporates, but has the potentiality to re-emerge. "Although the presumption may disappear, the facts on which it was based are still in the case, and any inferences arising from them may be considered and argued to the jury. The prudent course, however, is to be prepared with evidence rather than to rely on a presumption, except where proved impossible to attain."[86]

The law of presumptions is often troubling to trial judges. Judge Learned Hand, one of America's finest jurists, keenly interprets the law of presumptions:

> Judges have mixed it up until nobody can tell what on earth it means and the important thing is to get something which is workable and which can be understood and I don't care much what it is.[87]

## § 1.8 BURDENS OF PROOF

Definitionally, the burden of proof is an allocation, distribution, and measure of evidence. In going forward, meeting the burden of proof is a prosecutor's solemn responsibility. Before entering the courthouse doors, the attorneys plan a strategy sufficient to meet and exceed the evidentiary burden. When compared to presumptions, burdens are evidentiary obligations and duties. For a prosecutor to convict, a jury must be satisfied that sufficient evidence exists to convict. How much evidence meets the burden? Do burdens vary depending on the type or style of litigation? Do burdens vary depending on the damage or claim? Do burdens shift? Are burdens quantifiably measurable, or are they qualitative judgments?

The justice system constructs its very edifice on the evidentiary measure called a burden. The system asks whether there is enough evidence to convict, to declare a mistrial, to commit, to adjudge insane, or to be declared incompetent.

### Types of Burdens

The major classifications of burdens in criminal and civil cases are *beyond a reasonable doubt, by clear and convincing evidence,* and *by a preponderance of evidence.* Criminal cases at the felony level put the highest, most stringent burden—*beyond a reasonable doubt*—on the state, the commonwealth, the government, in proving its position. Some criminal cases use the *clear and convincing evidence* standard, but this is rare. Civil law employs only the latter two burdens. A plaintiff cannot merely allege harm, but must meet a burden. To win, the evidence must be either *clear and convincing* or *preponderantly* better than the opposition's. These burden classifications are a combination of objective and subjective criteria. One might attempt to quantify the burdens numerically. "In order to win, the plaintiff must satisfy his burden of persuasion that fact X is true. In other words, there must be more evidence tending to show that X is true than evidence against this proposition."[88]

More rationally stated, the advocate, if expecting to win, should have more than the opposition, but the advocate need not be perfect in overcoming the burden's threshold. Burdens are not infallible rules of evidence, only probable ones. Henry M. Hart and John I. McNaghten qualify the variable and relative nature of meeting a burden:

> The law does not require absolute assurance of the perfect correctness of a particular decision. While it is of course important that the court be right in its determinations of fact, it is also important that the court decide the case when the parties ask for the decision and on the bases of the evidence presented by the parties. A decision must be made now, one way or the other. To require certainty or even near certainty in such a context would be impracticable and undesirable.[89]

Is the demonstration of blood, a victim's clothing, and the actual victim's body sufficient to meet the criminal burden? Are noncriminal explanations possible? See Figures 1.9 and 1.10.

If absolute truth is not required in meeting burdens, what measuring stick elucidates the standards? First, the answer depends on the nature of the litigation. In criminal cases, the applicable burden, *beyond a reasonable doubt,* is admittedly the highest proof standard in the American justice system. But what does the term *beyond a reasonable doubt* mean? There is no controversy or confusion about the fact

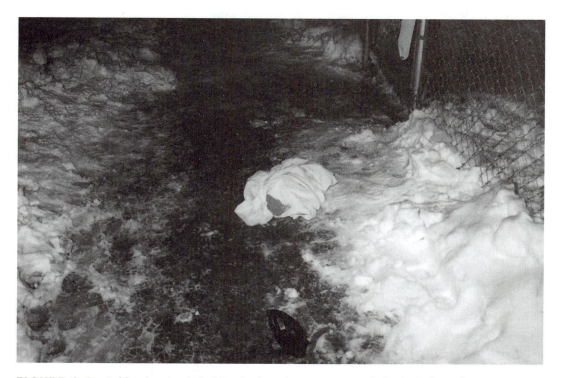

**FIGURE 1.9** Is blood-stained clothing in the winter snow proof of criminal conduct?

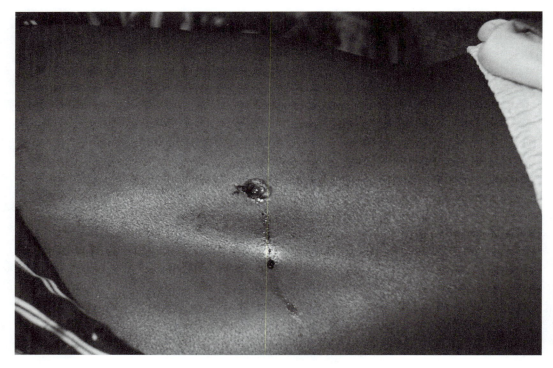

**FIGURE 1.10**    Can criminal conduct be inferred from a bullet in the back?

that the standard applies, but when the prosecutor has met the burden of *beyond a reasonable doubt* is open to debate. John Siffert, in his commentary *Instructing on the Burden of Proof in Reasonable Doubt,* relates precisely the definitional dilemma:

> What is surprising is the extent of the disagreement over the definition of the standard of proof that should be given and, if given what the standard should be. One district court has even suggested a numeric quantification of probability of truth for each of the generally applied standards, with preponderance of evidence being given the requirement greater than fifty percent, clear and convincing seventy percent, clear, unequivacable and convincing calling for eighty percent, and beyond reasonable doubt requiring approximately ninety-five percent.[90]

While the formula is instructive, is it measurable? Does *beyond a reasonable doubt* mean that only 5 or 10 percent of the overall case is doubtful?

A lack of precise definition for reasonable doubt may be advantageous to the legal system and more specifically to the nature and operation of a jury. "Given the impossibility of establishing with precision the meaning of reasonable doubt, that meaning should be resolved in practice through jury deliberation rather than by judicial fiat, because the reasonable doubt standard in a criminal trial calls for application of the very common sense, or community judgment, for which juries are prized."[91] Undoubtedly, there are more conservative jurors and judges who will be very satisfied with possibly 60 or 75 percent of the evidence being damaging to the defendant.

These numerical quantifications are helpful, but theoretically a dead end. Literal interpretation and construction of the term *reasonable doubt* is probably more helpful. The term *reasonable doubt* manifests its plain meaning. First, there is doubt, and second, the doubt is based on reasonable, not irrational, grounds and is not purely conjectural. Some equate doubt with moral guilt or certainty. In other words, doubt relates not only to particular fact, but to culpability.[92] Unquestionably, doubts persist in all types of litigation. Doubt that is reasonable is doubt residing not in triviality, but instead in serious substantive concerns. Reasonable doubt is appropriately defined as follows:

> It is a doubt that a reasonable person had after carefully weighing all the evidence. It is a doubt which would cause a reasonable person to hesitate to act in a manner of importance in his or her personal life. Proof beyond a reasonable doubt must, there- fore, be proof of such convincing character that a reasonable person would not hesi- tate to rely and act upon it in the most important matters of his own affairs.[93]

Adding to the impression of this definition is the lack of any uniform definition at the federal or state level.

Whether a criminal or a civil case, there is no doubt that the analysis of burdens is an exercise in probabilities. The question becomes whether something is more or less true. Judicial technicians and statisticians argue that the process is more quantifiable.

The same inquiry applies in the standards used in civil litigation, *by clear and convincing evidence* and *by a preponderance of evidence*. Mathematical theory and the fundamental maxims of probability calculus cannot accurately do justice to legal burden analysis. Two statements are said to be mutually exclusive if they cannot be true at the same time. Under all traditional definitions of probability, the probability that one of two mutually exclusive statements will be true is equal to the sum of their individual probabilities. That is, if A and B are mutually exclusive, then $P(A \text{ or } B) = P(A) + P(B)$.[94]

In an age of jurimetrics, when applied computer software and statistical analysis are elevated above human reason, attraction to these formulas is understandable. By contrast, subjective, nonscientific determinations at least have a human edge. The term *preponderance of evidence* means in lay English that something is more likely than not. The advocate in a civil case, the person who alleges negligence, must show that negligence probably occurred.

When all else is considered, analyzing any burden is a judgment of reason, the very element a juror uses in legal decision-making.

In cases where a jury instruction on burdens is needed, Form 1.5[95] outlines a useful design. Within the instruction, *preponderance of evidence* is synonymous with the "greater weight of evidence." The term *weight* means, just as if on a scale, that the party saddled with the burden tips the scale in his or her favor.

You are instructed that the terms "preponderance of evidence" and "greater weight of evidence" are terms of practically the same meaning. When it is said that the burden rests on either party or greater weight of evidence, it is meant that the evidence offered and introduced in support thereof to entitle such party to a verdict, should, when fully and fairly considered, be more convincing as worthy of belief when weighed against the evidence introduced in opposition thereto. Such preponderance is not always to be determined by the number of witnesses on the respective sides, although it may be thus determined, all other things being equal, but from the character of the evidence, the character of the witnesses, their intelligence, means of knowledge, and strength of memory, their interest and want of interest in the result of the suit, the probability or improbability of their statements, and all facts and circumstances in evidence affecting the question as a whole.

**FORM 1.5** Instruction to jury—preponderance of evidence—definition. (Reprinted by permission of West Group.)

If legal scholars and practitioners have difficulty determining the measurability of *beyond a reasonable doubt* and *by a preponderance of evidence,* how does the burden *by clear and convincing evidence* fit in the discussion? What is *clear* and what is *convincing?* How does one measure these descriptive standards? Be sensible; interpret wisely and with good horse sense.

Subjectively, the preponderance standard, or for that matter the clear and convincing evidence standard, calls for a jury to arrive at actual, though not infallible, beliefs. "The concept of *actual belief* being explored is obviously not a probabilistic or statistical concept. It is essentially a cultural or psychological question of when an individual is prepared, short of absolute certainty, to turn his innermost thoughts into a statement of 'I believe' on which others may judge both that of which he speaks as well as him personally."[96]

At ground level, burdens, however imprecise, should force an advocate and support staff to amass enough evidence to meet these subjective and objective criteria. "To meet the burden of proof, the advocate's cause of action or charge must be satisfactorily demonstrated to a jury or justice. If the jury rules in favor of a plaintiff, it can be stated that the burden has been met, at least from a factual perspective."[97] By way of analysis, remember these issues:

1. Has a prosecutor met the burden of *beyond a reasonable doubt* when the entire case in a charge of murder rests upon circumstantial evidence?

2. Has a plaintiff met the burden of *clear and convincing evidence* in a case of medical malpractice when the actions of the medical professional were allegedly negligent, where an array of experts produced at trial concurs in a judgment of negligence?

**3.** Has a plaintiff/victim injured in an automobile accident met the burden of proof, proving by *clear and convincing evidence* that the gas tanks were negligently installed and designed, resulting in a foreseeable explosion?

Whether in a civil or criminal case, burden analysis forces the advocate to decipher an evidentiary plan of proof. "Counsel must therefore consider the order of proof not only in the light of law governing presumptions, inferences, *res ipsa loquitur,* etc., but also according to the standard or quantum of proof required in a particular case, and the rules determining which party has the affirmative of the issues."[98]

## § 1.9 SUMMARY

The chapter's primary emphasis was the introduction of evidentiary concepts and definitions. What evidence is, and how it is grouped and classified, was initially analyzed. What qualities constitute good evidence, and whether evidence is competent, relevant, material, and probative, were underlying threads in this chapter. Forms of evidence, from direct to documentary, were analyzed. In addition, the influence of the hearsay rule and its many exceptions was posed, as well as other evidentiary policies involving presumptions, burdens, and the concept of legal weight.

## *Notes*

1. Professors David Schum and Peter Tiller, in their creative article *Marshaling Evidence for Adversary Litigation*, advise practitioners to use their imaginations when marshaling as much evidence as possible in the litigation process. In their view, the quality and content of evidence are directly correlated to one's level of imagination and creative thought. They state in part: "Our study of investigative discovery puts great stress on the role of imagination. Few investigative problems in law (or else) spring forth in well-posed form in which specific possibilities are immediately obvious and all relevant evidence is readily available. Hypotheses or possibilities and relevant evidential tests of those hypotheses and possibilities have to be constructed. In short, because the investigative discovery depends on the imaginative skills of investigators, imaginative reasoning plays a crucial role in investigative discovery. Despite its obvious importance, imaginative reasoning is not well-understood." David Schum & Peter Tiller, *Marshaling Evidence for Adversary Litigation,* 13 Cardozo L. Rev. 657, 659 (1991).

2. Evidence practice is a tough field to conquer. Schum and Tiller state: "Organizing evidence is one matter, but using it as a basis for one's choices or to persuade others is quite another." *Id.* at 678.

3. CHARLES P. NEMETH, Litigation, Pleadings and Arbitration 523 (2d ed. 1990).

4. EDWARD M. MORGAN, *Foreword* to Model Code of Evidence 4 (1941).

5. JOHN M. MCGUIRE et al., Evidence, Cases and Materials 1 (1973).

6. CHARLES P. NEMETH, The Paralegal Handbook, 225–226 (1986).

7. GUIDO CALABRESE, Common Law for the Age of Statutes (1982).

8. Edward Imwinkelried states the dilemma precisely: "The first year classes at the typical law school usually do a superb job of promoting the students' development of the fact- and case analysis skills required of a practitioner in a common-law system. Although statutes have become the dominant source of law in the United States, the time and intellectual energy most law schools devote to legisprudence pale in comparison with that still committed to common law processes. Law schools claim to be engaged in professional education; but if they are to fulfill their responsibilities to prepare graduates to practice law, they must devote far more resources and time to legisprudence." Edward Imwinkelried, *Evidence Pedagogy in the Age of Statutes,* 41 J. Legal Educ. 227, 241 (1991).

9. Carlisle v. United States, 517 U.S. 416 (1996).

10. Fed. Proc. R. Serv. (Law. Co-op) 755–756 (1992).

11. Model Code of Evidence Rule 1(12) (1942).

12. Fed. R. Evid. 401.

13. 1 JOHN H. WIGMORE, Evidence 410 (1940) (emphasis added).

14. Fed. R. Evid. 402.

15. Richard D. Friedman, *Anchors and Flotsam: Is Evidence Law "Adrift,"* 107 Yale L. J. 1921 (1998) (reviewing MIRJAN R. DAMAŠKA, Evidence Law Adrift (1997)). The U.S. Supreme Court allowed the admission of a battered child syndrome defense in the prosecution of a second-degree murder case. Holding the evidence relevant, the Court remarked: "Thus, evidence demonstrating battered child syndrome helps to prove that the child died at the hands of another and not by falling off a couch, for example; it also tends to establish that the 'other,' whoever it may be, inflicted the injuries intentionally. When offered to show that certain injuries are a product of child abuse, rather than accident, evidence of prior injuries is relevant even though it does not purport to prove the identity of the person who might have inflicted those injuries." People v. Jackson, 18 Cal. App. 2d 504, 506–508, 95 Cal. Rptr. 919, 921–922 (1971); People v. Bledsoe, 36 Cal. 3d 236, 249, 203 Cal. Rptr. 450, 458, 681 P.2d, 291, 299 (1984).

16. Fed. R. Evid. 401.

17. MICHAEL GRAHAM, Evidence, Text, Rules, Illustrations and Problems 13 (1983).

18. U.S. DEPARTMENT of JUSTICE, Handbook of Forensic Science 1–2 (1981).

19. Fed. R. Evid. 403.

20. Indeed, the polygraph continues to befuddle its proponents as it is locked out of courtrooms. The decision to ban is based on continuing disagreement about the accuracy of the polygraph technique. United States v. Scheffer, No. 96-1133 (March 31, 1998).

21. Dominic Massaro states: "In the realm of novelty, special challenges are presented. The risk of admitting as 'explanatory' a palpably untrustworthy opinion is deemed unacceptably high where the jury can be misled with an aura of certainty, glossed by a diploma and the facade of superior knowledge, to overestimate its probative value and obscure its merely conjectural nature. Lay jurors tend to give considerable weight to novel 'scientific' evidence when presented by 'experts' with impressive credentials. In any case, unreliable evidence does not satisfy the definition of relevancy." Dominic R. Massaro, *Novelty in the Courts: Grouping for Consensus in Science and the Law,* 65 N.Y. St. B.J. 46 (1993).

22. Mark Hansen, *Believe It or Not,* 79 A.B.A. J. 64, 67 (1993).

23. NEMETH, *supra* note 3, at 526–527.

24. *Id.* at 402.
25. Fed. R. Evid. 201(b) & (c).
26. Fed. R. Evid. 201 advisory committee's notes.
27. *See* Fed. R. Evid. 201(c) & (d).
28. *See* Fed. R. Evid. 201(e).
29. *See* Fed. R. Evid. 201(f).
30. *See* Fed. R. Evid. 201(g).
31. Pennsylvania Bar Institute, Evidence: A Statewide Institute 23 (1990).
32. 9A Am. Jur. Pl. & Prac. Forms § 71 (1984).
33. *Id.* at § 72.
34. Fed. R. Evid. 601.
35. Fed. R. Evid. 602.
36. Fed. R. Evid. 603.
37. Fed. R. Evid. 701.
38. Fed. R. Evid. 702.
39. Fed. R. Evid. 703.
40. Petruzzi's IGA Supermarkets, Inc. v. Darling-Delaware Co., Inc., 988 F.2d 1224 (3d Cir. 1993).
41. *See* Fed. R. Evid. 704.
42. "Keep these factors in mind when setting out to address character evidence.
    1. Have 'good faith' basis for questions relative to specific acts.
    2. Question witness's familiarity with people where witness lives, works, and spends his or her time.
    3. Question witness's familiarity with the reputation of those people.
    4. Ask specifically where, when, and from whom witness learned of the reputation.
    5. Show any bias on part of witness.
    6. Show any bias on part of those upon whom the reputation is based ('only black living in white neighborhood').
    7. Question witness's familiarity with reputation personally (investigator not allowed to testify as to what people told him).
    8. If you know of improper basis for reputation, PURSUE IT. 'Johnny was unpopular because he refused to perjure himself when the others were caught stealing, isn't that right?'
    9. If you know witness is concealing good character traits, PURSUE IT. 'Didn't you tell John everyone liked him and couldn't believe this about him?'
    10. Inquire about specific instances. 'Were you aware that he admitted . . .'
    11. Avoid arguing with witness. 'Would you change your mind if you assumed the defendant is guilty of this?'
    12. Argue importance of special instance if 403 argument advanced.
    13. Attack factual basis of an opinion.
    14. Limit cross-examination to character trait covered on direct examination.
    15. Where character is in issue, pursue the specific instances (opposing counsel is given thorough opportunity because of importance of character issue, so you should cross-examine with same thoroughness).

    16. Witness giving opinion should be required to comply with Rule 701 if lay wit-
       ness (perception) and if expert, then with Rule 702 (based on what experts in
       the particular field reasonably rely upon).

    17. Ask witness about statements made by party. 'Didn't defendant tell you he was
       involved in counterfeiting?' (Held proper—"other crime" admissible to show
       intent, etc.)

    18. Avoid testimony that can cause mistrial. 'Where were you when defendant told
       you that?' 'We were in prison.'

    EDWARD T. WRIGHT, Evidence: How and When to Use the Rules to Win Cases 61–62
    (1990).

43. NEMETH, *supra* note 3, at 402 (1990).

44. Fed. R. Evid. 412(a).

45. Fed. R. Evid. 412(b).

46. *See* Charles P. Nemeth, *Character Evidence in Rape Trials in 19th Century New York: Chastity and the Admissibility of Specific Acts,* 6 Women's Rts. L. Rep. 3 (Spring 1980); Charles P. Nemeth, *An Evaluation of New Jersey's Sexual Offense Statute: Judicial and Prosecutorial Perceptions in Rape Reform,* N.J. L. J. (1983).

47. Michigan v. Lucas, 500 U.S. 145, 152 (1991). Professor Toni Lester's fascinating study on sexual harassment delves into how the entire legal system weighs accusations based on gender differences. She uses rape law as a fitting analogy in her demonstration of the distinct evidence standard in cases that involve women. She relays: "A close examination of rape law reveals that judges who apply the reasonable person test have often focused to an unusually high degree on the actions, reactions, motives, and inadequacies of the victim . . . [as opposed to] those of the defendant. Support for this conclusion can be found in the following list of situations in which women were deemed to have given their consent:

    1. The woman did not physically resist the unarmed rapist;
    2. The woman assumed the risk of being raped by placing herself in what was deemed to be an obviously dangerous situation;
    3. The woman had the type of sexual fantasies and/or sexual life that demonstrated to the court that she had a propensity to want to have sex with the alleged rapist;
    4. The woman wore the type of clothing that demonstrated to the court the rapist was justified in finding her sexually provocative; or
    5. The woman's credibility was questioned because she failed to report the rape immediately after it occurred."

    Toni Lester, *The Reasonable Woman Test in Sexual Harassment Law—Will It Really Make a Difference?,* 26 Ind. L. Rev. 227, 234 (1993).

48. Fed. R. Evid. 608(a).

49. Fed. R. Evid. 608(b).

50. Fed. R. Evid. 609(a)(1).

51. Fed. R. Evid.. 609(a)(2).

52. Fed. R. Evid. 404(a).

53. Fed. R. Evid. 404(b).

54. Jeffery Cole, *Bad Acts Evidence Under Rule 404(b),* 14 Litig. 8, 9 (1988).

55. *See* Fed. R. Evid. 405.

56. Rowton L. & C. 520 (1865); Redgrave 74 Cr. App. 10 (1982).

57. *See* Fed. R. Evid. 901 & 902.

58. Fed. R. Evid. 1002.

59. Fed. R. Evid. 801(c).

60. PENNSYLVANIA BAR INSTITUTE, *supra* note 31, at 118.

61. JAMES MCCARTHY, Making Trial Objections 4-30 (1986).

62. Fed. R. Evid. 807.

63. David M. Gersten, *Evidentiary Trends in Domestic Violence,* Fla. B.J., July–Aug. 1998, at 65, 68 n.7.

64. Note, *Evidence Law—Hearsay Rule,* 110 Harv. L. Rev. 805 (1997).

65. Fed. R. Evid. 801(d)(2).

66. A 1992 U.S. Supreme Court decision reaffirmed the traditional rationale for this hearsay exception. "We note first that the evidentiary rationale for permitting hearsay testimony regarding spontaneous declarations and statements made in the course of receiving medical care is that such out-of-court declarations are made in contexts that provide substantial guarantees of their trustworthiness. But those same factors that contribute to the statements' reliability cannot be recaptured even by later in-court testimony. A statement that has been offered in a moment of excitement—without the opportunity to reflect on the consequences of one's exclamation—may justifiably carry more weight with a trier of fact than a similar statement offered in the relative calm of the courtroom." White v. Illinois, 502 U.S. 346, 355–356 (1992).

67. NEMETH, *supra* note 6

68. People v. Ortega, 672 P.2d 215 (Colo. App. 1983); P. Magarick, *Investigating Particular Civil Actions,* 2 Am. Jur. Trials 53 (Supp. 1993).

69. Bryan A. Liang, *Shortcuts to "Truth": The Legal Mythology of Dying Declarations,* 35 Am. Crim. L. Rev. 229, 277 (1998).

70. *See* Fed. R. Evid. 803(6) & (7).

71. KENT SINCLAIR, Trial Handbook 75 (2d. ed. 1992).

72. Fed. R. Evid. 803(11) & (12).

73. Edward J. Imwinkelried, *Forensic Science: Role of the Hearsay Doctrine in Litigating* Frye *Challenges to the Admissibility of Scientific Evidence,* 29 Crim. L. Bull. 158, 165-66 (1993).

74. Am. Jur., *supra* note 32, at § 78.

75. Pope v. Shalala, 998 F.2d 473 (7th Cir. 1993).

76. Am. Jur., *supra* note 32, at § 95.

77. Ronald Allen, *Presumption in Civil Actions Reconsidered,* 66 Iowa L. Rev. 843, 845 (1981).

78. *See* Edmund M. Morgan, *Instructing the Jury upon Presumptions in the Burden of Proof,* 47 Harv. L. Rev. 59, 78 (1933).

79. Allen, *supra* note 77, at 857.

80. *Id.* at 868.

81. Presumptions are not ethereal concepts. In a criminal case, a "[p]erson when first charged with crime is entitled to presumption of innocence, and may insist that his guilt be established beyond reasonable doubt; ...once defendant has been afforded fair trial and convicted of offense for which he was charged, however, presumption of innocence disappears." Herrera v. Collins, 506 U.S. 390, 398–399 (1993).

82. Model Code of Evidence Rule 701 (1942).

83. Lynne R. Kurtz, *Protecting New York's Children: An Argument for the Creation of a Rebuttable Presumption Against Awarding a Spouse Abuser Custody of a Child,* 60 Alb. L. Rev. 1345 (1997).

84. Model Code of Evidence Rule 704 (1942).

85. Fed. R. Evid. 301.

86. Donald Lay, *Mapping the Trial—Order of Proof,* 5 Am. Jur. Trials 505 (1991).

87. 13 LEARNED HAND, ALI Proceeding 217 (1941).

88. James Brook, *Inevitable Errors: The Preponderance of Evidence Standard and Civil Litigation,* 18 Tulsa L.J. 79, 81 (1982).

89. HENRY M. HART, JR. & JOHN T. McNAGHTEN, Evidence and Inference 53 (1959).

90. John Siffert, *Instructing on the Burden of Proof in Reasonable Doubt,* 8 Bridgeport L. Rev. 356, 366 (1987).

91. Note, *Reasonable Doubt: An Argument Against Definition,* 108 Harv. L. Rev. (1955).

92. Rolando V. Del Carmen, Craig Hemmens, & Kathryn E. Scarborough, *Grave Doubts About "Reasonable Doubt": Confusion in State and Federal Courts,* 25 J. Crim. Just. 231–254 (1997).

93. L. SAND & JOHN SIFFERT, Modern Federal Jury Instruction 401 (1984).

94. Brook, *supra* note 88, at 81–82.

95. Am. Jur., *supra* note 32, at § 99.

96. Brook, *supra* note 88, at 96. In federal corporate cases, like bankruptcy, there is a presumption that decisions are made according to the preponderance of evidence rather than the clear and concise standard. In *Grogan v. Garner,* the U.S. Supreme Court relayed: "The preponderance standard is presumed to be applicable in civil actions between private parties unless particularly important individual interests or rights are at stake, and, in the context of the discharge exemption provisions, a debtor's interest in discharge is insufficient to require a heightened standard." Grogan v. Garner, 498 U.S. 279 (1971).

97. NEMETH, *supra* note 43, at 422.

98. MAX R. ISRAELSON, Selecting the Jury—Plaintiff's View, 5 Am. Jur. Trials § 42 (1966).

# C H A P T E R  2

# *Real Evidence*

## § 2.1 THE NATURE OF REAL EVIDENCE

The study of real evidence involves the collection, preservation, and identification of real, tangible objects. Real evidence, for definitional purposes, is in actuality "the thing," the object or the instrumentality under inspection. Real evidence is not a representation, a testimonial impression or viewpoint, or the expert's opinion. It is the object itself (e.g., the gun, blood, etc.) "Real evidence involves producing an object which usually, but not necessarily, had a direct or indirect part in the incident."[1] Samples of real evidence are as boundless as nature itself. In rape cases, vaginal swabs of the victim are analyzed, and any omission or error in processing and storage will open doors of challenge for the defense advocate. Bloodstains, another form of real evidence, have been intensely analyzed.[2] Skeletonized human remains, another classic form of real evidence, have been the subject matter of the DNA tester.[3]

From the outset, it is important to distinguish the real from the demonstrative, or other secondary sources of evidence, as will be covered in Chapter 3. Dean John H. Wigmore, in his treatise on evidence, portrays the three-tiered sources of evidence:

> If for example, it is desired to ascertain whether the accused has lost his right hand and wears an iron hook in place of it, one source of belief on this subject would be the testimony of a witness who had seen the arm. . . . A second source of belief would be the mark left on some substance grasped or carried by the accused. . . . A third source of belief remains, namely the inspection by the tribunal of the accused's arm.[4]

As the trier of facts discerns truth, what form of evidence is most convincing during deliberation? Is the testimony of experts or lay witnesses regarding what they think, what they see, what they interpret the facts to be, more convincing than the introduction of the actual subject matter of their testimony? Is the plaintiff's testimony in a civil negligence case regarding pain and suffering more persuasive than the exhibition of actual injuries on the plaintiff's body? At first glance, the real and tangible evidence seems to have more bite. While this may be a general principle of evidentiary law—namely, that real evidence is the preferred source—in many circumstances the real evidence cannot and does not speak for itself. For example, a gun or ballistics test result sheds very little light on its agency in a murder charge. Other forms of evidentiary assistance are needed to buttress the real, such as the testimony of a ballistics expert, the test results from experiments conducted under substantially similar conditions, or the testimony of an eyewitness who saw the projectile's general trajectory.

Thus, while it is tempting to place real evidence at the apex of evidentiary quality, jurors and the court alike cannot possibly evaluate the real evidence without the aid of secondary sources, from the testimonial and the documentary, to the demonstrative and the expert. This caution does not relegate real evidence to a lower status, but exhorts the advocate to rely on various forms of evidence in proof at trial. Guns and other weaponry are a common form of real evidence, as portrayed in the photographic evidence below at Figures 2.1 through 2.4.

Real evidence reflects the reality of the case before the bar. Consider the extensive array of real evidence in a drug case. (See Figures 2.5 through 2.7.) The bare allegation by a police officer that a defendant took drugs will fall short of the necessary burden of proof. The drug itself is a more direct proof of the criminal act, or at least some proof of its existence, whether by trace, microscopic examination, or chemical evaluation. Similarly, in a burglary charge, a police investigator's allegation that a defendant used high-torque drill equipment to break

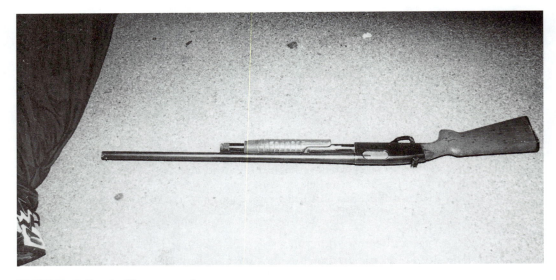

**FIGURE 2.1**   A rifle at a murder scene.

**FIGURE 2.2**   A broken knife found among bedsheets and clothing.

into a safe would be less influential in directing a juror's decision-making than the introduction of the actual tool.

An arson prosecutor depends heavily, if not primarily, on the demonstration of real evidence and its connection to criminality. The arson investigator looks for accelerants that intensify at the fire origination point. The collection and extraction of said evidence are a delicate exercise that requires not only skilled legal advocates, but also forensic specialists. Accelerants are real evidence; so, too, are fire patterns and chemical residues.[5]

In an auto negligence case, when an eyewitness asserts that the defendant's car came in contact with an injured victim, will the testimonial evidence be sufficient to prove contact or agency? Let's assume that a paint chip had, at the point of impact, been propelled onto the victim and was subsequently matched by comparative micrography. In the lab, the forensic specialist concluded that the paint chip on the victim matched the color and composition of the paint on the vehicle that was involved in this collision. Comparatively, which form of evidence tells a better story—the paint chip or the testimony of the witness?

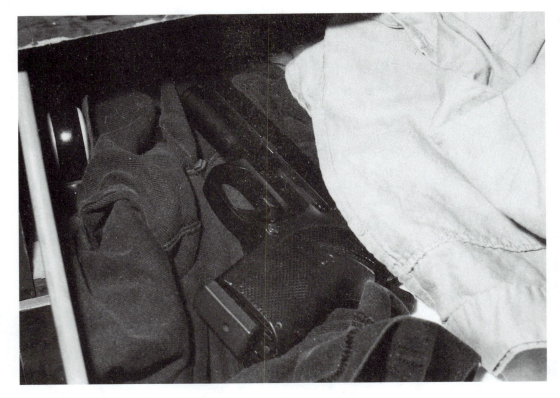

**FIGURE 2.3**    A handgun found during a search.

Another illustration is the comparison of typewriter faces in a case of consumer fraud, embezzlement, or civil conversion. A witness that simply testifies to the comparative similarities of the typefaces persuades less than the same witness armed with real evidence of the typefaces and the tests conducted. See Figure 2.8.[6] An analysis of glass fracture patterns, at Figure 2.9,[7] is also a real evidence exercise.

Whether used by investigators in a prosecutor's office or analyzed by a law firm's negligence team, the role that real evidence plays in litigation cannot be overemphasized. Cases that rely solely on secondary, circumstantial, and extraneous evidence generate healthy juror and judicial skepticism. Get the real evidence and combine it with sources that illuminate, elucidate, and make it live in the mind of the court or jury. Figures 2.10 through 2.13 illustrate several forms of real evidence that will need the assistance of secondary evidence.

As John Tarantino says in his masterful work, *Trial Evidence Foundations:*

Real evidence can have a very important effect on the trier of fact. It is something that can be seen, touched and, in some cases heard or smelled. Because of its appeal, it is necessary to master the elements of a foundation for its admission.[8]

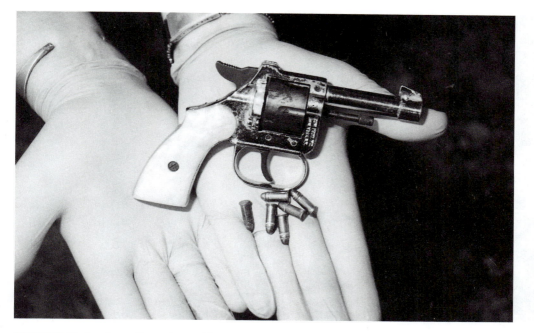

**FIGURE 2.4** A small revolver with ammunition.

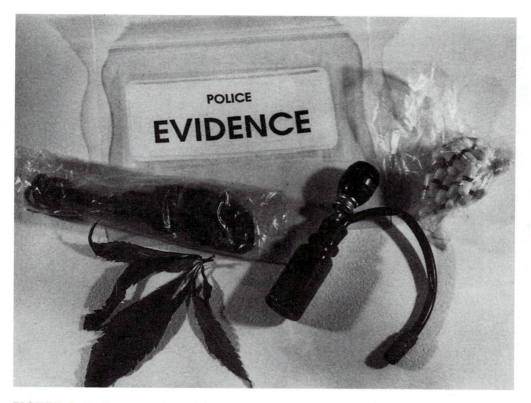

**FIGURE 2.5** Drug paraphernalia, marijuana, and prescription drugs seized as evidence.

**FIGURE 2.6**   Results of a drug seizure.

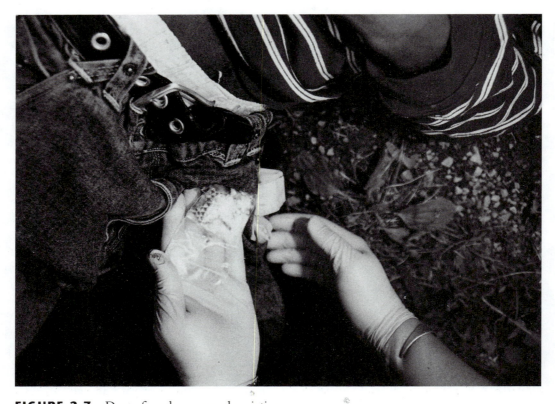

**FIGURE 2.7**   Drugs found on a murder victim.

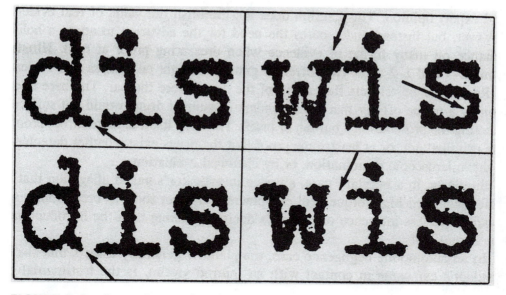

**FIGURE 2.8**    Comparing typefaces from two different typewriters.

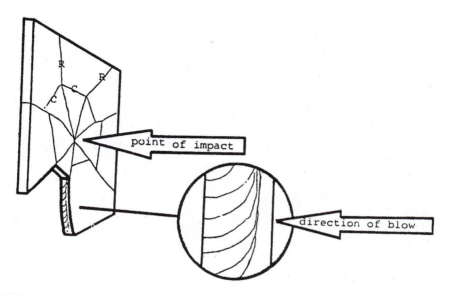

**FIGURE 2.9**    Glass fracture pattern analysic diagram.

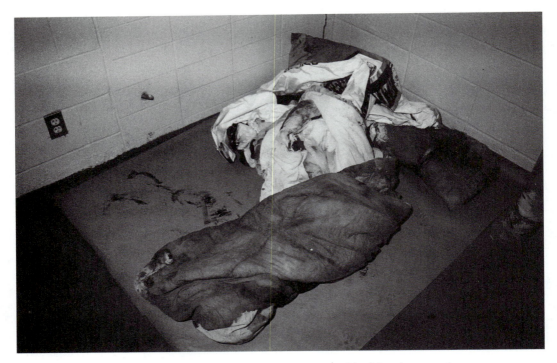

**FIGURE 2.10**   Photographic display of bloody clothing and bedding in a murder case.

**FIGURE 2.11**   Footprint imaging.

**FIGURE 2.12**  Forced entry point in burglary case.

**FIGURE 2.13**
Fingerprint lifted from gray duct tape.

## § 2.2 THE RELEVANCY OF REAL EVIDENCE

Real evidence, to be properly admissible, needs to be relevant, meaning evidence having any tendency to make the existence of any fact "that is of consequence to the determination of the action more probable or less probable than it would be without the evidence."[9] It is consequence that signifies relation. The evidence needs to relate to the matter at hand, that is, to be of consequence to the case presently litigated. In addition, in FRE Rule 402, relevant evidence is typecast as being generally admissible, with the contrary result accorded irrelevant evidence. FRE Rule 403 excludes relevant evidence "if its probative value is substantially outweighed by the danger of unfair prejudice, confusion of the issues, or misleading the juror, or by considerations of undue delay, waste of time, or needless presentation of cumulative evidence."[10]

To exemplify, review the essential elements of relevancy in *State v. Johnson,*[11] at Case Example 2.1, and *State v. Stone,*[12] at Case Example 2.2.

Is there a better form of evidence to prove a case of statutory rape? What other real evidence might be of use to the advocate of a claim? What about these real forms:

- Proof of penetration,
- Genital injury,
- Spermatozoa,
- Semen stains on underwear and/or other clothing, and
- Microscopic hairs and fibers.

Under the provisions of FRE Rules 401 and 403, each of these real forms of evidence would be relevant and readily admitted.

Real evidence, due to its proximity to truth and the reality of its subject matter, is usually deemed relevant. Dean Wigmore eloquently characterizes the judicial tendency of courts to admit it:

> [T]here is a general mental tendency, when a corporal object is produced as proving something, to assume, on sight of the object, all else that is implied in a case about it. The sight of it seems to prove all the rest. Thus, it is very easy for a jury, when witnesses speak of a horse being stolen from Doe by Roe, to understand, when Doe is proved to have lost the horse, that it still remains to be proved that Roe took it; the missing element can clearly be kept separate as an additional requirement. But if the witness to the theft were to have a horse brought in the courtroom and to point it out triumphantly, "If you doubt me, there is the very horse!" this would go a great way to persuade the jury of the rest of his assertion and to ignore the weaknesses of his evidence of Roe's complicity. The sight of the horse, corroborating in the flesh, as it were, a part of the witness' testimony, tends to verify the remainder.[13]

**CASE:** *State v. Johnson,* 316 Mo. 214, 234 S.W.2d 219 (1950).

**FACTS:** A charge of statutory rape was based upon the allegation that a 19-year-old man had sexual intercourse with a 15-year-old woman. As a result of the sexual intercourse, and subsequent sexual relations, a pregnancy occurred. As part of the state's case in chief, the prosecutor offered the baby as evidence for a comparative inspection for purposes of identifying the father. Note the direct examination conducted on the female victim.

   Q. And you testified that the baby was born of that intercourse?

   A. Yes.

   Q. Do you have that baby here today?

   A. Yes.

**BY COUNSEL:** If the court please, we would like to offer that baby in evidence for comparison in appearance between it and the alleged father.

**BY OPPOSING COUNSEL:** I object to the offering of the baby in evidence for comparison. The state alleges that the defendant is the father of it, and she alleges it is the result of the intercourse testified to here, and the defendant further objects for the reason that the child is now approximately one year old, and it is only being offered by the state to prejudice the jury, and it wouldn't shed any light on this case whatsoever at this time.

**THE COURT:** Under the plea of not guilty of the charge made, that has been held proper evidence. Overruled.

   Q. I will ask you if the baby you hold in your arms is the baby that was
      born as the result of the defendant?

   A. Yes.

**THE COURT:** Remove the cap.

   Q. Take the cap off and walk in front of the jury so they can observe the
      baby and don't make any comment. [Witness walking in front of the
      jury with baby in her arms.]

**QUESTIONS AND ISSUES:**

1. Do you think that a baby is real evidence?
2. Is it proper for the court to admit the baby as real evidence?
3. Is a baby, in the case of statutory rape, relevant evidence, that is, evidence having a tendency to make the existence of any fact that is of consequence more or less probable?
4. Even if the baby is relevant, is the introduction of the baby prejudicial or confusing?
5. How do you think the court resolved these questions?

**HOLDING:** The baby is not only real evidence, but relevant to a finding of paternity. The datedness of the case, circa 1950, belies modern scientific improvements in paternity and DNA analysis. In the case of statutory rape, a pregnancy likely indicates sexual intercourse, but cannot exclude any other feasible explanations, such as in vitro fertilization.

---

**CASE EXAMPLE 2.2**  *Relevancy*

**CASE:** *State v. Stone,* 240 N.C. 606, 83 S.E.2d 543 (1954).

**FACTS:** Defendant was convicted of assault with intent to commit rape and incest. On appeal, the defendant claimed that the rape complainant had testified that he had occasionally used prophylactics during sexual intercourse. Upon his arrest, the police found prophylactics in his billfold, which were offered and accepted by the court into evidence.

**QUESTIONS AND ISSUES:**

1. Is possession of prophylactics relevant in a charge of assault with intent to commit rape?
2. Does the existence of prophylactics within the wallet of a defendant tend to prove or disprove a fact or consequence?
3. Can it be argued that the admission of prophylactics can trigger undue prejudice?
4. How do you think the court resolved these questions?

**HOLDING:** The court reversed the conviction, stating that possession of prophylactics is irrelevant and does not tend to prove the defendant committed assault with intent to commit rape or incest.

---

In the absence of prejudice or bias, real evidence, whether a handgun or a blood sample, is approved depending on relevancy. In this legal environment, relevance is not a purely scientific exercise. Relevance consists of relational qualities, probability factors, the tendency to prove or disprove a specific fact or issue, and the contrast between tangential and central matters before the tribunal. Fundamentally, these questions determine whether evidence is relevant or not:

1. What is the offered evidence being used to show or demonstrate?
2. What is the material issue in this case?
3. Does the offered evidence establish or tend to establish the issues before the court?

From a judicial vantage point, relevancy is not a static standard, but one of both tradition and evolution. "Courts probably decide most relevance questions on the basis of (1) a 'feeling' about the offered evidence, and (2) subtle judicial precedent, if there is any. Judges sometimes have a feeling about the evidence and an intuitive reaction to it that is based on their experience, common sense, and a knowledge in the way the world turns."[14] Judgments concerning relevance should always be partisan to the laws of logic. As long as the proponent can demonstrate a nexus between the real evidence being offered and some significant issue before the court, a claim for admissibility is legitimate. Conceptually, relevancy is synonymous with neither sufficiency nor certainty. As the notes of the Advisory Committee to the Federal Rules of Evidence make clear:

> Relevancy is not an inherent characteristic of any item of evidence but exists only as a relation between an item of evidence and a matter properly provable in the case. Does the item of evidence tend to prove the matter sought to be proved? Whether the relationship exists depends upon principles evolved by experience or science, applied logically to the situation at hand.[15]

## § 2.3 THE AUTHENTICATION OF REAL EVIDENCE

In order for real evidence to be introduced, the proponent must lay a sufficient foundation and authenticate the evidence. Dean Wigmore classifies the requirements of authentication or identification as a condition precedent to the admissibility.[16] Meeting the requirements of authentication does not assure admissibility, since some other technical or substantive rule of evidence may bar admission, an example being hearsay. However, authentication encompasses these basic issues:

1. The real evidence is relevant and not to be excluded under theories of FRE Rule 403.

2. A witness can testify as to the unique and identifiable characteristics of that real evidence.

3. The witness can identify the proposed exhibit as that unique and identifiable real evidence.

4. The witness is able to identify the real evidence.

5. The witness can identify the real evidence as being in the same condition as it was when previously observed.

In Case Example 2.3, admission was possible only after authentication by a witness with personal knowledge.[17] When working with real evidence, it is necessary to find a suitable and capable authenticator.

Be mindful that most states have adopted procedural rules that can bypass authentication and identification requirements. Authentication is unnecessary when a pretrial agreement, admission, or stipulation from the opposing party has been approved by the court. See the examples in Forms 2.1 and 2.2.

Finally, be open and gracious with the opposition regarding the inspection rights of real evidence in one's possession. Discovery and disclosure rules are liberal in scope and decision. In criminal practice, constitutional issues may compel the discovery and disclosure of real evidence.

# CASE EXAMPLE 2.3    *Authentication*

**FACTS:** In a case of bank embezzlement, the prosecutor seeks to admit a series of memoranda or letters that show tampering with financial records by a former bank vice president. Following the courtroom formalities of marking and sharing a proposed exhibit with the court and opposing counsel, proponent's counsel seeks to introduce an actual original memorandum. One of the memoranda had been delivered to a witness, John Stevens, the bank president. Counsel examines the witness as follows:

Q. I will now present to you what has been marked as *Plaintiff's Exhibit 1* for identification and ask you to review it.

A. I have reviewed it.

Q. Have you ever seen *Exhibit 1* before?

A. Yes.

Q. When and under what circumstances?

A. I received it from the Vice President of Finance on May the 10th, 1992.

Q. Had you had any correspondence with the Vice President prior to that date?

A. Yes, the content of this letter had been discussed orally on other occasions.

Q. Was this letter a confirmation of previous conversations?

A. Yes.

Q. Are you familiar with the signature of the author of this letter, the Vice President?

A. Yes I am.

Q. Please look at the bottom of *Exhibit 1* and explain to the court and jury who that signature belongs to.

A. The Vice President.

Q. Has this letter been altered in any fashion or form since the date you received it?

A. No.

**QUESTION AND ISSUE:** Under this direct questioning, have authentication requirements been satisfied?

**HOLDING:** The real evidence is an original document authored by the alleged embezzler. The evidence will be accepted because the witness could identify and authenticate the signature and the content of the document. In a case of bank embezzlement, the real evidence would be admitted because

1. The exhibit is relevant;
2. The exhibit was identified as the same one in the case in question; and
3. A witness identified the real evidence as relevant to the case before the court and stated that the letter had not been altered and was substantially in the same condition as when previously observed.

It is stipulated by the parties hereto, through their respective attorneys of record, at the pretrial conference held on _____, 20_____, as follows:

1. That the following evidence for _____ is stipulated to:

   _____

2. That the judge appointed by the court may conduct such hearings and take such evidence and make such findings and report to the court as are usual and customary in such cases or as the court may direct in its order or reference.

3. That after hearing on the judge's findings and report, and making of such order based on said report as may be appropriate, the court may set this action for trial on the remaining issues at any time not less than _____ days after the hearing on said report.

Dated _____, 20_____


_____

[Signature]

**FORM 2.1**  Pretrial agreement on admissions.

It is hereby stipulated that all documents offered and admitted in evidence at the former and present trial of this case may be considered as offered and admitted at the retrial of the case, with the same force and effect as if the document gave testimony, subject to all objections and exceptions made by counsel to the admission of any such testimony as were made at the former trial.

Dated: _____, 20_____


_____

[Signatures and addresses]

**FORM 2.2**  Stipulation.

## § 2.4 REAL EVIDENCE IN THE CHAIN OF CUSTODY

Even if a piece of evidence is relevant, and does not foster substantial prejudice, undue delay, or waste, and can be properly identified and authenticated, its admission may still be barred or blocked because of a contaminated chain of custody. Chain of custody challenges implore the court to consider the unreliability of the proposed evidence due to its alteration. For example, opposing counsel might argue that the evidence proffered is not the evidence acquired initially or may allege that the evidence was switched or substituted. From another perspective, the chain of custody challenge can be upheld because of the evidence's poor packaging, maintenance, or preservation; inadequate refrigeration; or biological spoilization. With these conditions, the evidence is altered, changed, and thereby unacceptable.

The image of a chain is most appropriate, since any break in a chain or series of links on a chain eventually will result in the chain's destruction. By analogy, evidence with a checkered history, whether as to location or packaging, loses its inherent credibility. For this reason, the proponent of real evidence establishes that the condition of the real evidence being offered has remained basically unchanged—that it is substantially in the same condition as on the date of collection and has not been tampered with or suffered from unwarranted intrusion. Knowing the origin of any real evidence in question is a terminal practitioner concern. "It is the thing itself, and with it comes the tradition of the chain of custody."[18] James W. McElhaney provides a conceptional sequence to chain of custody analysis:

> To establish a proper chain you need to prove:
>
> - From whose custody the evidence is produced.
> - Who had custody of the evidence in a continuous chain back to the relevant time.
> - Is a chain of custody required to get real evidence admitted over the opponent's objection? Absolutely not. There is nothing magic about the chain of custody (although some judges do not understand that). It is simply circumstantial evidence of two facts:
>   - Identity. This is the real thing.
>   - No change. The evidence is in the same condition as when originally received.[19]

Opposing counsel challenging the quality and integrity of the real evidence will say not only that the evidence is contaminated, but also that it lacks a reliable historical record that assures its original state. Being responsive to the chain of custody argument safeguards the identity and the unencumbered state of evidence throughout its evidentiary life. "The relevant period for tracing the custody of physical evidence begins when the evidence is found at the crime scene and not when it leaves the hands of the accused."[20]

The chain of custody issue also embraces a constitutional dimension. The discovery and disclosure process, where defense and prosecution share most information prior to trial, mandates the automatic, compulsory disclosure of evidence exculpatory to a defendant. Labeled the *Brady doctrine*,[21] it requires prosecutors to disclose evidence that is favorable to and exonerative of a defendant. This theory is rooted in the U.S. Constitution's 6th Amendment's Confrontation clause and the Due Process portions of the 5th and 14th Amendments. By implication, destroyed or altered evidence not only violates the Due Process clauses, but also is so extreme a constitutional error that reversals of guilt are regularly witnessed. A corollary concern is an obligation to preserve and care for evidence that bears on critical facts in upcoming litigation. In *United States v. Bryant*,[22] a failure to safeguard evidence that may have been exculpatory to a particular defendant was deemed a constitutional error. The opinion held in part:

> It is most consistent with the purposes of [the *Brady doctrine*, Jencks Act, and Criminal Rule of Procedure 16] safeguards to hold that the duty of disclosure attaches in some form once the government first gathered and had taken possession of the evidence in question. Otherwise disclosure might be avoided by destroying the vital evidence before prosecution begins or before defendants hear of its existence. Hence, we hold that before a request for discovery has been made, the duty of disclosure is operative as a duty of preservation.[23]

Essentially, defendants in criminal cases have an implied right of preservation with respect to any form of real evidence, whether blood, drugs, urine, semen, or other forms of physical evidence.

At street level, chain of custody issues always involve real evidence. In DUI or DWI cases, the intoxicant frequently challenges Breathalyzer or other mechanical results that report intoxication levels. Defense counsel bases Breathalyzer litigation strategy on mechanical failure, maintenance of the measuring device, and a failure to replace the internal measuring ampoule. Similarly, defense counsel will frequently urge the court to disregard the results because the machine's maintenance and equipment logs are incomplete and manifest poor administrative practice. Famed attorney Jim D. Lovett of Texas, in his article *Defense on Charge of Driving While Intoxicated*,[24] issues excellent advice on the probability of breaks in the historical chain of evidence in DUI/DWI litigation:

> The classic chain of evidence problem in a driving while intoxicated case involves blood and urine samples taken by the police which must be conveyed in one

manner to a chemist. In such cases, the defense attorney should try to create a reasonable doubt in the minds of the jury as to its proper handling by emphasizing
how busy the prosecution chemist was and the possibility or human error.[25]

Prosecution of drug cases directly involves the chain of custody doctrine. Elic-
iting the testimony of police officers on the amount, condition, and original weight
of the drug seized is a frequent challenge to the chain of custody. Review the following sequence of cross-examination, the sole purpose being to undermine the integrity of the chain of custody.

Q. Officer Jones, in previous testimony you have indicated upon seizure of
drugs, after packaging, they were submitted to your forensic lab. Was this
correct?

A. Yes.

Q. Does your forensic laboratory have the capacity to store, safely and securely,
evidence for upcoming trials?

A. Yes. [Describes facility.]

Q. Is there a logging procedure?

A. Yes.

Q. Can you provide us with a copy of your signature on that log with the evidence in question?

A. Yes.

Q. Were you given a receipt?

A. Yes.

[Receipt is offered into evidence.]

Q. Officer, I now hand to you a package that is marked *Exhibit 9* for your
identification and ask that you review its contents.

A. Yes.

Q. Have you ever seen these items before?

A. Yes.

Q. Under what circumstances and conditions did you see this package and its
contents?

A. This package and contents were mailed to a government chemist. I see my
initials on the package, and the package number corresponds to the mail receipt that I have.

Q. Is this package in the same condition as the day you mailed it?

A. Absolutely, since the seal on the outside package is not broken. I had used an evidence tape which prevents premature opening.

Q. Did you receive a report back from the chemist who performed an examination on the contents?

A. Yes.

Q. I would like now to show you a document marked *Exhibit 10* for identification and ask you to review its contents.

A. Yes.

Q. Can I ask you the name of the document?

A. Yes, it's titled Forensic Lab Report.

Q. Can I ask you to look at the center of the page of this same exhibit and ask if you see the category at Number 9 called result?

A. Yes, I do.

Q. Are you familiar with what section 10 of this result means?

A. Yes, this is where the confirmation either affirmative or negative on drug content is made.

Q. Thank you very much.[26]

Chain of custody challenge is the surest path to debunking real evidence. Even if evidence is totally relevant, thoroughly unprejudicial, and procedurally authenticated, its admissibility is placed in question by the inference of a broken chain of custody. The Wisconsin Department of Justice's Crime Laboratory proposes an unrivaled suggestion regarding the protection of evidence and the custodial chain applicable in both criminal and civil litigation:

> In any criminal investigation the validity of information derived from examination of the physical evidence depends entirely upon the scrupulousness with which the evidence has been protected from contamination. If the evidence which has been submitted has been contaminated or is of uncertain origin, because of improper packaging or the introduction of extraneous materials into the crime scene, its value is almost entirely negated and no amount of laboratory work will be of any assistance. Therefore, it is of the greatest importance that the crime scene be protected from all intrusion of all extraneous factors until all physical evidence has been collected and that the evidence be recovered and packaged as outlined . . .[27]

## Packaging and Preservation of Evidence

Packaging and preservation of evidence, real or otherwise, are continuous responsibilities for the legal and justice practitioner. The techniques and methods

| Specimen | Standard | Evidence | Send By | Identification | Wrapping and Packaging | Remarks |
|---|---|---|---|---|---|---|
| Blood:<br>1. Liquid Known Samples. | One tube each (Sterile) 5cc–10cc blood only. No preservatives. | All | Registered mail. | Use adhesive tape on outside of test tube. Name of donor, date taken, doctor's name, name or initial of investigator. | Wrap in cotton, soft paper. Place in mailing tube or suitable mailing carton. | Submit immediately. Don't hold awaiting additional items for comparison. Keep under refrigeration, *not* freezing, until mailing. *No* refrigerants and/or dry ice should be added to sample during transit. Fragile label. |
| 2. Small quantities:<br>a. Liquid Questioned Samples. | | All | Registered mail. | Same as above. | Same as above. | If unable to expeditiously furnish sample allow to dry thoroughly on a nonporous surface, and scrape off; or collect by using eye dropper or clean spoon, transfer to nonporous surface and let dry; or absorb in sterile gauze and dry. |

**FIGURE 2.14** Packaging for various blood types as suggested by the U.S. Department of Justice.

**FIGURE 2.15** Handgun (Smith & Wesson Model 38 "Bodyguard") sealed in evidence bag.

employed largely depend on the type of evidence in question. The U. S. Department of Justice's, *Handbook of Forensic Science,*[28] lists suitable forms of packaging for the various blood types. See Figure 2.14.[29] Other examples of representative packaging are shown in Figure 2.15.

Tags for evidence identification and preservation are another crucial tool for justice professionals. See Figures 2.16, 2.17, and 2.18.[30] See Appendix A for a list of evidence supply companies.

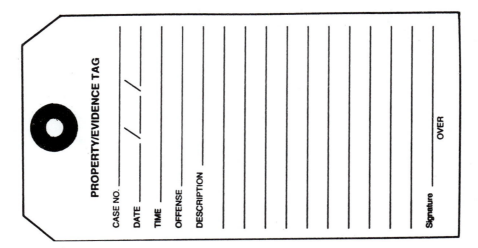

**EVIDENCE**

Case No. _____

☐ TO BE TESTED FOR DNA
☐ TO BE TESTED FOR FINGERPRINTS
☐ HANDLE WITH CARE
☐ UNPROCESSED EVIDENCE
☐ DO NOT HANDLE
☐ OTHER _____

Place evidence found _____
_____ date & time _____

Victim _____
Complainant _____
_____

Department                                    Signature, Rank

FORM E-TAG25  G.A. THOMPSON CO.  P.O. BOX 64681  DALLAS, TX 75206

**MISCELLANEOUS PROPERTY IDENTIFICATION**

☐ SAFEKEEPING          ☐ LOST & FOUND          ☐ OTHER

Description of item _____

Received from _____ Owned by (if known)_____

Address _____ Phone _____

Where item recovered/found _____
_____

Date & Time Received _____

Received by _____
                    Dept.                    Signature, Rank

FORM P-TAG25  G.A. THOMPSON CO.  BOX 64681  DALLAS, TX 75206

PROPERTY/EVIDENCE TAG

CASE NO.
DATE / /
TIME
OFFENSE
DESCRIPTION

Signature

OVER

**FIGURE 2.16** Three evidence tags.

62

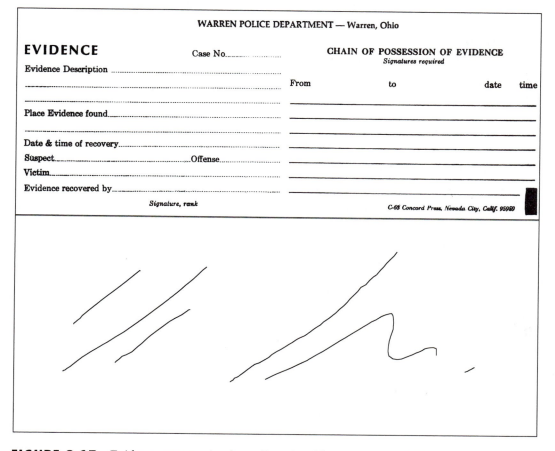

**WARREN POLICE DEPARTMENT — Warren, Ohio**

**EVIDENCE**  Case No.................. ...............

Evidence Description ..................................................................

----------------------------------------------------------------------------

----------------------------------------------------------------------------

Place Evidence found..........................................................

----------------------------------------------------------------------------

Date & time of recovery.......................................................

Suspect....................................................Offense....................

Victim..............................................................................

Evidence recovered by.........................................

*Signature, rank*

**CHAIN OF POSSESSION OF EVIDENCE**
*Signatures required*

| From | to | date | time |
|------|-----|------|------|

*C-63 Concord Press, Nevada City, Calif. 95959*

**FIGURE 2.17**  Evidence preservation bags. (Reprinted by permission of Concord Press.)

GRAYS HARBOR COUNTY SHERIFF'S DEPARTMENT

# EVIDENCE
Case No._____

Evidence Description _____

_____

Place Evidence found_____

_____

Date & time of recovery_____

Suspect_____Offense_____

Victim_____

Evidence recovered by_____
*Signature, rank*

### CHAIN OF POSSESSION OF EVIDENCE
*Signatures required*

| From | to | date | time |
|------|-----|------|------|

Item 60 Concord Press.    Nevada City, Calif. 95959

**FIGURE 2.17** *Continued*

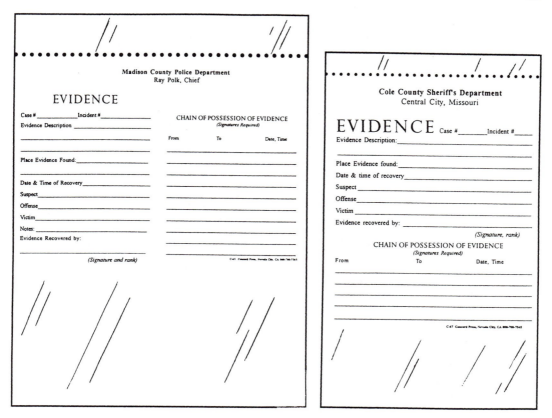

**FIGURE 2.18** Evidence preservation bags. (Reprinted by permission of Concord Press.)

## § 2.5 PRACTICE POINTERS ON REAL EVIDENCE

To ensure the integrity of real evidence and an unimpeachable chain of custody, tracking documentation is mandatory. A log that chronologically tabulates the evidence's time and date of admission, as well as its temporary release times, should be adopted. See Form 2.3. Use receipts to track the whereabouts of evidence. See Form 2.4. An exhibit list serves as a documentary catalog and tracing device for real evidence. See Form 2.5.[31]

**EVIDENCE LOG**

PAGE ——— OF ———

VICTIM—

CRIME (S)—

AUTHORITY—

FILE OR INVESTIGATION NO. ———

DATE—

| Item Number | Description of Items | Where found | Found by Whom | Date & Time | Turned Over to & Date (Lab #) |
|---|---|---|---|---|---|
| | | | | | |
| | | | | | |
| | | | | | |
| | | | | | |
| | | | | | |
| | | | | | |
| | | | | | |
| | | | | | |
| | | | | | |
| | | | | | |
| | | | | | |
| | | | | | |
| | | | | | |

**FORM 2.3**  A tool to track chain of custody.

**PROSECUTOR'S OFFICE
EVIDENCE RECEIPT**

Investigator's Name _____ File No. _____
(Signature)

Received from _____ Log No. _____
(Signature)

Date and Time Received _____ Location _____

Owner's Name and Address _____

| Item No. | Description of Item |
|----------|---------------------|
|          |                     |

**Relinquished by** _____ **Date** _____

**Received by** _____ **Date** _____

**FORM 2.4** Track the movement of evidence with receipts.

```
┌─────────────────────────────────────────────────────────────────┐
│                    ┌──────────────────────────────────┐         │
│                    │                                   │         │
│                    │          Name of Client           │         │
│                    │                                   │         │
│                    └──────────────────────────────────┘         │
│                                                                  │
│                        PLAINTIFF'S EXHIBITS                      │
│                                                                  │
│   offer      rec'd      no.                 description          │
│                                                                  │
│   ─────      ─────     ─────    ────────────────────────────     │
│                                                                  │
│   ─────      ─────     ─────    ────────────────────────────     │
│                                                                  │
│   ─────      ─────     ─────    ────────────────────────────     │
│                                                                  │
│   ─────      ─────     ─────    ────────────────────────────     │
│                                                                  │
│   ─────      ─────     ─────    ────────────────────────────     │
│                                                                  │
│   ─────      ─────     ─────    ────────────────────────────     │
│                                                                  │
│   ─────      ─────     ─────    ────────────────────────────     │
│                                                                  │
│   ─────      ─────     ─────    ────────────────────────────     │
│                                                                  │
│   ─────      ─────     ─────    ────────────────────────────     │
│                                                                  │
│   ─────      ─────     ─────    ────────────────────────────     │
│                                                                  │
│   ─────      ─────     ─────    ────────────────────────────     │
│                                                                  │
│   ─────      ─────     ─────    ────────────────────────────     │
│                                                                  │
│   ─────      ─────     ─────    ────────────────────────────     │
│                                                                  │
│   ─────      ─────     ─────    ────────────────────────────     │
│                                                                  │
└─────────────────────────────────────────────────────────────────┘
```

**FORM 2.5**   List exhibits for use at trial.

## § 2.6 SUMMARY

Appreciating the nature and utility of real evidence in litigation is the primary aim of this chapter. Analysis of the rules of admissibility in the offering of real evidence, the notion of relevancy, the technical requirements of authentication and identification, and chain of custody challenges were fully covered. Forms, checklists, and other tracking devices were included as tactical aids for justice professionals.

## *Notes*

1. MICHAEL GRAHAM, Evidence Text, Rules, Illustrations and Problems 419 (1983).

2. Ed. Shipp et al., *Effects of Argon Laser Light, Alternate Source Light, and Cyanoacrylate Fuming on DNA Typing of Human Bloodstains,* 38 J. Forensic Sci. 84 (1993).

3. Deborah L. Fisher et al, *Extraction, Evaluation, and Amplification of DNA from Decalcified and Undecalcified United States Civil War Bone,* 38 J. Forensic Sci. 60 (1993).

4. JOHN H. WIGMORE, Evidence 150 (1972).

5. Edward Imwinkelreid, as an example, portrays arson evidence extraction techniques: "One extraction methodology is immiscible phase flotation. The analyst soaks the fire scene debris in water and the accelerant then floats to the top of the water. However, this method often yields a poor recovery of accelerant; the concentration of the accelerant must be high for this procedure to yield an adequate sample for subsequent testing." Edward J. Imwinkelried, *Forensic Science: Forensic Evidence in Arson Cases: Part II,* 29 Crim. L. Bull. 70, 71–72 (1993).

6. WISCONSIN DEPARTMENT OF JUSTICE, Criminal Investigation and Physical Evidence Handbook 164 (1987).

7. U.S. DEPARTMENT OF JUSTICE, Handbook of Forensic Science 46 (1981).

8. JOHN TARANTINO, Trial Evidence Foundation 5–23 (1987).

9. Fed. R. Evid. 401.

10. Fed. R. Evid. 403.

11. 316 Mo. 214, 234 S.W.2d 219 (1950).

12. 240 N.C. 606, 83 S.E.2d 543 (1954).

13. JOHN H. WIGMORE, Evidence 704 (1978).

14. JOHN WALTZ, Criminal Evidence 51 (1975).

15. Fed. R. Evid. 401 advisory committee's notes.

16. *See* WIGMORE, *supra* note 4, at 150.

17. GRAHAM, *supra* note 1, at 420.

18. James W. McElhaney, *Proving Your Evidence Is Genuine,* 79 A.B.A. J. 96, 98 (1993).

19. *Id.*

20. MARK GREENBERG & ANTHONY BOCCHINO, Pennsylvania Evidence Objections and Responses 12–13 (1983).

21. Brady v. Maryland, 373 U.S. 83 (1963).

22. 439 F.2d 642 (D.C. Cir.), *aff'd on remand,* 448 F.2d 1182 (D.C. Cir. 1971).

23. *Id.* at 651

24. Jim D. Lovett, *Defense on Charge of Driving While Intoxicated,* 19 Am. Jur. Trials 123, 227 (1972).

25. *Id.*

26. *See also* Donald Cantor & Harry Hultgren, *Defense of Narcotic Cases,* 8 Am. Jur. Trials 573 (1965).

27. WISCONSIN DEPARTMENT OF JUSTICE, *supra* note 6, at 12.

28. U.S. DEPARTMENT OF JUSTICE, *supra* note 7, at 114.

29. *Id.* at 114–115.

30. CONCORD PRESS, Nevada City, Ca. 95959. See Catalog Numbers C-65 and C-67.

31. VERNE LAWYER, Trial by Notebook, A System of Trial Organization for the Modern Plaintiff's Attorney 14 (1982).

# CHAPTER 3

# *Demonstrative Evidence*

## § 3.1 THE NATURE OF DEMONSTRATIVE EVIDENCE

From its Latin derivative, *demonstro,* meaning "to show" or "to manifest," demonstrative evidence presents itself as neither the real thing nor an alternate form, but rather as a substitute form of evidence that educates the court, jury, and litigants. Demonstrative evidence amplifies the *real* evidence in question. Types of demonstrative evidence are presented at Figure 3.1.[1]

Real evidence, of course, is the thing itself (i.e., the gun, the blood, etc.). The *Demonstrative* is the Real's representation. Since the real is often microscopically unwieldy, and sometimes even too gruesome for the average person to contend with, a demonstration of said evidence is judicious. A corpse in a murder case, surely real evidence, is not palatable for the average person. A real autopsy, with a cutup cadaver that edifies the cause of death, may be evidentially accurate, but is too offensive for the court's chief players. Demonstrative evidence can present this same autopsy by less intrusive means, such as photographs, charts, diagrams, and medical models. Demonstrative evidence is a tool utilized to unfold the real.

In a case of product liability, how would plaintiff's attorney demonstrate the injuries caused by a defective glass windshield? If the glass is already shattered, possibly in hundreds of pieces, how does one reconstruct the real? How does a bag or box of broken shards of glass explain the defect? In this specific circumstance, demonstrative evidence effectively "illustrate[s] the difference between crystal glass and safety

| Models | Scale models, working or mechanical models, architectural models |
| Videotapes | "Day in the life," television news clips, documentaries |
| Computers | Graphics, reconstructions, simulations |
| Drawings | Medical/anatomical, technical/architectural, perspective, isometric, plan views, cartography |
| Medical | Skeletal preparations, anatomical charts, anatomical models |
| Experiments | Experiments and tests made under conditions and circumstances similar to those existing at the time of the incident in question |
| The View | Depiction of the scene involved in the case and the layout thereof |
| Photography | Computer-enhanced photographics, enlargements, vertical/fixed-wing aerial, oblique, slides-vuegraphs, motion pictures, stills, x-ray films, thermograms, human body, machinery and equipment |
| Charts | Two-dimensional displays, velcro exhibits, magnetic exhibits, graphs, diagrams, overlays and cells, titles, color for emphasis |

**FIGURE 3.1**   Types of demonstrative evidence. (JOAN M. BROVINS & THOMAS OEHMKE, The Trial Practice Guide: Strategies, Systems and Procedures for the Attorney 166 (1992). Copyright the American Bar Association. All rights reserved. Reprinted by permission.)

glass, or between tempered glass and wired glass, by bringing into court two panes of the same size and thickness and actually demonstrating the marked difference in their breaking propensities."[2]

Complementing the real is what demonstrative evidence is all about. Therefore, to prove the factual reality of stab wounds in the deceased, a secondary, demonstrative exhibition of said injuries, namely, photographs, is more instructive than the actual exhibition of the deceased or injured.

In its most favorable light, demonstrative evidence is a form of secondary reality that illustrates the actual evidence under legal scrutiny. Demonstrative evidence elucidates, clarifies, and is "evidence employed solely for illustrative purposes as distinguishing from substantive evidence."[3] Neither the Federal Rules of Evidence nor the Revised Uniform Rules of Evidence delineates a precise definition of what demonstrative evidence is. At best, the concept is defined inferentially. Peripherally addressing real and demonstrative evidence, FRE Rule 401 states that the evidence must be relevant—that it must have a "tendency to make the existence of any fact that is of consequence to the determination of the action more probable or less probable than it would be without the evidence."[4] Accompanying this is FRE Rule 403, which excludes evidence, even the demonstrative, "if its probative value is substantially outweighed by the danger of unfair prejudice, confusion of the issues, or misleading the jury, or by considerations of undue delay, waste of time, or needless presentation of cumulative evidence."[5]

Typically, courts evaluate whether the evidence offered is prone to generate prejudicial or biased thinking. To exemplify, apply FRE Rule 403 to a series of color autopsy photographs. Admittedly, autopsy photographs are, by nature of their content, grisly affairs. Certainly, these types of photographs are relevant and probative.

Despite achieving these evidentiary benchmarks, can this same evidence be excluded due to its gruesome and grisly content? The answer depends on the circumstances and the rationale of usage. If the photographic exhibits are employed to prove the cause of death or the direction of a projectile or are offered in response to an affirmative defense, such as self-defense or provocation, admission is sensible. However, if submitted to arouse and enrage the passions of the jury, rejection of said evidence, despite its relevance, materiality, and probativeness, is wise.

The use of and dependency on demonstrative evidence are now well established. Traditional litigation heavily relies upon it. Dean Charles T. McCormick's treatise on evidence captures this reliance:

> It is today increasingly common to encounter the offer of tangible items that are not contented themselves to have played a part in the history of the case, but which are instead tendered for the purpose of rendering other evidence more comprehensible to the trier of fact. Examples of types of items frequently offered for purposes of illustration and clarification include models, maps, photographs, charts, and drawings. If an article is offered for these purposes, rather than as real or original evidence, its specific identity or source is generally of no significance whatever. Instead the theory justifying admission of these exhibits requires only that the item be sufficiently explanatory or illustrative of relevant testimony in the case to be of potential help to the trier of fact.[6]

Useful demonstrative evidence aids the trier of fact in discerning the truth. It simplifies complex problems and convincingly portrays events.

Criminal and civil litigators have come to depend upon the appeal of demonstrative evidence to multiple sensory capacities. The great trial lawyer Melvin Belli finds demonstrative evidence indispensable:

> To say that demonstrative evidence is available in every case, to either the plaintiff or defendant's side, is merely to repeat that, in the trial of a lawsuit there is
>
> (1) the most dramatic way to try the case, and
> (2) there are more senses which to appeal [to] than the sense of hearing alone.[7]

In the sensory realm, the *hearing* of testimony has historically been the primary experience for juror and judge. Veteran litigators know that any attention span based on such a singular sensory experience is limited. Demonstrative evidence enlists "so many other sensory capabilities and is a powerful tool in courtroom communication and persuasion, and successful trial teams recognize that some form of demonstrative evidence is appropriate in almost every case."[8]

In the courtroom, demonstrative evidence amplifies, complements, and makes discernible the often boring or overly complex reality. For example, expert testimony regarding DNA, the genetic code system that supposedly matches itself to a singular individual, much like a molecular fingerprint, is tough to comprehend without demonstrative assistance. Testimony by itself would be sterile and incomprehensible. Look at the DNA direct examination below.

Q. Now, Dr. Gilligan, what are the results of your DNA testing?

A. My results confirm a genetic coding that is unique to the defendant.

Q. Please advise the court how the genetic coding matches the defendant?

A. By the complementary strands which match the strands of affinity.

Few can comprehend this testimonial subject matter. Accordingly, the propounder of sophisticated evidence should illustrate the reality by demonstrative means. In this scenario, the expert can deliver testimony, yet point out—more figuratively— these technical findings. How the evidence tells its story should concern every justice practitioner.[9]

Testimony alone does not achieve the complete education of the jury. Effective advocacy relies upon more than hearing, since understanding is aided by other senses, particularly sight, which lights up the mind. Newton Gresham's sterling contribution to the *Trials* series indicates that "[s]uccessful advocacy is largely the use of the teaching and explaining process, and it is generally easier to learn through the eyes than through the ear. . . ."[10]

Granting demonstrative evidence the due it deserves should lead to its unbridled use. The time and expense involved in designing such exhibits, the complications of the subject matter, and the need for expert witnesses to testify to content are all tactical considerations worth remembering.[11] For now, the task is to enumerate the traditional means of demonstrating the underlying real evidence.

## § 3.2 PHOTOGRAPHIC EVIDENCE

While it may be a cliche to state "A picture is worth a thousand words," it is undeniably true. For example, an allegation of adultery in a divorce proceeding is not as persuasively proven by mere testimony. Even more compelling is such testimony when coupled with photographic evidence. Aside from conveying a realistic portrait to a jury, photographic exhibitions unquestionably help witnesses who testify or experts who expound upon a scientific finding. Ultimately, photographic evidence corroborates facts within the testimony. The inadequacy of pure, unaided testimony is seen in many a personal injury action. The bald allegation of assault without confirming photographic support is a weak, flawed presentation. Does the testimony below do the job? Or would a picture better describe the contents?

He hit me hard, smashing my face with a beer mug. The fractures were on the top of my eye. The damage knocked me out.

Photographs like the ones that would be utilized in the above example amply demonstrate this gruesome reality. Words do not always adequately express the trauma.

Photographs, motion pictures, and videotapes are generally admissible. Legal challenges are seldom made on scientific grounds, since the field of photography and its related disciplines have long been recognized. Challenges are usually procedural, based more on the technique and methodology employed, but questions of relevancy still exist in the evidentiary arena. In the treatise *Scott on Photographic Evidence,* the standard of relevancy is met if the following occur:

1. Photographic evidence is admissible whenever it has a reasonable tendency to prove some material fact in issue.

2. Photographic evidence is admissible whenever it appears that it would have been competent for the trier of fact, court or jury, to have viewed or examined the subject of the pictures at the time they were taken had it been practical for them to do so at that time.

3. Photographic evidence is admissible whenever it assists the trier of fact, court, or jury, in understanding the case.

4. Photographic evidence is admissible as corroboration evidence of oral testimony or other evidence in both criminal and civil cases.

5. Photographic evidence which tends to disprove the testimony of a witness is admissible to contradict or impeach him.

6. Photographic evidence is admissible when it assists a witness in illustrating or explaining his testimony.[12]

See Case Example 3.1.

---

**CASE EXAMPLE 3.1**  **Demonstrative Evidence— Photographs**

**CASE:** *State v. Poe,* 21 Utah 2d 113, 441 P.2d 512, *appeal after remand,* 24 Utah 2d 355, 471 P.2d 870 (1970).

**FACTS:** Defendant Roy Lee Poe was convicted of first-degree murder. The sentence pronounced by the court was death. Defendant's appeal is primarily based on the trial court's admission of color slides that portrayed the autopsy of his murder victim. The photographic content was described by the court as follows:

> To describe them as being gruesome would be a gross understatement. One of them, for example, depicted the deceased's head showing the base of the skull after the skull cap and brain had been removed by the pathologist. The skin is peeled over the edge of the skull showing the empty brain cavity. Another is a top view of the empty cavity. They would have been gruesome in black and white but the color accentuated the gruesomeness.

**QUESTION AND ISSUE:** Despite relevancy, did the admission of said pictures cause prejudice in the juror analysis due to the inflammatory content?

**HOLDING:** The court ruled that the pictures should have been denied admission.

As with all types of demonstrative evidence, photography is received positively if its exhibition is helpful to the trier of fact in determining specific facts and issues:

> Photographs of persons, things, and places, when duly verified and shown by extrinsic evidence to be faithful representations of the subjects as of the time in question, are admissible in evidence, as aids to the jury in arriving at an understanding of the evidence, the situation or the condition of objects or premises, the circumstances of an accident, or the condition or identity of a person when any such matter is relevant to the issues being litigated.[13]

Examine the photographs in Figures 3.2 and 3.3. Do words adequately describe the damage caused by a violent accident (at Figure 3.2) or the path of a projectile in a murder case where the bullet traveled into the attic (at Figure 3.3)?

FRE Rule 1001 defines a photograph as a still work, x-ray film, videotape, or motion picture.[14] Within the same rule, the original of any photograph includes "the negative or any print therefrom."[15] Negatives should be made available for the

**FIGURE 3.2**   Photographic evidence of front-end collision.

**FIGURE 3.3** Path of a projectile.

opposing party's inspection, as well as the court's review. In order to be admitted, the photograph must

1. Be relevant,
2. Be an aid to the jury and the court, and
3. Be authenticated and supported by testimonial means.

## Laying the Foundation for a Photograph: Authentication

If a photographic exhibit is relevant, the advocate takes steps to lay a proper foundation for the exhibit's admission. "A foundation is laid for a still photograph or motion picture through testimony of any person or group of persons with personal knowledge, at a time relevant to the issues, of the subject matter depicted in the photograph."[16]

   Ponder the following before proceeding with the photo's usage:

1. Is there a witness who is familiar with the event or subject matter of the photo that is depicted?
2. Can that same witness explain in a meaningful way how he or she is familiar?
3. Can the witness intelligently identify the content of the photo?
4. Is the photo, in the witness's view, a fair and accurate depiction?

   Reflect on a case of arson. While testimony extensively covers the costs of the arson damage, the fire marshal's report, and assorted investigative processes, the prosecutor wishes to photographically portray the arson. View the photographs from an arson case in Figures 3.4 and 3.5. Who could attest to the content and accuracy of these photographs?

- A photographer?
- A crime scene investigator?

**FIGURE 3.4**   Firefighters can properly authenticate a photograph due to their presence.

**FIGURE 3.5**   Photograph of arson fire.

- An eyewitness?
- The owner of the property?
- A neighbor?
- A police officer?
- An employee?

Depending upon the experience of any of the above, all potentially can authenticate the content of the photograph.

The photograph, as graphically demonstrative as it is, cannot exist on its own—it needs a party to authenticate its subject matter. Mark Dombroff, a national expert on evidence law, gives wise advice when calling upon photographic users to establish the foundation:

In order to lay a foundation properly one must:

1.  call witnesses who will verify the photographs,
2.  have the photographs marked for identification by the clerk,

3.  if not already done, show the photograph to opposing counsel,

4.  lay a foundation by establishing the familiarity of the witness with the thing the photograph depicts.[17]

The authentication of each photograph should be conducted as follows:

Q. Mr. Doe, are you familiar with the subject matter?

A. Yes.

Q. Are you familiar with how it looked on [date]?

A. Yes.

> *Step 1.* Have the exhibit marked.
> *Step 2.* Show the exhibit to opposing counsel.
> *Step 3.* Ask the Court's permission to approach the witness.
> *Step 4.* Show the exhibit to the witness.
> *Step 5.* Elicit testimony on exhibit.

Q. I show you Plaintiff's Exhibit 1 for identification. Is this photograph a reasonably accurate representation of the [subject matter] as it existed on [date]?

A. Yes, sir, I'd say it is.

Q. Will this photograph help you in explaining your testimony to the jury?

A. I think so.

> *Step 6.* Move for admission of the exhibit into evidence.
> *Step 7.* Have the identification symbol struck.
> *Step 8.* Obtain permission to publish the exhibit to the jury.
> *Step 9.* Publish the exhibit.[18]

## Legal Challenges to Photographic Evidence

Photographic materials used during the investigative process are obviously not subject to the same level of scrutiny as at trial. At trial, once can expect legal challenges to arise on many fronts.

***Gruesome Content.*** The appellate courts are replete with cases involving gruesome photographic content, which is unsettling to the average person. Consider the case of *People v. Hoffman,*[19] where a court was confronted with pictures of a victim whose genitals were amputated and thereafter stuffed in his mouth, a tactic often employed by organized crime hitmen. If the trial judge has discretion to admit photographs such as these, how does the judge balance the competing interests of probativeness and prejudice? It is not always easy to resolve. Horrific pictures are not necessarily bad evidence. Gruesomeness reflects a distasteful reality, and in the absence of other suitable proof, pictures of amputation, dismemberment, and other severe injuries will never be comfortable coverages. Trial judges should not sanitize reality to the degree it becomes inaccurate, but on the other hand, they have certain evidentiary gatekeeping responsibilities. Prejudicial effect should not give way to evidentiary fantasy. Dombroff eloquently instructs practitioners on the nature of prejudicial impact:

> Demonstrative evidence, a powerful persuasive tool, has the capability of being highly prejudicial. The word *prejudicial*, however, is not synonymous with inadmissible. As used in this context, prejudicial means that the evidence is meant to persuade the trier of fact in favor of the side making [an] offer. Accordingly, the fact that the word prejudicial is associated with a particular piece of evidence is in itself of no significance.[20]

For a few advocates, any restriction on admission is improper, especially in criminal litigation. Criminal conduct is a reality fraught with gruesomeness. See Figure 3.6. As the court stated in *State v. Seehan,*[21] evidence of this nature tends to be gruesome because murder is gruesome. Similarly, in *State v. Jackson,*[22] the court exhibited little empathy to a defendant's appeal for the exclusion of said photographs, by stating: "If an accused does not wish the jury to see the blood which is criminal and has caused to flood, then he choose some method other than bloodshedding to commit his murder."[23]

Civil libertarians cringe at this form of hard-line, victim-oriented reasoning, but the suggestion is instructive. Gruesome fact patterns produce gruesome picto-

**FIGURE 3.6**
Detached finger with ring in a murder case.

rial displays. The question becomes not whether gruesome evidence is possible in any context, but whether the same evidentiary result can be achieved employing it. When mainstream television and news organizations rarely flinch at the presentation of the grotesque and the appalling, the gruesomeness doctrine may have lived out its useful life. In *People v. Long,*[24] the court poignantly addresses the modern insensibility of this rule.

**FIGURE 3.7**   A double-exposed photograph.

A jury is not some kind of dithering nincompoop, brought in from never-never land and exposed to the harsh realities of life for the first time in the jury box. There is nothing magical about being a member of the bench or bar which makes these individuals capable of dispassionately evaluating gruesome testimony. . . . Jurors are our peers, often as well educated, as well balanced, as stable, as experienced in the realities of life as the holders of law degrees. The average juror is well able to stomach the unpleasantness of exposure to the facts of a murder without being unduly influenced. The supposed influence on jurors of allegedly gruesome or inflammatory pictures exists more in the imaginations of judges and lawyers than in reality.[25]

***Tampering/Alteration.*** The entire darkroom process is replete with opportunities to alter, tamper with, and modify photographic evidence. An image can be reversed, lightened, darkened, and made coarser or harsher by the development process. The image can also be double exposed while being photographed. See Figure 3.7.

Even with the most rudimentary understanding of the photographic and development processes, it is amazing how readily photographic evidence is admitted. "Although photographic evidence is an asset to the adept trial lawyer neither courts nor lawyers fully understand the capacity of photographic evidence for deception and improper influence."[26] Commencing with the subject matter of the photographic display and the photographic locations, to the intricacies of the darkroom, development process, and artistic imagery, photos can be altered without much intentionality. Add to this lens variations, camera styling, film, content of the developer, angle, lighting, camera manufacturer, focal lengths, length of exposure, and speed, it is frankly astounding that more objections are not upheld.

Figures 3.8 and 3.9 illustrate how deceptive focal lengths can be. So subtle are changes in lighting that they seem to produce different effects and results. Other variables influencing the photographic result are film types and lens filters, improper exposure, reversing of negatives, retouching, and other chemical influences. In truth, photography is a form of artistry subject to the moods of the artist.[27]

The potential for alterations is as varied as the chemical and human processes involved in photography. Even the layman experiences the wide differentiation of colors, lighting, and background when 35 millimeter pictures are developed at different locations. Photographic results markedly differ in color, brightness levels, heights, depths, distances, omissions of scene due to focal point, and overall projection. Reverse negatives are commonly witnessed. See Figure 3.10.

Although its reputation and general usage are formidable,

photographic evidence has numerous potential deficiencies that affect not only its admissibility, but also its evidentiary weight. Variations of lenses and camera position can render a photograph dangerously deceptive. Other variables such as lighting, film type, lens filters, camera quality, exposure, development techniques, and perceptional errors, can also render a photograph misleading.[28]

**FIGURE 3.8**   Focal lengths can be deceiving.

***Chain of Custody.***   Be sure the photographer and the photographic process have a clear-cut, impeccable chain of custody. By asserting a break in the chain, the advocate implies that the display has been altered or tampered with. A parallel argument may be that the photograph being offered into evidence could not be accounted for, for a certain period of time and, thus, had been switched with another. From another angle, the challenger to a photograph may argue that the photograph being offered does not fairly or accurately portray the condition, person, or location in question because it was taken at a time previous to the

**FIGURE 3.9** Would the damage appear as devastating from a different position?

**FIGURE 3.10** Reverse negative.

event or subject matter before the court. The justice operative is well advised to track, log, and meticulously describe case photographs. Use a photo data tracking record that records scene or object, place, date, distance from named object, direction the camera was pointed, picture number, and development history. See Form 3.1.

***The Silent Witness Theory.*** In an age when mechanical devices perform surveillance and other automatic security systems track movements, the traditional precepts of photography are being tested, specifically the identification requirements. Assume a customer writes a check at a local store and, as part of the check validation process, stands in front of a regiscope, which takes a picture. So automatic is the equipment (the regiscope) and so unaware is the operator of its target that the personal knowledge of authentication is lacking. Who confirms that the photograph from the surveillance camera, regiscope, ATM machine, or other mechanical device is a fair and accurate representation? Certainly, a witness can corroborate the results, but in most of these cases, no one actually witnesses or remembers the events. The case of Rodney King explains the phenomenon. Assume that the alleged beating of Rodney King by police officers had been taped by a bank surveillance camera in the parking lot. Assume that there were no other witnesses to the event outside of the police officers who refused to testify. Would an objection be upheld due to a lack of identification and authentication under traditional rules?

Recognizing the anomaly that would result, some courts permit the admission of a bank's surveillance pictures, ATM photographs or videotapes, and regiscope pictures, while foregoing these historical requirements. Under a theory of recent popularity, known as the *silent witness theory,* courts are admitting photographic evidence from mechanical devices not for purposes of illustration, but for purposes of substantive evidence. The evidence is being admitted not only because it is relevant, but also because it speaks for itself. In *State v. Pulphus,*[29] the Rhode Island Supreme Court admitted photographs from a bank surveillance camera by considering a diversity of novel factors and abandoned the long-standing tradition of providing an authenticating witness. The court was convinced that bank surveillance camera results are in a sense almost self-authenticating if a proponent can establish the following:

1. No alterations or tampering,
2. Testimony as to the automatic nature of camera activation,
3. Evidence concerning time intervals between frames,
4. Evidence establishing the dates of the photographs,
5. Chain of custody evidence, and
6. Testimony explaining what the photo portrays.[30]

## PHOTO DATA TRACKING RECORD

Case Name: _____     Case Number: _____
                                         Photo Number: _____

Firm Name: _____
Address: _____
Phone Number: _____
Attorney Name: _____

Client's Name: _____

Case Information:
  Location of Incident: _____
  Time of Incident: _____
  Date of Incident: _____
  Individuals Involved: _____
  _____

Photographer Information:
  Photographer: _____
  Address: _____
  Phone Number: _____
  Years of Experience: _____
  Used Services Before? _____
  Available for Court Apearance? _____

Photograph Information:
  Type of Camera: _____
  Film:
    Brand: _____
    ISO Number: _____
    Number of Exposures: _____
    Number of Rolls: _____
  Subject Description: _____
  _____
  _____
  _____

  Subject Location: _____
  Time Photograph Was Taken: _____
  Date Photograph Was Taken: _____
  Distance from Subject: _____
  Direction Camera Was Pointed: _____
  Development Laboratory: _____
  Location of Laboratory: _____
  Time of Development: _____
  Date of Development: _____

**FORM 3.1**    Track scene photographs with various information.

If anything, the court accepts the self-authenticating nature of a picture created by purely mechanical means.[31] "By treating photographs as substantive evidence, the silent witness theory simply removes the percipient witness testimony obstacle to their admission. Criticism that this theory opens the door to admission of falsified pictures is misplaced."[32]

James McCarthy's seminal work, *Making Trial Objections,* states that, to benefit from the silent witness theory, counsel must establish

1. The date the photograph was taken,
2. That the photograph has not been altered, and
3. The identification of persons depicted in the photograph.[33]

But this general comfort with the machine causes some jurists consternation. Does a surveillance tape speak for itself? Can authentication be assumed because of the mechanistic nature of the video camera? New York's Court of Appeals[34] has now mandated the pretrial disclosure of surveillance tapes. "In settling the question, the high court noted that films are so convincing that once the jury has seen them, to show later that they were distorted might not undo the damage. And without a chance to study and authenticate films before trial, plaintiffs would often have to ask for a continuance, disrupting the trial and further clogging the courts."[35]

The unbridled usage of surveillance tapes under the silent witness theory seems to have seen its day. Counsel is now urged to undercut the integrity of the surveillance process.[36]

## § 3.3 VIDEOTAPES AND MOTION PICTURES

Under the Federal Rules of Evidence, videotapes and motion pictures fall within the definition of a photograph and, as a result, are subject to the same evidentiary tests and rules. Videotapes and motion pictures need to fairly and accurately portray the subject matter and be relevant.

To assure a proper foundation for the use of a videotape or a motion picture, the proponent of the evidence should offer proof of the following:

1. That the device was capable of taking testimony;
2. That the operator of the equipment was competent;
3. That the recording is authentic and correct;
4. That no deletions, changes, or additions have been made;
5. How the recording has been preserved;
6. Identification of the speakers; and
7. That the testimony was voluntarily made.[37]

## Tactical Uses of Videotapes

Under FRE Rule 1001(3), any print of a videotape is an original and therefore is not subject to the complexities of the best evidence rule. Comparatively, photographs are trapped in time, while videotapes animate life. Videotapes afford a more comprehensive view of injuries. Videotapes resolve a variety of logistical problems by bringing to the jury's view accident scenes, hospital settings, calamities or catastrophes, and day-in-the-life summaries of injured parties. "The variety of potential views is all but limitless."[38] Under FRE Rule 1006, a videotape may limit or reduce its content to summary form. Rule 1006, in calling for a fair and accurate portrayal, requires that

1. The underlying tapes be voluminous,
2. The summary tape fairly reflect their contents,
3. The summary also fairly portray the subject matter that it depicts,
4. The underlying tapes be admissible, and
5. Opposing counsel be given every opportunity to review the underlying tapes in advance.[39]

In addition, videotapes are used to give insight into damages and to record tests, experiments, demonstrations, and simulations of events that are too large in scope for jury visitation or re-creation.

The question of whether or not videotapes are admissible in court is recent. It is well established that motion pictures, when properly authenticated and relevant to the issues, are usually admitted.[40]

## The Day-in-the-Life Videotape

Proving damage claims relating to one's occupation, one's quality and enjoyment of life in the home, pain and suffering, and general trauma has historically been done by direct testimony. Of recent interest has been the use of video diaries, which chronicle extended periods of time in the normal living routine of an injured party. If a picture is worth a thousand words, what are 48 hours of video worth that intimately depict the many effects of injury?

In extreme cases of injury, defense attorneys claim such presentations are inflammatory or highly prejudicial. Excessive anguish may cause the court to construe prejudicial impact over probative value. "Thus, films which show matters like the plaintiff repeatedly grimacing or yelling in pain or growling menacingly or uncommunicatively, have not been admitted. If the court finds some portion of a videotape inadmissible, you should request permission to edit out the offensive portion and show the remainder."[41] Such videotapes are vigorously challenged because the opposition is not a party to their production, is suspicious of their content, and is aware of their obvious slant in presentation. This is particularly true in personal injury cases.[42] Day-in-the-life videos, such as those produced by B. and B. Enterprises (2 Half Mile Common, Westport, CT 06880), have been on the receiving end of serious legal challenges. In a case of medical malpractice, a videotape produced by B. and B. Enterprises was admitted into court. The hospital objected on the theory of prejudicial impact and, upon appeal, urged the court to overturn the damage finding. However, the court, in *Pisel v. Stamford Hospital,*[43] rejected the objection and, in its opinion, stated, "[A]fter examining the videotape with the above principles in mind, we agree with the trial court that the 'tape' while not pleasant viewing, fairly presented to the jury Miss Pisel's condition and type of care she was required to receive."[44]

Companies that focus on the continuous agony of the plaintiff and adopt an overdone, tear-jerking approach in the guise of an objective appraisal of the plaintiff's injuries are to be shunned. Evaluate day-in-the-life videotapes with these criteria in mind:

1. The film fairly depicts the day-to-day activities of the plaintiff,

2. The film demonstrates the plaintiff's adaptation to his or her injury,

3. The film does not unduly distract the jury, and

4. The plaintiff who is the subject matter of the film can be cross-examined as to his or her self-serving portrayal on film—his or her conduct in the film.[45]

Other recommendations for the enlightened practitioner hoping to benefit from this demonstrative tool follow:

- Deal with a reputable filmmaker.
- Purge subjectivity in the videotape's production.
- Examine the videotape far in advance of litigation for editorial purposes.
- Disclose the content of the videotape during pretrial discovery.
- Summarize the technique or chronology used in the production of the videotape.
- Assure honesty and accuracy; do not belabor and repeat the negative reality.
- Do not be cumulative in your approach.
- Afford opposing counsel the right to review the videotapes.
- Eliminate stipulations, if possible.
- Request cautionary or limiting instructions of the court.
- Prepare the videotape exhibits.
- Check jurisdictional rules.

The videotape as a form of demonstrative evidence has made substantial inroads into the litigation process.[46] While there is some dichotomy in the federal courts,

---

**CASE EXAMPLE 3.2**   *Demonstrative Evidence—
Day-in-the-Life Videotape*

**CASE:** *Scisarik v. Palos Community Hospital,* 193 Ill. App. 3d 41, 549 N.E.2d 840 (1989), *appeal allowed,* 131 Ill. 2d 558, 553 N.E.2d 394 (1990).

**FACTS:** In a medical malpractice case, defense counsel became aware that plaintiff was producing a "day-in-the-life" film for presentation to the jury. Defense counsel requested the opportunity to be present during the filming to assure the videotape's integrity. Plaintiff refused to allow defense presence. The defense counsel petitioned the court for an order permitting on-site location during filming. The court entered an order allowing presence during filming. Plaintiff's counsel refused to comply and was subsequently held in contempt and fined the sum of $100.00. The court order included the following three conditions:

1. The defendants were to be given notice of the making of the film.
2. The film was to be preserved in it entirety.
3. The film was to be made available to all the defendants.

**QUESTION AND ISSUE:** Do you agree with the court?

---

the majority of state courts have adhered to historical underpinnings of photographic evidence and will permit the admission of videotapes unless unduly provocative, inflammatory, or prejudicial. See Case Example 3.2.

Seeing increasing companion use with the videotape is the *life-plan report.* A life-plan report documents the present condition of an injured party, as well as the long-term prognosis for the party. A comprehensive life-care plan involves the consideration of the many areas that impact on the life of a catastrophically injured person. See Table 1.

Curiously, modern judicial decision-making is not wholeheartedly supportive of the use of videotape, and rightfully so. Besides, filmmaking is at least a quasi–art form, influencing emotions and creating empathies far more dramatic than do still photographs, paper documentation, and other competing formats. Evaluate *Thompson v. D. G. Tate Construction Company,*[48] in which a badly burned auto accident victim was videotaped during an excruciating physical therapy session. The court refused to admit the videotape, echoing the extreme influence the tape had. The court's opinion notes:

During the entire process plaintiff was grunting, groaning, and crying and his face forming various contortions and grimaces evidencing much pain.

It is impossible in the foregoing brief summary to completely depict what is revealed by the audio and visual presentation of the tape. The tape positively shows

## TABLE 1. Elements of Life-Care Plan

*Evaluations*

| | | |
|---|---|---|
| Rehabilitation | Psychological | Music |
| Physical | Vocational | Hearing |
| Occupational | Speech | Visual |
| Educational | | |

*Therapies*

| | | |
|---|---|---|
| Physical therapy | Group counseling | Recreation therapy |
| Occupational therapy | Marital counseling | Audiological training |
| Speech therapy | Sexual therapy | Cognitive training |
| Individual counseling | Visual perception therapy | Behavioral therapy |
| Family counseling | Music therapy | Remediation therapy |

*Education and Development*

| | | |
|---|---|---|
| Infant stimulation | Tutoring | Educational games and toys |
| Early childhood education | Prevocational training | Work activity center |
| Preschool education | Vocational training | Sheltered workshop participation |
| Special education (both public school and residential facility) | | |

*Drugs and Supply Needs*

*Specialists*

| | | |
|---|---|---|
| Orthopedist | Internist | Pediatrician |
| Neurologist | Psychiatrist | Dentist |
| Urologist | Family physician | |

*Equipment to Allow the Catastrophically Disabled Person More Independence*
Architectural renovations
Home care/facility care area

*Potential and Future Complications*[47]

the plaintiff is experiencing extreme pain and mental anguish. During the viewing of this tape, one has a tendency to try to disregard it and direct his attention to something more pleasant, and if one has the slightest tendency to be squeamish, a feeling of nausea arises.

The tape definitely incites extreme sympathy for the plaintiff and would inflame the average person.[49]

Undeniably, a videotape of an accident victim experiencing trauma during physical therapy is relevant to the case. Indeed, the videotape has probative value. To no one's amazement, the videotape likely meets procedural requirements relative to laying a foundation and authentication. However, the content's inflammatory nature potentially bars the videotape's admission.

## § 3.4 X-RAYS

X-rays are included in the definition of a photograph under FRE Rule 1001(2) and are mentioned directly in the authentication requirements covered in FRE Rule 901(B)(9). Traditionally, authenticators of x-rays are doctors, radiology technicians, or experts qualified in the interpretation of x-rays. Few restrictions exist on the admissibility of x-rays as long as foundational requirements are met. Nevertheless, the technical nature of the x-ray equipment shifts the burden to the scientific and technical proficiency of the machine's operator. On occasion, chain of custody arguments do come up regarding alteration.

The largest area of evidentiary concern for x-rays at trial is foundationally related. The areas that must be addressed are listed:

1. The x-ray technician's qualifications,
2. That the operator x-rayed a specific part of the body at a specific time and place,
3. The type of equipment used and the fact that it was in good working order,
4. The procedures used by the operator,
5. How the subject was identified on the x-ray cassette,
6. That the particular x-ray cassette being offered is the one used at the time the injury was filmed,
7. The chain of custody between the time of filming and its introduction into evidence.[50]

A typical questioning sequence that establishes a suitable foundation for admissibility is outlined below:

- I show you exhibit Y; do you recognize it?
- How do you recognize this particular x-ray, exhibit Y?
- Are you familiar with the circumstances under which it was made?
- What were the general qualifications and experience of the technician who prepared exhibit Y?
- When was exhibit Y taken?
- Where was it made?
- What equipment was used to make exhibit Y?
- What kind of film was used to make exhibit Y?
- How do you know that this is the film taken on that occasion (what identification procedures were used to label the x-ray)?
- Who developed the x-ray, exhibit Y?
- Does the development process change the x-ray at all?

---

[Caption]

The parties to the above-mentioned action, through their respective under-signed attorneys, stipulate as follows:

1. Each party shall be entitled to submit x-rays such as may be desired pertaining to the foregoing.
2. After the examination has been made, the x-rays shall be preserved and shall remain in the custody of the court.

Dated _____, 20_____

_____

[Signature and address]

---

**FORM 3.2**   Stipulation—requesting submission of an x-ray.

- Where has the x-ray, exhibit Y, been since the date on which it was made?
- Who has had custody of exhibit Y prior to today?
- Who obtained exhibit Y from the hospital file for use here in court?
- Your honor, I offer exhibit Y into evidence at this time.[51]

Stipulations are routinely agreed to between opposing parties. See the pertinent stipulation request at Form 3.2.

## § 3.5 MODELS

When physicians explain a condition to a patient, they often use an anatomical model. When counselors seek the testimony of a child in a suspected case of sexual abuse, they employ doll-like models children more easily interact with. In these and other cases, models serve to illustrate, amplify, and supplement the underlying evidence. Often, models are used for testimonial assistance, rather than for evidentiary admission. Medical Legal Art is a premier supplier of custom-made medical exhibits. See Figure 3.11.[52]

Few restrictions exist regarding the admission of models. FRE Rules 401 and 403—bearing on the question of relevancy, probative value, and prejudicial impact—coupled with FRE Rule 901—dealing with authentication—regulate the admission of models. The model's construction has to be fair, accurate, and unprejudiced in its portrayal.

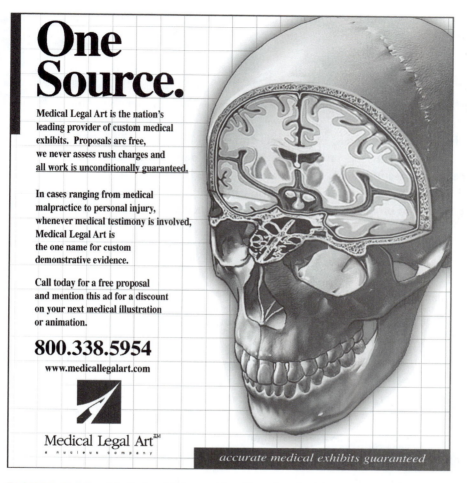

**FIGURE 3.11** Medical exhibit provider. (Reprinted with permission. © 2000, Medical Legal Art, www.medicallegalart.com.)

## Accuracy

Courts expect the model, by its scale design, to accurately mirror the original. Presentation of a model that is distorted, out of scale, or blatantly misaligned properly results in rejection. Models are to be realistic, accurate representations. Misleading and confusing evidence is contrary to justice. Slight deficiencies may be tolerated, but substantial deviance from the thing represented is never acceptable. Models should be substantially similar in operation, function, and composition. "Even a model with slight inaccuracies may still be admitted if the parties stipulate to it which, of course, they would do only if the inaccuracies were not material to the case issues."[53]

While some litigators insist that a model should be crafted to architectural perfection, infallible scale is not necessary. Closeness to dimension, space, and actuality is essential. The model should be miniaturized to scale, be modified by practicality, and, if possible, be an exact replica.

## Authentication

The admission of a model largely depends on whether or not a proper foundation is laid for its admission. Models are authenticated by the testimony of a qualified witness who has actual knowledge of the facts and issues relevant to the model's representation. Consider this general principle in a case of child sexual abuse. Testimony by experts, court-appointed psychiatrists, and related witnesses involves the technical and emotional challenges of extracting evidence from small children. Often, these experts and other interrogators utilize anatomical dolls. Such a doll obviously cannot gain admission by its own force. The court, in order to grant its admission or permit its use in testimonial delivery, must minimally be apprised of the following:

1. Who is the manufacturer of this anatomical model?
2. When was the model made?
3. How was the model made?
4. Is its doll-like structure normative in design, specification, and measurements for children at these age levels?
5. Is the doll's depiction of sexual organs to scale, reasonably placed, or prejudicially designed?
6. Is the model substantially similar to the human constitution of a small child?
7. Does the model aid in the delivery of testimony?
8. Does the model confuse, mislead, or clarify issues before the court?
9. Is the model a fair and accurate representation of a child's anatomical structure?

Given the recent rash of child abuse cases, is it any wonder that courts are searching for evidentiary items that promote free-flowing and accurate testimony? The national scandal of child abuse, however, should not permit an ungovernable liberalization of admissibility rules. It is equally known that both the dolls and the interrogators who employ them, at least in some selected cases, have elicited testimony from children that is less than reliable.

## Acquiring Models

Many sources, both private and public, exist for demonstrative evidence. In some government agencies, larger law firms, and law enforcement entities, illustrators and artists are on staff. Private consulting firms can assist the litigation team with a wide

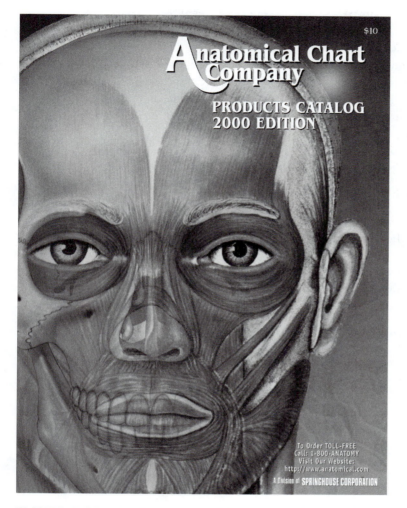

**FIGURE 3.12** Another medical exhibit provider. (Reprinted with permission of Anatomical Chart Company.)

array of products. Legal Graphic Communicators[54] provides numerous products, including charts, graphs, medical exhibits, computer animation, diagrams and illustrations, casts, maps, and models. In the anatomical sector, the Anatomical Chart Company, a division of Springhouse Corporation, has been a leader in the development and production of illustrated charts covering human anatomy and physiology, pathological conditions, medical discoveries, and demonstrative evidence. See Figure 3.12.[55] Companies that are reliable sources for medical models include Markham Anatomical, 211 Atlantic Street, P.O. Box 950, Stamford, CT 60901, 1-800-242-2449, and Medical Plastic Laboratory, Professional Health Educators, P.O. Box 38, Gatesville, TX 76528, 1-800-433-5539.

## Models and Litigation

Properly mixed into the litigation strategy, models enhance the case theme because they strikingly stand out in the combative landscape of litigation. The model has to be a first-rate production, something that tends to augment the jury's understanding of the proponent's case. A model that runs the risk of making the proponent's case less believable, less credible, or less moving is a model that needs to be cast aside.

The model can be used as either the focal point of the jury's analysis or to illustrate a single fact amongst an array of others. For example, models may be appropriate only in those circumstances when experts testify or as an aid to a lay witness struggling to describe an injury or wound. Level of usage is clearly a strategic concern for the legal team.

Models should be prepared well in advance of trial and cataloged. See Form 3.3.

Models, like every other form of demonstrative evidence, clarify the testimony of witnesses, give meaning to scientific explanation, and permit the trier of fact a more educated view of unwieldy evidence. Even if not offered into the court's formal record, models offer a witness a way of amplifying his or her testimony. Milford Meyer suggests their regular employment to buttress expert testimony:

> Medical models, charts, diagrams, casts, or skeletons may be used by an expert during his testimony even though they need not be admissible in evidence. The witness should be prepared to testify that he can best illustrate his testimony to the court and jury by the use of such aids.[56]

---

Name of Case: _____

Exhibit Number Assigned: _____

Model: _____

Model Description: _____

_____

Manufacturer: _____

Witnesses Who Will Testify as to the Contents of the Model:

_____

Time of Introduction: _____

_____      Photographic Evidence

_____      Corroborating Model

Special Equipment Necessary for Presentation: _____

---

**FORM 3.3**   Demonstrative model evidence record.

Models of buildings, products, and machinery are equally helpful. When a witness is describing the layout of a building, a scale model paints a more realistic picture. When alleging a product defect or mechanical failure in a personal injury case, the mechanical model furnishes a clearer image of the defect. Injuries due to the defective design of a football helmet can be demonstrated most effectively by a model exhibit.

## § 3.6 CHARTS, MAPS, DIAGRAMS, ILLUSTRATIONS, AND OTHER DRAWINGS

Less exacting and less multidimensional are the demonstrative chart, map, diagram, and illustration. If properly offered, these demonstrative means amass complex scientific and testimonial evidence into a particularized graphic. Information is more smoothly interpreted, categorized, and comprehended. Like other forms of demonstrative evidence, the chart, map, diagram, and illustration are readily admitted if relevant and probative. The content should not be prejudicial, inaccurate, or so confused that it will mislead the jury. The demonstrative form should "fairly and accurately portray what it proports [sic] to depict and its relevance so requires, to do so at the period of time relevant in litigation."[57]

> Before a map or blueprint becomes admissible in evidence, it must be shown to be relevant and be verified by testimony under oath that it is a fair and accurate representation of what it purports to portray. Thus, a map or plat, even though kept in a public office and in general use there for reference, cannot be admitted as evidence without verification by proof of its correctness as to the matter for which it is sought to be used.[58]

Phillip Anthony and Donald Vinson's *Demonstrative Exhibits: A Key to Effective Jury Presentations* relays seasoned guidance on what graphics can accomplish:

> The first rule to remember in developing a graphic display is that the display must convey a clear and understandable message.
>
> The second rule of any exhibit is that it must be simple and straightforward.
>
> A third rule concerns the use of what are called cues. Cues can take two forms. They can come before an exhibit is seen by jurors, or they can come just after. Cues given before an exhibit is seen, or just as it is seen, are signposts pointing to what is significant in the exhibit.[59]

Foundational responsibilities and the authentication requirements, as guided by FRE Rule 901, are identical to those for other demonstrative forms.

The range of possibilities for this demonstrative method is impressive. The intricacies of human anatomy are ably served by a medical chart or diagram. Customarily, litigation teams have relied on works that clearly diagram the human body. See Figure 3.13[60] for an example of one of the many providers of anatomical charts.

Fingerprint typification in a criminal case would be an impossible exercise without charts or diagrams. Interpreting loops, whorls, and arches on real fingers requires micrographic examination. The demonstrative exhibit, in the form of a chart or diagram, naturally edifies this miniature condition, making possible the interpretation of fingerprint classifications.

Charts, posters, and illustrations are a primary means to advance a theory or factual proposition in civil or criminal litigation. Injuries to the human body are more easily understandable with a graphic aid than through testimony alone.[61]

Demonstrative evidence provides an intelligible presentation of any medical condition. The craft of medical illustration blends both art and science in the drafting. Medical illustrators can be found in many locations, including colleges and universities, local hospitals, medical facilities, medical libraries, and specialty publishers. For information on medical illustrators in your region, write to the Association of Medical Illustrators, 1819 Peach Tree Street NE, Suite 560, Atlanta, GA 30309, 404-350-7900. The firm Legal Graphic Communicators specializes in the production of medical illustrations that convey information about complicated medical problems, delicate surgical procedures, and the effects of medication on specific parts of the body. See Figure 3.14.[62]

Charts and illustrations are equally helpful in defective product cases. Expert and lay witnesses describing the defective nature of a product are made more credible by the demonstrative display. Technical illustrations demonstrate the inner workings of mechanical or electronic devices, machinery, heavy equipment, power tools, office equipment, vehicles, and farm equipment. Cutaways and glass imaging techniques supplement the often dull factual recitation. Overhead views of larger environments are even available. Legal Graphic Communicators also specializes in these types of technical illustrations. See Figure 3.15.[63]

Charts and illustrations can compile the results of technical analysis, testings, and design. In general, statistics and raw data are incomprehensible to the average person. Charts and graphs accurately present statistical facts in an easily discernible format and are designed to attract and hold the attention of the court and jury. In the development of any statistical presentation, the educational level and interest of the jury should be given significant consideration.

On the more informal and impromptu side, courts frequently see witnesses chart testimony or attorneys advocate cases utilizing a simple blackboard. Trial attorney Jack A. Olender says, in *Showing Pain and Suffering*, that he is most comfortable outlining damages on the blackboard:

> The blackboard can be used for detailing the various elements of damages. This can be done during testimony establishing the elements and during argument. Intangibles such as pain and suffering can be computed on the blackboard in the presence of a jury.[64]

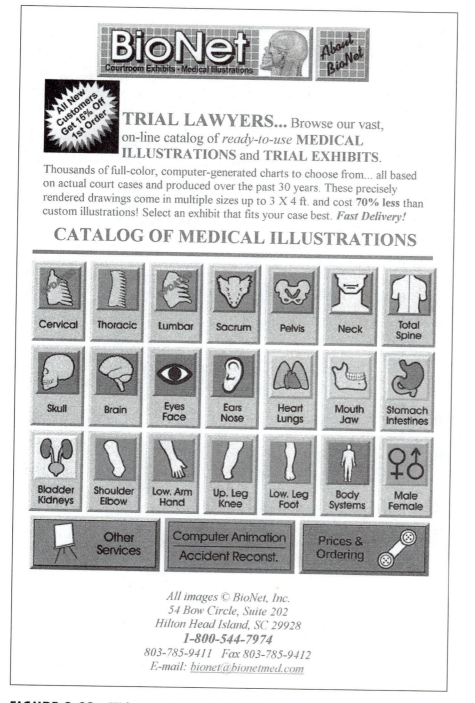

**FIGURE 3.13**   Web page of a medical exhibit company. (Reprinted with permission of BioNet, Inc., 1-800-544-7974.)

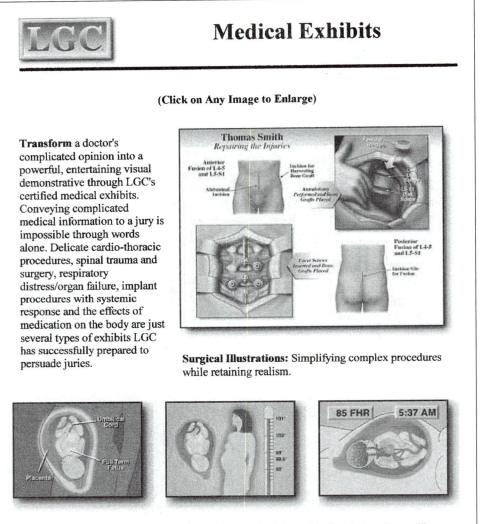

**FIGURE 3.14** Would these exhibits help explain a condition better than testimony alone? (Reprinted with the permission of Legal Graphic Communicators.)

The blackboard and other visual mediums can be employed to calculate damages and to outline opening and closing arguments, testimony, the theory of a case, and other related matters. By emphasizing the use of these visual aids, the demonstrative evidence acts as a "road map."[65]

Aside from clarifying the issues, charts, posters, and diagrams have a perma-nency to them, being both tangible and stationary; their presence indelibly im-

**Anatomy/Injuries:** Highligthing areas where injuries occurred to help visualize an expert's testimony.

**Anatomy/Pathology:** Depicting abnormalities that are difficult to understand or see in x-rays.

All medical exhibits are produced under the direction of our certified medical illustrator who is well versed in all specialties. He will work one on one with your medical expert to develop accurate and compelling exhibits.

LEGAL   GRAPHIC   COMMUNICATORS

| Accident Reconstruction | **Medical** | Mechanical & Technical | Architecture & Construction | Environmental | Timelines, Diagrams & Charts |

Why LGC? | Products and Services | **Gallery of Work** | LGC Staff | More Information?

*Please send comments regarding this site to fuller@legalgraphic.com.*
*Copyright © 1996, 1997, 1998 Legal Graphic Communicators.*

LGC

**FIGURE 3.14**   *Continued*

presses upon a juror's mind the advocate's position. Milford Meyer appreciates this subconscious effect:

> You have to keep in mind that the purpose of putting anything on the blackboard is to stimulate the memory of the jurors by having whatever it is in front of them for a long period of time, preferably the entire trial.[66]

In this way, these demonstrative forms continuously bombard the senses. For example, auto negligence cases often involve multiple parties at road intersections. What better way to make an intellectual impression than by a diagram of the intersection? Accident reconstruction diagrams minister to this purpose.

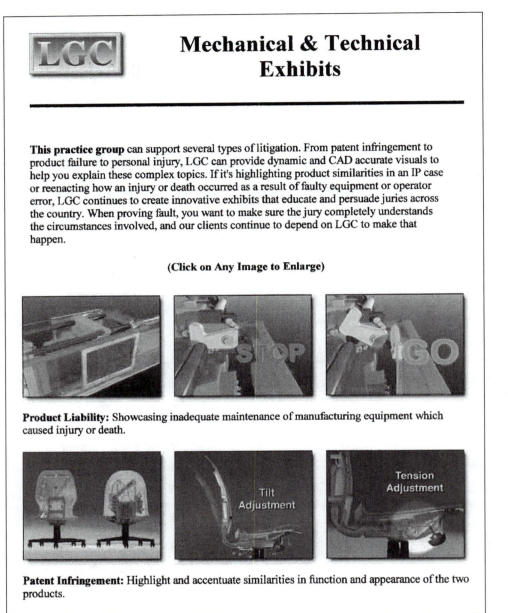

**FIGURE 3.15** Would you understand the mechanics of equipment without these illustrations? (Reprinted with the permission of Legal Graphic Communicators.)

Maps, surveys, and other drawings can range from sophisticated topographical representations to rough-view drawings. Evidence of this type, which exemplifies a scene or transaction (i.e., an accident or other occurrence) or the placement of objects—if presented in a reasonably accurate fashion—is admissible into court.[67] If

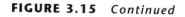

**Product Failure:** Simplifying the machinery by breaking it down to its basic components, then focusing on the area of concern.

L E G A L   G R A P H I C   C O M M U N I C A T O R S

| Accident Reconstruction | Medical | **Mechanical & Technical** | Architecture & Construction | Environmental | Timelines, Diagrams & Charts |

Why LGC? | Products and Services | **Gallery of Work** | LGC Staff | More Information?

*Please send comments regarding this site to* fuller@legalgraphic.com.
Copyright © 1996, 1997, 1998 Legal Graphic Communicators.

LGC

**FIGURE 3.15** *Continued*

the court is satisfied that the exhibits submitted will help the trier of fact, admissibility questions are rare. Maps can be admitted under various legal principles, including the ancient document rule[68] or as an official government document. The map, for admission purposes, needs to be an accurate representation of the area represented. This accuracy must be supported and authenticated by a witness familiar with its content. Maps can be intersectional, such as a police officer's hand-drawn or computer-aided accident diagram. Criterion Press produces the Blaq Boxx system used by police departments desirous of uniformity in accident reporting.

Making a diagram of a particular scene is an effective strategy in legal cases involving environmental hazards, zoning violations, real property disputes, accidents, OSHA violations, trespass, nuisance, and negligent design of traffic systems. Diagrams are helpful in depicting key components of a case, such as equipment, accident scenes, products, or defects. This type of demonstrative evidence allows the witness to explain the intricacies of a topic, holding the audience's attention and focusing it on the diagram.

Maps are available from numerous sources, including bookstores, commercial surveyors, government agencies, real estate offices, convention or visitors' information booths, libraries, county recorders of deeds or tax offices, and university libraries.

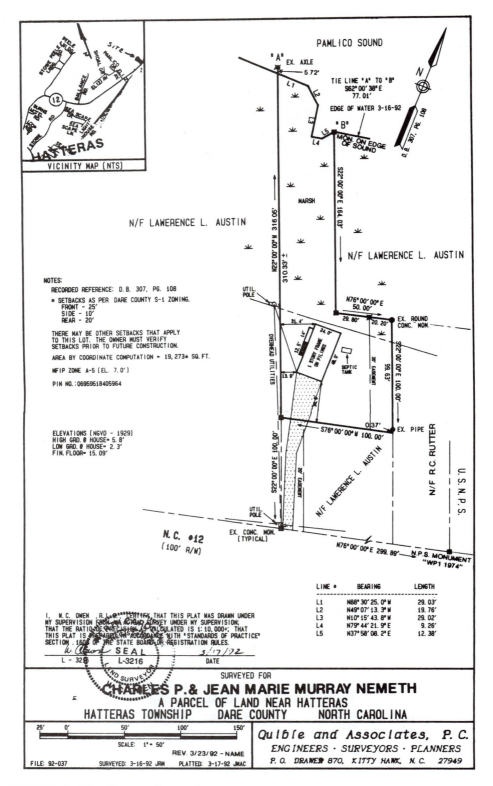

**FIGURE 3.16** Survey of property.

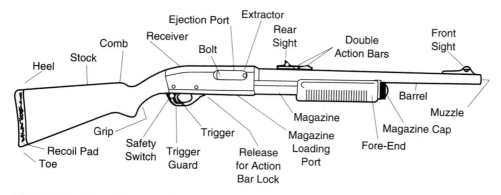

**FIGURE 3.17**   Diagram of a shotgun.

Surveys are demonstrative representations of actual real property.[69] See Figure 3.16.

Another justification for the use of diagrams often relates to the nature of the evidence involved. As noted earlier, it is unlikely that a cadaver would be submitted to the jury for inspection, but photographic or documentary evidence would be presented. The same is true in a case involving handguns or weaponry. Prosecutors in criminal cases are generally hesitant to hand jurors firearms. A diagram explaining weaponry is beneficial in ballistics interpretation. See Figure 3.17.

## § 3.7  COMPUTER GRAPHICS AND ANIMATION

Computers are increasingly playing a role in the litigation process, using software that produces everything from lifelike depictions to artfully reproduced imitations. Such "evidence purporting to re-create events at issue in a lawsuit [or crime] must reflect conditions that are *substantially similar* to the actual events giving rise to the suit to be admissible at trial."[70] Modern attorneys familiarize themselves with these various tools, the scope and applications of which are beyond enumeration. Computers have clearly opened up a new demonstrative dimension, with simulations, re-creations, and enactments; edited capsulizations or summaries; high-resolution photos or slides; enhanced imagery; video-adapted microscopy; video animation; anatomical charts; and identification systems now being available. One of the earliest examples was developed by the Sirchie Company. *Photo-Identi Kit,* a product popular with many major police departments, catalogs human descriptions on acetate sheets for identification purposes. More than 900 face components are available, permitting the intermixture and matching of facial features, namely, hair, eyes, nose, lips, chin, and related accessories. This type of software animation has, for the most part, replaced the traditional artist's rendition of a suspect, but some investigators use both methods. Not unexpectedly, this acetate-based identification system is perceived as less subjective than the artist rendition. "When computer aided evidentiary tools are produced by experienced demonstrative firms, they have been shown to increase jurors' retention of important information and shorten the duration of trials."[71]

In the anatomical arena, computer-based graphics are establishing a stronghold. Forensic Art Services provides a web site, which describes the different facets of forensic art and provides informational resources to interested parties. Examples of composites on the site are at Figure 3.18.

Computer graphics depicting aircraft, vehicular, maritime, structural, medical, and product-related incidents have gained a foothold in most courthouses. These engineered simulations allow exploration and display of such critical factors as relative position, speed, timing, visibility, response time, and design features pertaining to an accident.

Wolf Technical Services, Inc., is a leader in computer graphics relating to railroad accidents, product liability, and aviation cases. See Figure 3.19.[72]

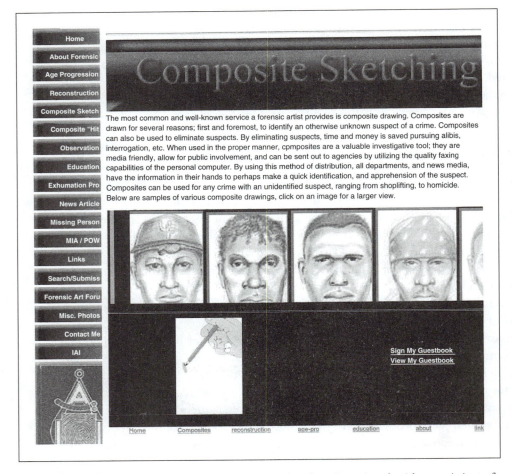

**FIGURE 3.18**  Examples of various composite sketches. (Reprinted with permission of Neville's Forensic Art Service.)

Technology continues to exert its influence in the field of animated graphics. A new technique labeled *photorealistic computer graphics* provides a startling reflection of the reality it seeks to image. "Photorealistic depiction of a dynamic environment with many moving objects, terrain features, clouds, and flowing water, for example, requires enormous computing power still available only on dedicated mainframe

## WTS WOLF TECHNICAL SERVICES, INC.

### Accident Reconstruction

WTS personnel have accumulated extensive experience in the investigation and reconstruction of all types of vehicular accidents involving cars, trucks, motorcycles, railroads and pedestrians. The technical committee assigns cases to ensure that the best qualified engineer receives the assignment. In addition, engineers, at any time, can draw on the expertise of other staff members. The corporate review procedure for reconstructions makes certain that every facet of the available information is analyzed.

WTS has developed in-house programs to reinforce commercially available accident reconstruction programs. WTS provides a complete reconstruction service including field investigation, written reports, court testimony and computer simulation.

SEMI WITH 4-WAY FLASHERS ONLY (TOP) THE TRAILER DISAPPEARS IN THE GLARE OF THE SEMI'S HIGH BEAMS (BOTTOM)

### Vision

Driver visual acuity, light conditions at the scene, and vision obstruction caused by scene objects or a car's design can all be contributing factors to a traffic accident.

The training and experience in vision issues permits a determination to be made of which visibility issues are significant in a crash. These might range from effects of local weather conditions such as fog or snow to whether glare from a windshield had an effect on the outcome of the accident.

WTS evaluates visual obstructions caused by the design of the car body. Examples of such obstructions are: inside rearview mirrors mounted at the driver's eye level, thick door and window pillars that can blot out passed or overtaking cars, windshield reflections and high, rear head restraints.

While night vision issues are most common, a bright sunny day can also bring vision problems. An object as big as a truck can be lost in the glare of the sun. Pedestrians can virtually disappear in the shade of a tree. Electrocutions often happen when victims misperceive the distance to overhead wires.

The specialists at WTS also have background in the relationship between vision and photography and can, therefore, determine whether photographic evidence accurately represents the conditions at the time of the accident.

**FIGURE 3.19**   Would an accident reconstruction be more useful than testimony? (Reprinted with permission of Wolf Technical Services, Inc.)

**Trucking**

Other specialized investigations include laboratory and field investigations of damage caused to truck cargo by shock and vibration, the design and maintenance of braking systems and other components of passenger cars and heavy trucks; also the training and evaluation of safe driving practices of over-the-road truck drivers. WTS' trucking experts have extensive qualifications, including commercial drivers licenses and certification by the National Safety Council as instructors and trainers of drivers (automobiles and trucks).

In addition to examining the maneuvers and actions and reactions of truck drivers, WTS also scrutinizes their performance in terms of the Federal Motor Carrier Safety Regulations and industry standards. The experts survey logs showing hours of service, specific routes followed, load, type of equipment and all facets of the driver's actions and duties. The motor carrier operations are evaluated for selection, screening, hiring and qualification of drivers.

WTS Home | Introduction
Accident Reconstruction | Forensic Technologies | System Safety
Materials, Metallurgy & Chemistry | Fire & Explosion Investigation
Smoke & Fire Hazard Analysis | Photogrammetry | Image Analysis
Computer Graphics | Contact WTS

WTS Techbits newsletter

**FIGURE 3.19**  *Continued*

computer graphics systems. These systems draw on multiple databases to obtain the necessary information, which then is simultaneously processed for terrain and other features. The information is combined only in the final stage to achieve photorealistic appearance."[73]

While it is indisputable that computer graphics and computer animation have advanced rapidly in recent years, the same rules of evidence still apply. No matter how tempting the animated result, admissibility questions remain central. "If defense counsel decides to use computerized demonstrative evidence, they must prepare in advance for objections to the admissibility."[74]

The same foundational requirements as for other demonstrative forms are called for:

• The original source data,
• All calculations and assumptions used in processing the data,
• The method of inputting data into the graphics computer,
• The operation and capability of the graphics computer and all associated software,
• The output process for the computer graphics,
• The medium by which the graphics are reproduced for presentation at trial, and
• The final presentation itself.[75]

Whatever the case in question, new forms of technologically advanced demonstrative evidence deliver a host of benefits to any litigation team.

## § 3.8 MISCELLANEOUS DEMONSTRATIVE EVIDENCE

As technology improves, so, too, does the range of demonstrative products and services. Every case will have some need for demonstration of an underlying reality.

### Recordings/Tapes/Voiceprints

In patent, trademark, or copyright infringement cases, recordings and tape evidence are frequently needed. Criminal cases rely on taped conversations in proving extortion, obscenity, harassment, terroristic threats, bookmaking, and a myriad of organized criminal activities. As a form of demonstrative evidence, the spectrogram, the comparative assessment of voice patterns, has come under attack for being an unreliable form of scientific evidence. If your local jurisdiction has accepted this evidentiary concept, be certain of foundation and authentication requirements.[76] Positive identification of a taped voice can, at least according to some experts, be accomplished by a voice spectrogram.

### Experiments and Reconstructions

The central judicial consideration governing the admissibility of experiments is whether or not the experiment or demonstration is probative and helpful to the court. The court has broad discretion to allow or even order a demonstration or experiment. Issues of fairness, accuracy, and similarly situated circumstances and conditions are fundamental for the court's determination on admissibility. "Such experiments and demonstrations must be made subject to a control that makes them reliable proof of the facts they purport to prove, which facts must be relevant and competent to the issues in the case."[77]

Think of the many types of cases in which experiments may prove indispensible:

1. Proving product liability
2. Product defects in product liability cases
3. Proving a company's knowledge of a defective design in an automobile (remember the Ford Pinto case and GM side gas tank cases)
4. Accident reconstruction
5. Railroad collision cases
6. Electrical and fire protection systems

7. Television defect
8. Elevator accidents
9. Lighting and heating cases
10. Motor defect
11. Ineffective signs and warnings
12. Industrial machinery accidents
13. Mobile and agriculture machine accidents
14. Emergency system malfunctions
15. Arson cases
16. Industrial safety
17. Machine guarding
18. Truck loading and unloading

An example of experimental services provided by consultant Wolf Technical Services, Inc., can be seen at Figure 3.19.

Similarity of events and conditions, in as close a fashion as possible, is required. Accident reconstruction is a classic example of times when experiments work well. "If re-creation is decided on, then great care must be taken to reproduce the occurrence with substantial similarity. Any differences in the roadway, vehicles or other instrumentalities must be carefully documented and explained at trial. Small insubstantial differences will not prevent admissibility if fully explained."[78] While re-creation is more cumbersome in an evidentiary sense, its results are powerful evidentially. Consider a case in which a stuntman operates a vehicle on a ramp to demonstrate the rollover capacity at a specific speed. This type of demonstration is used not necessarily to re-create the incident, but to simply show the potentiality for rollover in a particular vehicle.[79] Motor vehicle accident reconstruction experiments tell a story jurors find hard to forget. Combined with an expert in accident reconstruction, the evidence is compelling. Be sure the proposed expert is qualified. See Form 3.4.[80]

## Transparencies

With the use of an overhead projector, a transparency has even greater effect on the viewer than a chart or poster. Whether the darkened room, soft light, or multiple color schemes are more pleasing to the eye is debatable. What is certain is the transparency's eye-catching quality.

## Thermogram/MRI Results

A modern medical means of measuring injury and specific pathology is the thermogram or the results from magnetic resonance imaging (MRI). Elementally, the test

_____ (1) Complete biographical information (name, age, home address and telephone number, work address and telephone number).

_____ (2) Complete educational background:

    _____ (a) Formal education (colleges, universities, courses of studies, degrees—scientific, engineering, mechanical, etc.),

    _____ (b) Practical education (training as mechanic, engineer, automobile troubleshooter, automotive designer, road designer, race car driver, traffic planner, or city planner),

    _____ (c) Fellowship and honorary degrees,

    _____ (d) Teaching positions (university level and trade shop schools),

    _____ (e) Licenses held,

    _____ (f) Certifications.

_____ (3) Complete employment history (including employment in engineering, traffic planning, city planning, automotive field, physics, and human factors analyses):

    _____ (a) Position presently held (title, description, name of employer, duties, duration, and relation, if any, to accident reconstruction),

    _____ (b) Past experience (titles, descriptions, employers, duties, durations; and relations, if any, to accident reconstruction),

    _____ (c) Consulting work related to accident reconstruction (when, for whom, duties, and compensation).

_____ (4) Professional society memberships:

    _____ (a) Name and address of society in which membership is held,

    _____ (b) All criteria of membership,

    _____ (c) Any special honors or recognition (committee chairmanship, special duties, and responsibilities).

_____ (5) Complete list of publications, texts, and treatises:

    _____ (a) Articles,

    _____ (b) Doctoral dissertations,

    _____ (c) Seminar papers,

    _____ (d) Government reports and studies,

    _____ (e) Texts of speeches,

    _____ (f) Research (published and unpublished).

_____ (6) Complete list of all speeches, lectures, and seminars given:

    _____ (a) Title and topic,

    _____ (b) Date,

    _____ (c) Location,

    _____ (d) Group or organization lectured before.

**FORM 3.4**    Checklist: Qualifications of accident reconstruction expert.

\_\_\_\_\_ (7) Complete list of all licenses held (including requirements for obtaining and maintaining licenses and effective dates).

\_\_\_\_\_ (8) Previous qualifications as expert in accident reconstruction (list particulars of each case):

    \_\_\_\_\_ (a) Prior court experience,

    \_\_\_\_\_ (b) Prior deposition experience,

    \_\_\_\_\_ (c) All areas in which qualified as an expert (traffic engineering, mechanical engineering, electrical engineering, road design, traffic planning, automotive repairs, etc.),

    \_\_\_\_\_ (d) Recognition as expert by government or municipal authorities.

\_\_\_\_\_ (9) Recognition of other authority:

    \_\_\_\_\_ (a) All experts recognize as qualified and authoritative in the field,

    \_\_\_\_\_ (b) All texts, treatises, journals, articles, reports, or studies recognized as authoritative and accepted in the field,

    \_\_\_\_\_ (c) All organizations, committees, groups, or other organizations recognized as qualified and authoritative in the field,

    \_\_\_\_\_ (d) Whether the expert recognizes, is familiar with, and/or accepts the qualifications of the opponent's expert, and the extent of any such familiarity or acceptance.

\_\_\_\_\_ (10) State knowledge of the present case, including all information reviewed:

    \_\_\_\_\_ (a) Tests or measurements (method, areas tested, objects tested, photographs, videotapes, motion pictures, etc.),

    \_\_\_\_\_ (b) Results of tests or measurements,

    \_\_\_\_\_ (c) Findings and opinions,

    \_\_\_\_\_ (d) Demonstrative aids to be used at trial to amplify, explain, or supplement testimony.

\_\_\_\_\_ (11) Identify sources of information relied on:

    \_\_\_\_\_ (a) Histories,

    \_\_\_\_\_ (b) Police reports,

    \_\_\_\_\_ (c) Witness statements,

    \_\_\_\_\_ (d) Manufacturer's literature,

    \_\_\_\_\_ (e) Government reports,

    \_\_\_\_\_ (f) Government studies,

    \_\_\_\_\_ (g) Other studies, analyses, or tests,

    \_\_\_\_\_ (h) Texts, treatises, periodicals, or other literature.

\_\_\_\_\_ (12) Opinion and conclusion:

    \_\_\_\_\_ (a) All test results, facts, and studies on which opinion and conclusion are based,

    \_\_\_\_\_ (b) Specifics of each finding and its relevance to the conclusion,

    \_\_\_\_\_ (c) Degree of certainty of conclusion,

    \_\_\_\_\_ (d) Means of independent verification in support of conclusion.

**FORM 3.4** *Continued*

measures for heat distribution in the human body, with the more prominent heat distributions being correlated to pain or injury centers. "Thermography detects and measures variations in the heat transmitted by various regions of the body and transforms them into visible signals that can be recorded photographically. The basis of thermography is that blood pools in and around an injury to allow healing. The pooling produces hot areas—often called hot spots—on the body."[81] The credibility of the test is established, though challenges on the mechanical principles are still heard.

## § 3.9 PRACTICE POINTERS ON DEMONSTRATIVE EVIDENCE

### Prepare Early

Demonstrative evidence needs advance preparation time. It is not the stuff to think of two days before the trial commences. "Also the opportunity to obtain certain types of demonstrative evidence is often lost by waiting; collision scenes change, automobiles involved in collisions can't be located, documents are lost, etc."[82]

### Deal with Reputable People/Reputable Companies

The world is full of sharks who claim to have expertise in demonstrative services. Stick with the tried and true, the reputable companies. In complex medical fields, precision in the design of products and services is absolutely essential. Trade and professional groups have emerged that grant admission only to the companies meeting certain industry standards.

### Organize the Evidence

Whether by trial notebook, exhibit dividers, or other method, organize each demonstrative exhibit. Sloppiness and disorganization diminish the evidence's value.

### Don't Overdo It!

Salespersons are aware that oversell kills the deal. Overuse of demonstrative evidence minimizes its punch.

### Prepare the Witnesses

Each witness, from the witness to an accident who authenticates photographs or a radiologist confirming an x-ray, to the police officer inspecting the crime scene, needs preparation. Never use demonstrative evidence without sufficiently preparing the witness whose testimony is elicited on the exhibit's content.

## Obtain Admissions/Stipulations

The more pretrial admissions and stipulations acquired from opposing counsel, the fewer evidentiary disputes there will be. Pretrial stipulations "alleviate problems with improper foundation, speed the trial along, and halt interruptions by objection."[83] If the opposition is recalcitrant, make a pretrial request or motion on admissibility, similar to Form 3.5,[84] with the assigned judge. By and large, most attorneys cooperate.

## Prepare Exhibit Lists

Compile a list of all demonstrative exhibits with corresponding identifications and exhibit numbers.

---

[Caption and title]

1. Any of the instruments listed below or the record thereof, or a copy of the record thereof certified by＿＿＿＿＿＿＿＿ [identify certifying officer], or an abstract thereof, may be introduced and admitted in evidence on the trial of this cause. However, the opposing party may, should any question arise respecting the content of any instrument of which an abstract only has been introduced, require production of the complete instrument, or the record thereof, or a certificated copy of the record thereof.

2. Each of the undersigned further waives any requirement of the rules or statutes that notice of intention to introduce the instruments be given, or that a copy of the instruments be filed in the papers in authentication or identification as a condition precedent to the introduction of documentary evidence.

3. The instruments referred to are ＿＿＿＿＿＿＿＿＿＿.

Dated ＿＿＿＿＿＿＿, 20＿＿.

＿＿＿＿＿＿＿＿＿＿

[Signatures and addresses]

---

**FORM 3.5** Stipulation—admitting documents or copies of abstracts thereof and waiving rules relating to introduction of documentary evidence. (Reprinted by permission of West Group.)

## Be Sure to Lay a Foundation

Be certain that the evidence helps the court and the jury understand its case. Be able to relate how the evidence fits the facts and law in the case litigated. Most demonstrative evidence is admitted when its purpose and form are clearly enunciated.

## Authenticate, Authenticate, Authenticate

Never forget demonstrative evidence is generally inadmissible without an authenticating witness.

## Make Sure the Evidence Accomplishes Its Purpose

Discern whether the demonstrative form achieved its goal. Make sure that the evidence speaks to the *truth*.

## § 3.10 SUMMARY

The tools of demonstrative evidence are essential to practicing attorneys, prosecutorial and defense teams, and support personnel. Explaining the real underlying evidence by clarifying, elucidating, and making it more understandable is the chief purpose for demonstrative evidence.

The chapter covered in depth the diverse types of demonstrative evidence. Substantial attention was given to photographic evidence, models, charts, diagrams, illustrations, reconstructive materials, easels, blackboards, and other imaging techniques. X-rays, day-in-the-life films, thermograms, experiments, and re-creations were analyzed. Each of these demonstrative forms was scrutinized in light of its utility and function, as well as its admissibility. Numerous forms, checklists, and exhibits were sprinkled throughout the content.

### Notes

1. JOAN M. BROVINS & THOMAS OEHMKE, The Trial Practice Guide: Strategies, Systems and Procedures for the Attorney 166 (1992).
2. Julian O. Von Kalinowski, *Actions for Unfair Competition—Trade Secrets,* 14 Am. Jur. Trials 63 (1968).
3. PHILIP H. CORBOY & ROBERT A. CLIFFORD, *Demonstrative Evidence, in* Master Advocate Handbook 177 (D. Lake Rumsey ed., 1986).
4. Fed. R. Evid. 401.
5. Fed. R. Evid. 403.
6. CHARLES T. McCORMICK, McCormick on Evidence 528 (1972).
7. MELVIN BELLI, Modern Trials 926 (1954).

8. BEVERLY HUTSON, Paralegal Trial Handbook 4-5 (1991).

9. As the National Institute of Trial Advocacy comments, "The general test for admitting demonstrative evidence is whether it will truly help the jury understand relevant matters." CORBOY & CLIFFORD, *supra* note 3, at 179.

10. Newton Gresham, *Action on Fire Insurance Policies,* 10 Am. Jur. Trials 301, 368 (1965).

11. HUTSON, *supra* note 8, at 4-6.

12. CHARLES C. SCOTT, Scott on Photographic Evidence 319 (1969).

13. 8 STANDARD PA. PRACTICE 2d § 52.5. *See also* S. Ehrlich, *Preparing and Using Photographs in Civil Cases,* 3 Am. Jur. Trials 1 (1965).

14. Fed. R. Evid.1001(2).

15. Fed. R. Evid. 1001(3).

16. Michael Graham, *Evidence and Trial Advocacy Workshop: Demonstrative Evidence—Photographs of Victims and "Mugshots,"* 40 Crim. L. Bull. 333, 335 (1984).

17. Mark Dombroff, *Utilizing Photographs as Demonstrative Evidence,* 18 Trial 71 (Dec. 1982).

18. Graham, *supra* note 16, at 334.

19. 32 Ill. 2d. 96, 203 N.E. 873 (1965).

20. MARK DOMBROFF, Dombroff on Unfair Tactics 465 (1988).

21. 258 N.W.2d 374 (1977).

22. 22 Utah 2d 408, 410, 454 P.2d 290, 291 (1969).

23. *Id.,* 454 P.2d at 291.

24. 38 Cal. App. 3d 680, 689, 113 Cal. Rptr. 530, 536 (1974).

25. *Id.,* 113 Cal. Rptr. at 536.

26. Benjamin Mattison, *Seeing Can Be Deceiving: Photographic Evidence in a Visual Age—How Much Weight Does It Deserve?,* 25 Wm. & Mary L. Rev. 705 (1984).

27. As Benjamin Mattison points out in his exceptional article *Seeing Can Be Deceiving: Photographic Evidence in a Visual Age,* "A catalog of optical illusions is unnecessary to establish that one image may convey different ideas to different people. Perceptional errors result not so much from defects in the human optical system as from the process from which the mind interprets visual stimuli. The mind interprets stimuli according to past experiences and prejudices both of which are unique to the individual. Because of this subjective perception process, jurors can misinterpret the contents of an undistorted photograph." *Id.* at 733.

28. *Id.* at 738.

29. 465 A.2d. 153 (R.I. 1983).

30. Steven Bergel, *Evidence—"Silent Witness Theory" Adopted to Admit Photographs Without Precedent Witness Testimony,* 19 Suffolk U. L. Rev. 256, 257 (1985).

31. The silent witness theory has its share of critics. In *Bergner v. State,* in response to an objection under the silent witness theory, the court held "that a strong showing of the photograph's competency and authenticity must be established where a sufficiently strong foundation has been laid..." The photograph's inadmissibility "is left to the sound discretion of the trial court, reviewable only for abuse." 397 N.E.2d 1012, 1015 (1979). *See also* CHARLES C. SCOTT, Photographic Evidence (1969).

32. Bergel, *supra* note 30, at 358.

33. JAMES McCARTHY, Making Trial Objections 4-7 (1986).

34. DiMichael v. South Buffalo Railway Co. and Poole v. Consolidated Rail Corp., 80 N.Y.2d 184 (1992).

35. Georgia Sargeant, *Watching the Watcher: Surveillance Films Must Be Disclosed Before N.Y. Trials,* 29 Trial, 118 (1993).

36. For cross-examination suggestions on surveillance evidence, see Stewart M. Casper, *Looking Fraudulent Surveillance in the Eye: How to Refute Distorted Evidence,* 29 Trial 137, 140–141 (1993).

37. McCARTHY, *supra* note 33, at 4-8.

38. Greg Joseph, *Demonstrative Videotape Evidence,* 22 Trial 60, 61 (1986).

39. Fed. R. Evid. 1006.

40. SCOTT, *supra* note 12, at 1297.

41. CORBOY & CLIFFORD, *supra* note 3, at 183.

42. Greg Joseph, in his discussion *Demonstrative Videotape Evidence,* calls vigorously for the admission of day-in-the-life videotapes: "Day-in-the-life tapes document the effects of severe injury. They attempt to communicate the extent of injury by focusing on routine daily activities in the life of severely injured plaintiffs. The tapes are usually unpleasant and often emotionally draining to watch." Joseph, *supra* note 38, at 63.

43. 430 A.2d 1 (Conn. 1980).

44. *Id.* at 8.

45. JOHN TARANTINO, Trial Evidence Foundations 5-27 (1987).

46. *See* Robert D. Peltz, *Admissibility of "Day in the Life" Films,* 63 Fla. B. J. 55 (1989); Martha A. Churchill, *Day in the Life Films Subject to Court Challenge,* 32 For the Def. 24 (1990). The cases most often cited at the federal bench are Grimes v. Employer Mutual Liability Insurance Co., 73 F.R.D. 607 (D. Ala. 1977) (upheld the admissibility of video-tapes) and Bolstridge v. Central Maine Power Co., 621 F. Supp. 1202 (D. Me. 1985) (de-nied entry).

47. Edmond A. Provder, *Life Care Plan—Documenting Damages in Catastrophic Injury Cases,* 16 Trial Dipl. J. 5, 9–10 (1993).

48. 465 F. Supp. 566 (D.S.C. 1979).

49. *Id.* at 569.

50. EDWARD J. IMWINKELREID, Evidentiary Foundations 89–91 (1980).

51. KENT SINCLAIR, Trial Handbook 78 (2d ed. 1992).

52. Medical Legal Art, 900 Circle 75 Parkway, Suite 720, Atlanta, GA 30339.

53. HUTSON, *supra* note 8, at 4-34.

54. Legal Graphic Communicators, 2660 Horizon Drive, SE., Grand Rapids, MI 49506, 616-956-9009.

55. Anatomical Chart Company, 8221 Kimball Avenue, Skokie, IL 60076, 1-800-621-7500, <http://www.anatomical.com/anatomical/index.html>, visited January 19, 2000. Its free anatomical products catalog offers interesting representations of the human body.

56. MILFORD MEYER, Pennslyvania Trial Advocacy Handbook, 222 (1976).

57. MICHAEL GRAHAM, Evidence, Text, Rules, Illustrations and Problems 427 (1983).

58. 8 STANDARD PA. PRACTICE 2d, 52:17 (1994).

59. Philip K. Anthony & Donald E. Vinson, *Demonstrative Exhibits: A Key to Effective Jury Presentation*, 26 For the Def. 13, 15 (Nov 1986).

60. Bionet, Inc., 54 Bow Circle, Suite 202, Hilton Head Island, SC 29928, <http://www.bionetmed.com>, visited January 19, 2000.

61. PENNSYLVANIA TRIAL LAWYERS ASSOCIATION, Skeletal Anatomy and Fracture, A Personal Injury Handbook 42 (n.d.).

62. Legal Graphic Communicators, 2660 Horizon Drive, SE, Grand Rapids, MI 49546, <http://www.legalgraphic.com/medical.html>, visited January 19, 2000.

63. *Id.* at <http://www.legalgraphic.com/mechanical.html>, visited January 19, 2000.

64. Jack Olender, *Showing Pain and Suffering,* 5 Am. Jur. Trials 921 (1985).

65. Melvin Belli, *Use of Blackboard and Related Visual Aids*, 5 Am. Jur. Trials 584 (1985).

66. MEYER, *supra* note 56, at 223.

67. Annotation, *Admissibility of Evidence of Ancient Maps and the Like,* 46 A.L.R.2d 1318 (1990).

68. *Id.*

69. *Use of Maps, Plats and Charts to Show Change in Shoreline by Accretion or Avulsion,* 21 Am. Jur. Trials 2d 147 (1980).

70. Mark C. Joye, *Computer Animations,* 34 Trial 47 (Nov. 1998).

71. Brown, *Visual Evidence, Animation Adds a New Dimension,* Nat'l L.J. 2 May 27, 1991, at 2.

72. Wolf Technical Services, Inc., 16828 Hawthorn Park Drive, Indianapolis, IN 46220, 317-842-6075, <http://www.a1.com/wts/accident.html>, visited August 31, 1999.

73. Roy W. Krieger, *Photorealistic Computer Graphics: New Horizon for Evidence*, 29 Trial 46 (1993).

74. Joseph Ryan, *Techniques for Success in Preparing and Using Demonstrative Evidence*, Def. Couns. J. 189, 194 (1991). *See also* Robert Seltzer, *The Keys to Admissibility*, 10 Cal. L. Rev. 78 (1990); Lehr, *Admissibility of a Computer Simulation*, 32 For the Def. 8 (1990).

75. Krieger, *supra* note 73, at 49.

76. *See* ANDRE MOESSENS, Scientific Evidence in Criminal Cases (1998); CHARLES T. MCCORMICK, McCormick on Evidence (1984).

77. 8 STANDARD PA. PRACTICE 2d § 52.18.

78. John Merritts, *Re-creation, The Tool of a Winning Lawyer*, 15 Trial L.Q. 64, 66 (1983). *See* Lample v. Vaygood, 422 S.W.2d 708 (Tenn. 1967).

79. Breimon v. General Motors Corp., 509 P.2d 398 (Wash. App. 1973).

80. JOHN TARANTINO, Strategic Use of Scientific Evidence 566 (1988).

81. Gregory G. Jones & Lorin M. Subar, *Proving What Seems Unprovable*, 32 Trial 47 (Dec. 1996).

82. CORBOY & CLIFFORD, *supra* note 3, at 185.

83. TARANTINO, *supra* note 45, at 5-32.

84. 1 Fed. Proc. Forms L. Ed. 516 (1975).

# CHAPTER 4

# Documentary Evidence

## § 4.1 INTRODUCTION

The role documents play in civil and criminal litigation is noteworthy. Whether a criminal or civil case of fraud, forgery, or kidnaping is before the bar, documents are prime movers in meeting evidentiary burdens. Outside the litigation arena, documentary evidence is the centerpiece of the investigative process, from collecting medical and hospital reports in a malpractice case, to deciphering the contents of an arrest warrant in a defendant's constitutional challenge. Why documents receive such favorable status is obvious—they are permanent instruments that memorialize and trap thoughts, ideas, and proposed actions and by their content, both directly and indirectly, trap history. Documents like stock certificates or mortgages are prima facie evidence of ownership and control. Oral or other testimonial assertions are inferior to the document's content, since memory fades, while documents are intact.

Examples of documentary evidence include *business records, wills, trusts, deeds, contracts, hospital records, state and federal tax records,* and other official documents. The integrity of a document is always subject to challenge. Notice the alteration at Figures 4.1 and 4.2.

Evidentiary guidelines regarding the content, quality, and general admissibility of documents are this chapter's central focus.

## § 4.2 RULES OF ADMISSIBILITY

Assuming relevancy, nonprejudice, and technical sufficiency, documentary evidence rarely confronts evidentiary hurdles it cannot scale. However, technical rules are many. FRE Rule 1001 defines a document as follows:

> "Writings" and "recordings" consist of letters, words, or numbers, or their equivalent, set down by handwriting, typewriting, printing, photostating, photographing,

---

### AGREEMENT TO SELL PERSONAL PROPERTY

Purchase and Sales Agreement made by and between _John Q. Seller_
of _Anytown, USA_ (Seller), and _Mary Q. Buyer_
of _Anytown, USA_ (Buyer).

Whereas, for good consideration the parties mutually agree that:

1. Seller agrees to sell, and Buyer agrees to buy the following described property:

   _1 (one) 19" color TV, Panasonic, with remote control_

2. Buyer agrees to pay to Seller and Seller agrees to accept as total purchase price the sum of $ _200.00_ , payable as follows:

   $ _50.00_ deposit herewith paid
   $ _150.00_ balance payable on delivery by cash, bank or certified check

3. Seller warrants it has good and legal title to said property, full authority to sell said property, and that said property shall be sold by warranty bill of sale free and clear of all liens, encumbrances, liabilities and adverse claims of every nature and description whatsoever.

---

**FIGURE 4.1**   Original agreement to sell.

magnetic impulse, mechanical or electronic recording, or other form of data compilation.[1]

The Federal Rules of Evidence recognize the elaborate and often eccentric means of recording information, and, hence, "writing" is broadly defined. Complications arise in the content and quality of the evidence, rather than its nature. Examples of these legal difficulties include the following:

- Has the writing or document been altered, changed, or modified in any way?
- Has the writing or document been forged or altered for a criminal purpose?
- Is the writing or document an original, a copy, a duplicate, or other secondary representation?
- Is the writing or document hearsay and thus objectionable?
- Is the writing or document in need of authentication and identification?

---

### AGREEMENT TO SELL PERSONAL PROPERTY

Purchase and Sales Agreement made by and between ___John Q. Seller___
of ___Anytown, USA___ (Seller), and ___Mary Q. Buyer___
of ___Anytown, USA___ (Buyer).

Whereas, for good consideration the parties mutually agree that:

1. Seller agrees to sell, and Buyer agrees to buy the following described property:

   I (one) 19" color TV, Panasonic, with remote control

2. Buyer agrees to pay to Seller and Seller agrees to accept as total purchase price the sum of $ ___2,000.00___ , payable as follows:

   $ ___500.00___ deposit herewith paid
   $ ___1,500.00___ balance payable on delivery by cash, bank or certified check

3. Seller warrants it has good and legal title to said property, full authority to sell said property, and that said property shall be sold by warranty bill of sale free and clear of all liens, encumbrances, liabilities and adverse claims of every nature and description whatsoever.

---

**FIGURE 4.2**  Altered agreement to sell.

- Is the writing or document self-authenticating?
- Is the writing or document as submitted for the court's consideration the best evidence available?
- Are the format and composition of the writing or document sufficiently reliable if submitted in summary form?

Arguments involving the content and quality of documentary evidence are multifaceted. Under FRE 1008, an attempt is made to differentiate the purposes of a document's admission under the evidentiary rules:

> When the admissibility of other evidence of contents of writings, recordings, or photographs under these rules depends upon the fulfillment of a condition of fact, the question whether the condition has been fulfilled is ordinarily for the court to determine in accordance with the provisions of rule 104. However, when an issue

is raised (a) whether the asserted writing ever existed, or (b) whether another writing, recording, or photograph produced at the trial is the original, or (c) whether other evidence of contents correctly reflects the contents, the issue is for the trier of fact to determine as in the case of other issues of fact.[2]

In other words, documents can be offered to prove far more than the document's content alone. Is the document being admitted to prove the content within, or is the document being submitted for purposes of identification of a handwriting? Is the document being offered to prove notice of waiver of rights or other legal matter? Is the document being submitted to prove a substantive element of a crime, such as threat in a kidnaping case or a contract breach? Why documentary evidence is preferred has much to do with the evidentiary review the document will undergo.

## The Best Evidence Rule

The *best evidence rule* mandates a preference for original documents, rather than duplicates and other secondary sources. FRE 1002 emphasizes this inclination: "To prove the content of a writing, recording, or photograph, the original writing, recording, or photograph is required, except as otherwise provided in these rules or by Act of Congress."[3]

The best evidence rule derives its support from the conventional wisdom that originals are more reliable than duplicates. Alterations or other modifications are more difficult in original material. Dean John H. Wigmore is predictably eloquent on the subject:

> The reasons are simple and obvious enough and dictated by common sense and long experience. They may be summed up in this way:
>
> (1) As between a supposed literal copy and the original, the copy is always liable to errors on the part of the copyist, whether by willfulness or by inadvertence; this contingency wholly disappears when the original is produced. Moreover, the original may contain, and the copy will lack, such features of handwriting, paper, and the like, as may afford the opponent valuable means of learning legitimate objections to the significance of the document.
>
> (2) As between oral testimony, based on recollection, and the original, the added risk, almost a certainty, exists, of errors of recollection due to the difficulty of carrying in the memory literally the tenor of the document.[4]

The best evidence rule is a preferential rather than mandatory rule. The rule's intent and ultimate desire are for the production of originals. Realistically, the rule accepts that originals are not always available. FRE Rule 1004 sets out the distinction of original and duplicate requirements:

> The original is not required, and other evidence of the contents of a writing, recording, or photograph is admissible if—

(1) Originals lost or destroyed. All originals are lost or have been destroyed, unless the proponent lost or destroyed them in bad faith; or

(2) Original not obtainable. No original can be obtained by any available judicial process or procedure; or

(3) Original in possession of opponent. At a time when an original was under the control of the party against whom offered, that party was put on notice, by the pleadings or otherwise, that the contents would be a subject of proof at the hearing, and that party does not produce the original at the hearing; or

(4) Collateral matters. The writing, recording, or photograph is not closely related to a controlling issue.[5]

In this context, the Federal Rules of Evidence, as well as most state jurisdictions, prefer the primary document, although they are not inherently adverse to secondary evidence. The best evidence rule merely prefers the original, if at all possible to obtain, since it is the most convincing evidence available. FRE Rule 1003 categorically permits the admissibility of duplicates: "A duplicate is admissible to the same extent as an original unless (1) a genuine question is raised as to the authenticity of the original or (2) in the circumstances it would be unfair to admit the duplicate in lieu of the original."[6]

In cases of forgery, consumer fraud, extortion, or embezzlement, as illustrations, the rule's wisdom permits challenges to the original by giving preferences to a duplicate that manifests alterations or changes in the original document. Review the alteration at Figure 4.3.[7] In this circumstance, since the original has been altered, an infrared copy will be admitted as proof of the original's alteration.

The Federal Rules of Evidence also attempt to precisely define what an original is under the principles of the best evidence rule. At FRE Rule 1001, an original is "the writing or recording itself or any counterpart intended to have the same effect by a person executing or issuing it. An 'original' of a photograph includes the negative or any print therefrom. If data are stored in a computer or similar device, any printout or other output readable by sight, shown to reflect the data accurately is an 'original.'"[8] Under the same FRE Rule 1001, one of the most interesting nuances of the best evidence rule emerges at part (4), entitled "Duplicate." The rule suggests with irony that a proponent of the documentary evidence should provide an original, but simultaneously accepts a sweeping duplicate definition:

A "duplicate" is a counterpart produced by the same impression as the original, or from the same matrix, or by means of photography, including enlargements and miniatures, or by mechanical or electronic re-recording, or by chemical reproduction, or by other equivalent techniques which accurately reproduces the original.[9]

Hence, a literal reading of the duplicate definition describes a copy as being an acceptable substitute for an original. Copies are given the status of originals unless, as

**FIGURE 4.3**   Infrared copy of altered document. (Reprinted by permission of IISI, Ltd.)

was noted in FRE 1003, there is an issue as to the authenticity of the original or the admission of the duplicate would prejudice the proceedings or cause some unfair results. In an age of mechanical reproduction, both commonplace and highly sophisticated, the Federal Rules policy on the admission of duplicates seems wise. However, as a practical matter, even when the rules provide for exceptional circumstances, the justice professional should always yearn for the original. Under the Model Code of Evidence of the American Law Institute, the preferential inclination to the original is reinforced at Rule 602:

> As tending to prove the content of a writing, except in an official record, no evidence other than the writing itself is admissible unless:
>
> (a) evidence has been introduced sufficient to support a finding that the writing once existed and is not a writing produced at trial, and the judge finds

that, assuming that the writing once existed and is not a writing produced at trial,

(i) it is now unavailable for some reason other than the culpable negligence or wrongdoing of the proponent of the evidence or

(ii) it would be unfair or inexpedient to require the proponent to produce the writing; or

(b) the writing is one authorized by statute to be recorded in a public office of a state or nation and the offered evidence is admissible evidence of the content of the official record of the writing.[10]

These same rules can be applicably interpreted when the content of the document is the aim of the admission. In other cases—say, to refresh a witness's recollection or as an admission—the rule may not be applicable.[11] With these types of exceptional circumstances, it is uncanny how the best evidence rule has earned its reputation as an onerous legal barrier. Again, the desire and mandate for an original will be triggered only when the contents of the writing and the terms and conditions as enunciated within the writing itself are the bases for the writing's admission. From a secondary angle, if an original is not available for good-faith reasons (such as its proponent can prove that it is lost or unavailable or that its whereabouts are inexplicable), the best evidence rule will accept the next best evidence, which would be a copy or a duplicate. Upon closer reading of the Federal Rules of Evidence, duplicates—that is, exact reproductions or replications of the original—fall within the guidelines of the definition of an original. Examples of duplicates that are readily given the status of an original are copies of an originally impressed search warrant, duplicate sales slips that are carbonized, leases executed in duplicate, and other mechanically reproduced originals.

Viewed objectively, the best evidence rule is a principle of flexibility, rather than absolute dogma. While the original may be preferred, the rule recognizes that the original may be unavailable, or that the proponent has been unable to secure an actual original from the opposing party, or that the original is unnecessary, since the writing's contents are not in dispute. Professor Robert Barker sums up all the legal implications of the best evidence rule:

> Thus, where the Best Evidence Rule applies, the original must be produced unless its absence can be satisfactorily accounted for, in which case secondary evidence will be admissible. Questions arise concerning the application of these common law rules. First, is the content of the writing sought to be admitted for its substantive value? Second, what constitutes an original? Third, if the contents are sought to be proved and there is no original, what is a sufficient foundation for the introduction of secondary evidence? Fourth, what constitutes admissible secondary evidence?[12]

## The Best Evidence Rule: Exceptions

Under federal and most state guidelines, exceptions automatically admit copies or at least grant equal legal status to documents that fall within the following classifications or categories.

***Official Documents / Public Records.***   Explicitly accorded an "original" status at FRE Rule 1005 are official public records. The rule states:

> The contents of an official record, or of a document authorized to be recorded or filed and actually recorded or filed, including data compilations in any form, if otherwise admissible, may be proved by copy, certified as correct in accordance with Rule 902 or testified to be correct by a witness who has compared it with the original.[13]

Documents recorded or imprinted with a government seal are acceptable replacements for an original. Examples include copies of deeds, releases, mortgages, notes, and judgments. Certain jurisdictions accept, without reservation, copies that have been acknowledged by any notary or other government officer. Examples of acknowledgments that might be appended to a copy of an original document are shown at Forms 4.1 and 4.2.[14]

> Richardson's *Treatise on Evidence* approves the flexibility of the public records exception. In the case of public records, the importance of preserving the security of public records, coupled with a convenience afforded all parties concerned, prevails over the *Best Evidence Rule,* allowing copies to be produced in lieu of the original.[15]

***Summaries.***   For the sake of clarity, summarized or digested versions of huge collections of documents, or as the Federal Rules so designate, "voluminous writings, recordings, or photographs which cannot conveniently be examined in court may be presented in the form of a chart, summary, or calculation."[16] Employing a pragmatic tone, FRE Rule 1006 recognizes the impossibility of asking members of a jury or a witness to comprehend deposition tomes, or crates of governmental, medical, or business records that are often so weighty that an intelligible review in examination is impractical. Exercising their discretion, courts can permit summarized, condensed versions thereof as long as the originals are made available. If summaries are being introduced, make sure the underlying evidence matches the summarized work.

***Testimony or Written Admission of a Party.***   Under FRE Rule 1007, "[c]ontents of writings, recordings, or photographs may be proved by the testimony or deposition of the party against whom offered or by that party's written admission, without accounting for the nonproduction of the original."[17] Whether a court transcript, a deposition format, or a confession, Rule 1007 creates an exception to the best evidence rule by not requiring the original document. The rationale for the exception holds that testimony under oath is considered reliable enough to eliminate the demand for the original. A challenge to a copy under these circumstances will be rejected. However, the party against whom the admitted document is being used may challenge the accuracy of the copy relative to the original in rebuttal or cross-examination.

State of _____

County of _____

    On this, the _____ day of _____, [20] _____, before me _____, the undersigned officer, personally appeared _____, known to me (or satisfactorily proven) to be the person whose name _____ is subscribed to the within instrument, and acknowledged that _____ he _____ executed the same for the purposes therein contained.

    In witness whereof, I hereunto set my hand and official seal.

_____

_____

Title of Officer

**FORM 4.1** Acknowledgment of instrument executed by individual. (Reprinted by permission of West Group.)

State of _____

County of _____

    On this, the _____ day of _____, [20] _____, before me _____, the undersigned officer, personally appeared _____, known to me (or satisfactorily proven) to be the person whose name is subscribed as attorney in fact for _____, and acknowledged that he executed the same as the act of his principal for the purposes therein contained.

    In witness whereof, I hereunto set my hand and official seal.

_____

_____

Title of Officer

**FORM 4.2** Acknowledgment of instrument executed by attorney in fact.

*Hearsay.* Documents proposed for admission often contain the declarations, commentary, affirmations, or statements of unavailable witnesses. Documents may be business records, medical or hospital notations, notes, charts, records, marriage and divorce documents, birth records, or other regular vital data. In some circumstances, the content of the documents can be attacked as hearsay, since the content of the document is not being attested to by the declarant and the information contained therein is being proffered to prove the truth of the declaration or the assertion within the document. The restrictiveness of the hearsay rule has long promoted creative approaches in the forging and formulation of exceptions. Under FRE Rule 803, the availability of the declarant to attest as witness is completely immaterial in these documentary situations:

- Written statement regarding mental, emotional, and physical condition;
- Written statement involving medical diagnosis or treatments;
- Recorded recollections in a memorandum or other record;
- Records of regularly conducted activity;
- Public records and reports;
- Records of vital statistics;
- Records of religious organizations;
- Marriage, baptismal, and similar certificates;
- Family records;
- Statements and records of documents indicating an interest in property;
- Statements and ancient documents;
- Market reports;
- Commercial publications; and
- Learned treatises.

For example, in a deed dispute, will counsel be required to have the recording officer of the deed available to authenticate and attest to the content of the deed? Since the document falls within one of the hearsay exceptions, the recording officer need not be present.

Under the Federal Rules, the discretionary authority granted to a judge to determine hearsay exceptions in matters involving documentary evidence is liberal. At FRE Rule 807, the provision affords the admissibility of literally any form of hearsay if certain requirements are met. The rule relays specifically:

> A statement not specifically covered by Rule 803 or 804 but having equivalent circumstantial guarantees of trustworthiness, is not excluded by the hearsay rule, if the court determines that (A) the statement is offered as evidence of a material fact; (B) the statement is more probative on the point for which it is offered than any other evidence which the proponent can procure through reasonable efforts; and (C) the

---

> **CASE EXAMPLE 4.1**    *Admission of Hearsay Evidence*
>
> **CASE:** *McKinnon v. Skil Corp.,* 638 F.2d. 270 (1st Cir. 1981).
>
> **FACTS:** In an action under a product liability theory, plaintiff's counsel sought the admission of various studies authored by a government agency, the Consumer Product Safety Commission (CPSC). The CPSC regularly conducts safety tests and analyses on various products offered to the public. Victims of product accidents are routinely interviewed. In this case, testimony of the accident victim relayed how she was injured by the product. The reports also contain the conversations and commentary of a CPSC investigator. Both the investigator and the accident victim gave detailed information on how the accident occurred. Victim's counsel seeks admission of the reports. Defense counsel objects, claiming the documentary evidence is hearsay.
>
> **QUESTIONS AND ISSUES:**
>
> 1. Is the content of the CPSC report hearsay?
> 2. Assuming the writing is hearsay, is there an exception that permits its admission?
>
> **HOLDING:** In the absence of the declarants, namely, the accident victim and the CPSC investigator, the writing, as submitted, is hearsay.

general purposes of these rules and the interests of justice will best be served by admission of the statement into evidence.[18]

See Case Example 4.1.

Under Rule 803 of the Federal Rules of Evidence, entitled "Public Records and Reports," an exception may exist. If the public record is trustworthy, it may be admissible under Section (8)(C) of the same rule "in civil actions and proceedings and against the Government in criminal cases, factual findings resulting from an investigation made pursuant to authority granted by law, unless the sources of information or other circumstances indicate lack of trustworthiness."[19] In this case, the court viewed this writing as nothing more than double hearsay, and hence untrustworthy, since neither of the declarants was available. The court also considered the reports as being less than a factual finding.

A state trooper's standard accident report was admissible, despite the lack of trooper testimony at trial, under a theory of business or public record.[20]

## § 4.3 AUTHENTICATION AND IDENTIFICATION

Once the barriers of the best evidence rule, the hearsay rule, and relevancy have been overcome and before the evidence is admitted, the proponent needs to authenticate the document. Authentication is the process of establishing that a writing,

---

The parties to this action, through their undersigned attorney, stipulate:

1. Any of the instruments listed below, or the record thereof, or a copy of the record thereof certified by _____ [identify certifying officer], or an abstract thereof, may be introduced and admitted in evidence on the trial of this cause. However, the opposing party may, should any question arise respecting the content of any instrument of which an abstract only has been introduced, require production of the complete instrument, or the record thereof, or a certified copy of the record thereof.

2. Each of the undersigned further waives any requirement that notice of intention to introduce the instruments be given, or that a copy of the instruments be filed in the papers in this cause, or compliance with any other requirements relating to the authentication or identification as a condition precedent to the introduction of documentary evidence.

3. The instruments referred to are: _____

Dated _____, [20]_____.

_____

[Signatures and addresses]

---

**FORM 4.3** Stipulation admitting documents or copies or abstracts thereof and waiving requirements relating to introduction of documentary evidence. (Reprinted by permission of West Group.)

document, photograph, or other instrument is genuine and that it is exactly what the offering party claims that it is. Stipulations provide a shortcut in the authentication. See Form 4.3.[21]

Another avenue that minimizes the procedural demands of authentication is the function of self-authentication under FRE Rule 902. Extrinsic evidence of authentication as a condition precedent is not required with respect to the following writings or other documentary forms:

1. Domestic public documents under seal,
2. Domestic public documents not under seal,
3. Foreign public documents,
4. Certified copies of public records,
5. Official publications,
6. Newspapers and periodicals,
7. Trade inscriptions and the like,

8. Acknowledged documents,

9. Commercial paper and related documents, and

10. Presumption under acts of Congress.

In these classifications, authenticity is inherently established for purposes of admissibility. For reasons of public policy and practicality, governmental documents under seal are self-authenticating.

Another classification of documents that meets the criteria of self-authentication is the "ancient" document. Documents that are of sufficient antiquity are presumed to be credible simply because of their maturity. The Model Code of Evidence at Rule 601 suggests a codification:

A writing, offered in evidence as authentic, is admissible, if

(a) sufficient evidence has been introduced to sustain a finding of its authenticity or

(b) the judge finds that the writing
    (i)   is at least thirty years old at the time it is so offered and
    (ii)  is in such condition as to create no suspicion concerning its authenticity and
    (iii) at the time of its discovery was in a place in which such document, if authentic, would be likely to be found.[22]

## Authentication by Author

A document can be authenticated by its author, and if the writer/author is not available, subscribing witnesses in the case of sealed or notarized instruments may substitute. One who subscribes or attests to an instrument's content asserts the competency of its maker to understand and execute it. The rule requiring that "an attested writing be authenticated by the testimony of the subscribing witness whenever possible has been applied to various types of attested writings such as bonds not executed pleaded in court, instruments under seal, assignments of choses in action, contracts not under seal, attested negotiable instruments, and attested receipts."[23]

If neither the author nor a subscribing witness is available, look to other means of authentication. FRE Rule 901 highlights a series of alternatives to the actual author:

1. Testimony of a witness with knowledge,

2. Nonexpert opinion on handwriting,

3. Comparison by the trier or an expert witness,

4. Distinctive characteristics and the like,

5. Voice identification,

6. Telephone conversations,

7. Public records or reports,

8. Ancient documents or data compilations,

9. Process or system, and

10. Methods provided by statute or rule.[24]

## Authentication of Business/Medical Records

A witness who composed the record, is knowledgeable as to its content, or can attest to its accuracy and validity is capable of authentication. Yet gaining personal access to a business or medical record's preparer is not always feasible. In most jurisdictions, evidentiary rules of authentication have been relaxed. The authenticator can be a person who is custodian of the document or in control of the record. "Thus business records of large mercantile establishments may be authenticated by the testimony of the persons who either made the original memoranda or the book entries, or who are officers of the establishment in charge and custody of the books and memoranda in question."[25] The requirement for authentication of these types of records is that someone be familiar with the record's content and that the record be made in the regular course of business. At FRE Rule 803(6), a definition of records of regularly conducted activity is set out:

> A memorandum, report, record, or data compilation, in any form, of acts, events, conditions, opinions, or diagnoses, made at or near the time by, or from information transmitted by, a person with knowledge, if kept in the course of a regularly conducted business activity, and if it was the regular practice of that business activity to make the memorandum, report, record, or data compilation, all as shown by the testimony of the custodian or other qualified witness, unless the source of information or the method or circumstances of preparation indicate lack of trustworthiness. The term "business" as used in this paragraph includes business, institution, association, profession, occupation, and calling of every kind, whether or not conducted for profit.[26]

Under this definitional standard, the record's authenticator can be a party beyond the record's author. Since regularly kept business records are compiled by rote and repetition, and with a certain level of mechanical regularity, the actual author is not required. Due to its mechanical nature, the record's probability for trustworthiness and credibility far outweighs its potential for alteration. Thus, the authenticator can be the file clerk, the secretary, or the paraprofessional in charge of the documents. Trial attorney John Tarantino summarizes the foundational elements necessary for the admission of a business record:

- The witness has personal knowledge of the business filing or record-keeping system,

- The witness removed a record from a particular file or catalog retrieval system,

- The witness recognizes the exhibit as the record he or she removed from the file or catalog retrieval system, and

- The witness explains how he or she recognizes the exhibit.[27]

Those wishing to bar the admission of business records should inquire whether or not the record fits definitionally. Relevant questions might include the following:

1. Is the record a form of data regularly kept by the business or organization?

2. Does the record merely contain "rote" data, raw information without interpretation or opinion?

3. Are the records made at irregular intervals, rather than on consistent dates?

4. Were the entries in the business records made at or near the time at which they were to be inserted?

The regularity of the record demonstrates whether a record is a business record or not. For example, case notes authored by a social worker investigating a suspicious fire were deemed a normal business record not subject to hearsay restriction;[28] a letter of foreclosure from attorney to insuree was deemed a business record.[29] To the contrary, a mental health progress report was deemed untrustworthy and therefore inadmissible, due in large part to its interpretive quality.[30]

## Authentication by Handwriting Analysis: Lay Witnesses

In most legal circles, authentication of a document or writing is permissible by an examination, evaluation, and subsequent identification of the handwriting style. The opinion of a layperson as to the identity of the author can be based upon the content and style of writing. FRE Rule 901(b)(2) permits "[n]onexpert opinion as to the genuineness of handwriting, based upon familiarity not acquired for purposes of the litigation."[31] Lay theory identification must be based on certain foundational elements:

1. The witness is familiar with and has experience in the view and observation of the author's handwriting.

2. The witness can correlate that experience to the specific document in question.

3. The authenticator can prove familiarity with that handwriting.[32]

Sufficient familiarity may be demonstrated by seeing the author's writing, by exchanging correspondence, or by any other means that affords a basis for identifying the document at a later date.[33]

As in many other areas of the law, the historical preference granted to a lay witness has been replaced by an unwavering and sometimes unlimited authority bestowed on the "experts." Historically, in the area of documentary evidence and analysis, there was a reticence to admit expert testimony. Instead, the preferred means was for a lay witness to attest to a familiarity with the handwriting of the document's author. To the consternation of some legal scholars, courts continue to succumb to the seemingly unassailable qualifications of expert witnesses regarding this and other forms of evidentiary matter.

## Authentication by Handwriting Analysis: Expert Witnesses

The Federal Rules recognize that a document can be evaluated by qualified experts in the field of handwriting analysis and questioned documents. FRE Rule 901 permits "[c]omparison by the trier of fact or by expert witnesses with specimens which have been authenticated."[34] "The use of expert testimony is now the common and preferred means of offering evidence on the issues of document authentication."[35] Document examiners and handwriting analysts are interchangeably labeled calligrapher, graphologist, graphoanalyst, questioned document analyst, and handwriting examiner. Nanette Galbraith, in her work *Trends in the Field of Questioned Document Examination*, attempts to quantify handwriting and document examiner expertise.[36] For the period from 1956 to 1980, a survey was conducted of individuals who claimed to be experts. The conclusions reached are summarized:

> There have been two trends in the field of questioned document examinations as observed in the literature over the last twenty-three years: Training for examiners and increased use of scientific methods and equipment. There has been a continuous drive for properly trained and experienced document examiners. . . . The present trend is toward more advanced methods and techniques that can be applied in the field of questioned document examination. If the present trend continues, the application of current technology together with free exchange of new ideas and progress, will propel the field even further into the arena of modern scientific methodology.[37]

The range of educational qualifications and skills required of a document examiner or handwriting analyst is impossible to quantify, since colleges and universities rarely offer advanced study in the forensic field. How does one acquire the skills of critical examination, comparison, and analysis of documents and the stylistic aspects of handwriting? James Miller warns practitioners of the variation in skills and attributes of individuals who claim to be experts in this field. The questions he finds most helpful in determining expertise are these:

1. Where he trained?
2. How often and in what states and countries he has testified?

3. For what law firms he has worked?

4. Whether he is a member of the American Society of Questioned Document Examiners or the American Academy of Forensic Sciences or certified by the American Board of Forensic Document Examiners?

5. Which universities and professional groups he has lectured?

6. In which professional journals he has been published?

7. What the terms of his client agreement are?

8. If he has state of the art equipment?[38]

As in all fields of scientific endeavor and consultant services, the proponent of the expertise can be either a charlatan or the most skilled of authorities. Determine expertise for handwriting authentication using the checklist at Form 4.4.[39]

## Process of Comparison

Comparative handwriting analysis requires the test document and an exemplar. Handwriting experts cannot attest to the authenticity of a specific signature or other handwriting specimen without an objective, fair, and accurate comparative exemplar. The court must be satisfied that the exemplar is authentic, and the expert witness must be able to ground his or her opinion upon those similarities between the exemplar and the questioned document. To obtain an exemplar in criminal cases, a consent document is suggested. See Form 4.5.

If an expert is not testifying strictly on the matter of authentication, then the expert may be called upon to deal with matters of tampering, alteration, or change in the underlying document. The legal and factual issues involved in documentary analysis include numerous queries:

• Is the signature on a document genuine or an imitation?

• Who wrote the signature or other writing on this document?

• Was this legal form signed or prepared on the date the document shows?

• What kind of typewriter was used to execute this document?

• Was the typewriter in existence on the document's date?

• Was the document prepared on the suspect's typewriter?

• Were all the entries on the document executed during the same time interval, or were some entries added at later times?

• Have pages been substituted in this multipaged document?

• Does this document show indented replicas or impressions of writings written on a document that was laying on top of this document?

• Can you restore or decipher the text of the original entries that have been erased, eradicated, or obliterated?

_____ (1) Biographical background (name, age, and address).

_____ (2) Educational qualifications:

    _____ (a) Formal education (basic degree in the physical sciences, advanced degree in the physical sciences, criminalistics, special course, seminars);

    _____ (b) Practical education (apprenticeship with an expert examiner, years of active experience, association with government agencies, police departments and Federal Bureau of Investigation, training, seminars);

    _____ (c) Teaching experience (name of institution, years of teaching, position, and subjects taught);

    _____ (d) Honors or recognition for services;

    _____ (e) Certifications (American Board of Forensic Document Examiners).

_____ (3) Memberships in professional societies:

    _____ (a) Name of society in which membership is held (American Academy of Forensic Sciences, American Society of Questioned Document Examiners);

    _____ (b) How was membership earned (criteria of membership);

    _____ (c) Committee positions (leadership or membership positions, responsibilities, and interests).

_____ (4) Employment experience:

    _____ (a) Present position (title, employer, description, duties, years held);

    _____ (b) Past positions (title, employer, description, duties, years held);

    _____ (c) Consulting work;

    _____ (d) Employment history in association with government agencies;

    _____ (e) Employment history in forensic sciences.

_____ (5) Authorship:

    _____ (a) Texts and treatises (date, title, publication, area of interest);

    _____ (b) Articles (date, title, publication, area of interest);

    _____ (c) Miscellaneous (seminar papers, texts, or speeches);

    _____ (d) Research and studies (date, published/unpublished, area of interest, results).

_____ (6) Lectures:

    _____ (a) Title and topic;

    _____ (b) Date;

    _____ (c) Location;

    _____ (d) Group or organization lectured before.

_____ (7) Qualifications as expert in questioned document examination:

    _____ (a) Court experience;

    _____ (b) Deposition testimony;

    _____ (c) Training;

    _____ (d) Areas in which qualified as expert.

**FORM 4.4** Document expert questionnaire.

You are being asked by [name] of the [agency] to give your consent for/to [type of exemplar] which is an/are exemplar(s).

1. Do you understand that you have the right to refuse to allow us to take the exemplar(s) from you? _____

2. Do you understand that this (these) exemplar(s) can be used against you as evidence in a court of law? _____

3. Do you understand that you have the right to consult with an attorney before the exemplar(s) is/are taken? _____

4. Do you understand that if you cannot afford an attorney one will be provided to you free of charge, prior to the exemplar(s) being taken from you? _____

    I, _____, do authorize law enforcement officer(s) _____ and any other person designated to assist, to obtain from me the following exemplar(s):

_____

    I hereby give my consent for the exemplar(s) as indicated above. I certify that I am giving this consent for exemplar(s) without fear and without any threat or promise (expressed or implied) having been made by the above law enforcement officer(s) or any other person. I give this consent freely and voluntarily after having been informed of my rights to refuse to consent and to consult with an attorney before the exemplar(s) is/are taken, which rights I am giving up, after reading and understanding the complete contents of the Consent of Exemplar form.

_____

Signature of person consenting to the taking of exemplar(s)

Witnessed by:

_____

_____

DATE: _____

TIME: _____

**FORM 4.5**   Consent for exemplars.

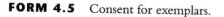

- Can you decipher the entries on these burned documents?
- What is the sex and age of the unknown writer of this document?
- What was the mental and physical condition of the writer when this document was executed?
- What can you tell me about the writer's personality?[40]

Next, the handwriting analyst, document examiner, or questioned document expert looks to the content, circumstances, and conditions of the document in order to determine its authenticity. "Every facet of a document might yield evidence that could either establish its validity or challenge its authenticity. With experience, special equipment, and photographic techniques, the qualified expert will be able to examine a document in many ways and determine its authenticity."[41]

The federal district court cases involving Timothy McVeigh, the Oklahoma bomber, and Unabomber Ted Kaczynski included arguments on handwriting evidence. In McVeigh's case, the court questioned the reliability of handwriting analysis, though it did "allow the expert to testify about similarities between handwriting samples produced by the defendants and the handwriting on several documents, including motel registration forms, a note found in McVeigh's car after his arrest, and a rental agreement for the truck allegedly used to carry the bomb."[42] Exemplars are sure to be discovered in the comprehensive list of handwriting samples and standards at Figure 4.4.[43]

Once a sample has been obtained, utilize the following guidelines to ensure an accurate view of the handwriting sample:

A. Reproduce the original conditions as nearly as possible as to text, speed, slant, size of paper, size of writing, type of writing instrument, etc.

B. Obtain samples from dictation until it is believed normal writing has been produced (the number of samples necessary cannot be determined in advance).

C. Do not allow the writer to see either the original document in question or a photograph thereof.

D. Remove each sample from the sight of the writer as soon as it is completed.

E. Do not give instructions in spelling, punctuation or arrangement.

F. Use the same writing media, such as type and size of paper, writing instruments, printed forms such as checks or notes.

G. Obtain the full text of the questioned writing in word-for-word order at least once, if possible. Signatures and less extensive writing should be prepared several times, each time on a different piece of paper. In hand printing cases, both upper case (capital) and lower case (small) samples should be obtained.

H. In forgery cases the Laboratory should also be furnished with genuine signatures of the person whose name is forged.

I. Obtain samples with both the right and left hands.

J. Obtain samples written rapidly, slowly, and at varied slants.

K. Obtain samples of supplementary writings such as sketches, drawings, manner of addressing an envelope, etc.

L. Writer should initial and date each page.

M. Witness should initial and date each page.

N. If readily available, samples of undictated writing should be obtained, such as application for employment, social or business correspondence, school papers, etc.[44]

**Bank Records**
  Canceled Checks
  Deposit Slips
  Microfilm
  Mortgages
  Safety Deposit Vault Register
  Withdrawal Slips

**City Records**
  Building Department
    Building Permits
  City Auditor
    Canceled Checks
  City Clerk
    Voters' Registration Lists
  Personnel Department
    Civil Service Applications

**County Records**
  County Clerk
    Civil Service Applications
    Claims for Service or Merchandise
  Purchasing Department
    Bids and Contracts
  Register of Deeds
    Deeds
    Birth Certificates
    ID Card Applications
  Selective Service
    Registrations
  Department of Taxation
    State Income Tax Returns
  Treasurer
    Canceled Checks

**Department Store Records**
  Applications for Credit
  Complaints and Correspondence
  Receipts for Merchandise
  Signed Sales Checks

**Drug Store Records**
  Register for Exempt Narcotics, Poisons

**Employment Records**
  Canceled Payroll Checks
  Credit Union
  Personnel Jackets, Letters, Memoranda
  Receipts for Bonds, Salary, etc.
  Withholding Exemptions Forms
  Work Product

**Federal Records**
  Civil Service Regional Offices Applications
  Department of Justice
  Post Office Department
    Application for P.O. Box
    Registered and Special Delivery Receipts
  Social Security Administration
    Applications for Numbers, Benefits
  Veterans Administration
    Applications for Benefits
  U.S. Treasury
    Canceled Payroll Checks

**In The Home**
  Books
  Canceled Checks, Notes
  Correspondence
  Diaries
  Notebooks
  Receipts
  Wills

**Hospital Records**
  Admissions, Releases

**Hotel and Motel Records**
  Registrations, Reservations

**Insurance Records**

**Library Records**
  Applications for Cards

*cont.*

**FIGURE 4.4**  Types of documentary evidence.

*On The Person*
  Contents of Wallet
  Letters, Post Cards
  Notebooks

*Police and Sheriff's Department Records*
  Complaints
  Canteen Slips
  Statements Written by the Suspect

*Public Utility Records*
  Applications for Service
    Electricity
    Gas
    Telephone
    Water

*Real Estate Records*
  Property Listing Agreements

*Relatives*
  Letters, Post Cards

*School and College Records*
  Applications for Entrance
  Daily Assignments
  Registration Cards

*State Records*
  Conservation Files
  Workmen and Unemployment Files
    Workman's Compensation
    Unemployment Compensation
    Canceled Checks
  Motor Vehicle Files
  Personnel Files
    Civil Service Applications and
    Examinations
  Corrections Files
  Secretary of State
  Taxation Files
  State Treasurer
    Canceled Checks

*Miscellaneous*
  Building After-Hours Registers
  Express Company, Cartage, Mover's
    Receipts
  Rent Receipts to Tenants

**FIGURE 4.4**  *Continued*

## § 4.4 PRACTICE POINTERS ON DOCUMENTARY EVIDENCE

Documents are overwhelming the criminal and civil justice systems. Attorneys, investigators, police officers, and other justice personnel are swamped with documentary demands. File organization and chronological tracking are necessary. Marcy Davis Fawcett unreservedly recommends the necessity of an organizational philosophy:

> The important thing is to choose one of them and be consistent with it, do not let documents mount up before integrating them into the filing system. That is a sure-fire way to lose something. Everyday, as documents become available see that they are indexed and abstracted immediately and made part of the file.[45]

A *document profile form*, which organizes and identifies documents, is mandatory. See Form 4.6.[46]

**DOCUMENT PROFILE FORM**

DOCUMENT NO. _____

AUTHORS _____

ADDRESSES _____

DATE OF DOCUMENT (YEAR, MONTH, DAY) _____

EXHIBIT NO. (Where applicable) _____

TITLE OR SUBJECT OF DOCUMENT _____

_____

PROGRAMMER'S NAME _____

REVIEWER'S NAME _____

ISSUES RELATIVE: (PREDETERMINED)

1) ☐ (damages, etc.) _____ 4) ☐ _____

2) ☐ (liability, etc.) _____ 5) ☐ _____

3) ☐ _____ 6) ☐ _____

PERSONS MENTIONED IN DOCUMENT:

1) _____ 4) _____

2) _____ 5) _____

3) _____ 6) _____

KEYWORDS:

1) _____ 4) _____

2) _____ 5) _____

3) _____ 6) _____

REVIEWER'S REMARKS _____

_____

_____

**FORM 4.6**   Identify and organize documents with a document profile form.

A *document index* is also of immeasurable assistance to practitioners responsible for the organization, labeling, tracing, and production of documents. See Form 4.7.[47]

Covered in a previous chapter, courts ask counsel to produce, at a pretrial hearing, settlement conference, or other preliminary process, a list of exhibits to be introduced at trial. Documentary evidence certainly is part of that list. Bills and statements relating to damages; photographs and x-rays; medical, hospital, and x-ray reports; physician's findings; depositions or affidavits; drawings or diagrams; loss of earnings documentation; and proof of salary and wages[48] are representative examples.

Compilation of a master *trial exhibit list* is good practice. See Form 4.8.[49]

Document collection will vary according to the kind of case. The checklist at Form 4.9[50] lists the document needs in an auto accident case.

### DOCUMENT INDEX

| Document # | Date | Primary Addressee | Author | Description |
|---|---|---|---|---|
| | | | | |
| | | | | |
| | | | | |
| | | | | |
| | | | | |
| | | | | |
| | | | | |
| | | | | |
| | | | | |
| | | | | |
| | | | | |
| | | | | |
| | | | | |
| | | | | |
| | | | | |
| | | | | |
| | | | | |
| | | | | |
| | | | | |
| | | | | |
| | | | | |
| | | | | |

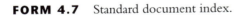

**FORM 4.7** Standard document index.

**MASTER TRIAL EXHIBIT LIST**

| Exhibit Number | | Marked for Identification | Received into Evidence | Witness | Exhibits Sent to Jury Date & Time |
|---|---|---|---|---|---|
| Pl. Ex. 1 | 1/4/00 police report, with supplemental reports and field notes attached | 12/1/00 | 12/1/00 | Officer T. M. Johnson | 12/5/00, 3:00 p.m. |
| Pl. Ex. 2 | 8 × 10 police photograph of both cars immediately following impact | 12/1/00 | 12/1/00 | Officer T. M. Johnson | 12/5/00, 3:00 p.m. |
| Pl. Ex. 4 | John Doe's WIIC medical records, 1/1/00–2/17/00 | 12/3/00 | 12/3/00 | Dr. R. T. Smith | 12/5/00, 3:00 p.m. |
| Pl. Ex. 7 | 8 × 10 eyewitness's photograph of John Doe immediately after impact | 12/4/00 | rejected-inflammatory | Paul Drake | rejected-inflammatory |
| Def. Ex. 2 | 8/9/00 medical report of Dr. Mitchell (independent medical exam) | 12/4/00 | 12/4/00 | Dr. T. G. Mitchell | 12/5/00, 3:00 p.m. |

**FORM 4.8**  An example of a completed master trial exhibit list.

---

1. Police agency—accident report—statements, maps, diagrams, photos, parts of vehicles.

2. Police officers—see their notes.

3. Prosecutor—see statements.

4. Proceedings in traffic court—what plea entered—if not yet held—prepare witnesses and consider obtaining Court Reporter. If held, check to see if defendant's insurer had court reporter present.

5. Motor vehicle licensing authority—for checking owner and driving record of driver.

6. Newspapers—for photographs and witnesses (most newspapers hold photos for limited time only).

7. Department of streets and traffic—for time cycle of lights and records of traffic control devices and signs.

8. City engineer or state highway department—for maps, including aerial maps.

9. Defendants—interview them and get policy limits.

---

**FORM 4.9** Documentary evidence in auto negligence case.

In some jurisdictions, a *trial exhibit index* or other listing format is required. Copies of the trial exhibit index should be given to the opposition, judge, court reporter, and other required parties. The index organizes the exhibit designation or identification number and a description of the exhibit, including the date and the author. See the trial exhibit index format at Form 4.10.

Those skilled in evidence organization will thrive in the analysis of documentary evidence. The burden of documentation need not overwhelm the investigative and litigation team. Recognize and treat documentary evidence as the proof that assures victory.

## § 4.5 SUMMARY

Documentary evidence or writings serve multiple purposes in the investigation and litigation of cases. Within this topical construct, specific attention has been given to the nuances of the best evidence rule, the influence of the hearsay rule on admissibility of writings and documents, and the role that both lay and expert witnesses play in the identification and analysis of handwriting and questioned documents. Authentication and identification requirements to assure admissibility were also covered. Finally, suggestions regarding document organization and production, as well as words of encouragement for those entrusted with documentary evidence, were offered.

```
IN THE COURT OF COMMON PLEAS OF _____, ____,

TAMMY YEAGER, et al.                    CASE NO. _____
                Plaintiffs,             JUDGE _____

v.

WILLIAM MILLER, et al.                  INDEX TO PLAINTIFFS'
                Defendants              TRIAL EXHIBITS
```

| EX.# | DESCRIPTION | DATE |
|------|-------------|------|
| 1. | Official Accident Report—Police Dept. | 2/5/00 |
| 2. | Copy of ticket issued to William Miller by Police Dept. for Failure to Signal | 2/5/00 |
| 3. | Emergency Room Record—General Hospital | 2/5/00 |
| 4. | Admission Records—General Hospital | 2/5/00 to 3/10/99 |
| 5A. | Photograph of Yeager automobile—Police Dept. | 2/5/00 |
| 5B. | Photograph of Yeager automobile—Police Dept. | 2/5/00 |
| 6. | Medical Report by Kevin Williams, M.D. | 3/1/00 |
| 7. | Neuropsychological Evaluation Report on Tammy Yeager —Steve Lawrence, Ph.D. | 3/8/00 |
| 8. | Summary of Medical Expenses—with copies of bills | |
| 9. | Back brace worn by Tammy Yeager | |
| 10. | W-2 forms and IRS form 1040 for 1999—Tammy Yeager | |
| 11. | Affidavit of Tammy Yeager's employer | 4/24/00 |

**FORM 4.10**   Index to plaintiffs' trial exhibits.

## Notes

1. Fed. R. Evid. 1001(1).
2. Fed. R. Evid. 1008.
3. Fed. R. Evid. 1002.
4. 4 JOHN H. WIGMORE, Evidence 417 (1972).
5. Fed. R. Evid. 1004.
6. Fed. R. Evid. 1003.
7. Forensic Imaging Systems, 1146 Walker Road, Great Falls, VA 22066, <http://members. aol.com/dbarnesphd/signatur.jpg>, visited September 9, 1999.
8. Fed. R. Evid. 1001(3).
9. Fed. R. Evid. 1001(4).

10. Model Code of Evidence Rule 602 (1942).

11. James W. McElhaney, *Using a Business Record,* 84 A.B.A. J. 66. (Feb. 1998).

12. Robert Barker, *The Best Evidence Rule: Article 10,* 47 Brook. L. Rev. 1391, 1391 (1981).

13. Fed. R. Evid.. 1005.

14. 8 STANDARD PA. PRACTICE 2D § 53.30.

15. J. PRINCE, Richardson on Evidence 583 (10th ed. 1973).

16. Fed. R. Evid. 1006.

17. Fed. R. Evid. 1007.

18. Fed. R. Evid. 807.

19. Fed. R. Evid. 803(8)(C).

20. Simmons v. Chicago & Northwestern Transp. Co., 993 F.2d 1326 (8th Cir. 1993).

21. 8 STANDARD PA. PRACTICE 2d § 53.38.

22. Model Code of Evidence Rule 601 (1942).

23. 8 STANDARD PA. PRACTICE 2d § 53.56.

24. Fed. R. Evid. 901(b).

25. 8 STANDARD PA. PRACTICE 2d § 53.64.

26. Fed. R. Evid. 803(6).

27. JOHN A. TARANTINO, Trial Evidence Foundations 5-7 (1987).

28. Malek v. Federal Ins. Co., 994 F.2d 49 (2d Cir. 1993).

29. Haygood v. Auto-Owners Ins. Co., 995 F.2d 1512 (11th Cir. 1993).

30. Romano v. Howarth, 998 F.2d 101 (2d Cir. 1993).

31. Fed. R. Evid. 901(b)(2).

32. Fed. R. Evid. 901(b)(2), advisory committee's notes.

33. Fed. R. Evid. 901, advisory committee's notes.

34. Fed. R. Evid. 901(3).

35. JOHN A. TARANTINO, Strategic Use of Scientific Evidence 439 (1988).

36. Nanette Galbraith, *Trends in the Field of Questioned Document Examination,* 25 J. Forensic Sci. 132, 134 (1980).

37. *Id.* at 139.

38. James Miller, *Document Examiners,* 23 Trial 44, 45 (1987).

39. TARANTINO, *supra* note 35, at 442.

40. WILLIAM G. ECKERT, Introduction to Forensic Sciences 186 (1980).

41. Miller, *supra* note 38, at 47.

42. Mark Hansen, *Evidence,* 83 A.B.A. J. 77 (May 1997).

43. WISCONSIN DEPARTMENT of JUSTICE, Criminal Investigation and Physical Evidence Handbook 173 (1987).

44. NATIONAL INSTITUTE of JUSTICE, Handbook of Forensic Science 75–76 (1981).

45. MARCY DAVIS FAWCETT, Paralegal's Litigation Forms 6-2 (1987).

46. *Id.* at 6–12.

47. NANCY SCHLEIFER, Litigation Forms and Checklists 6–15 (1987).

48. CAROLE BRUNO, Paralegal's Litigation Handbook 319 (1980).

49. BURGESS ELDRIDGE, Personal Injury Paralegal 1613 (1987).

50. FRED LANE, Lane's Goldstein Trial Techniques § 2.62 (3d ed. 1984).

CHAPTER 5

# Lay Witnesses

## § 5.1 INTRODUCTION

How witnesses are defined and classified is a major concern in criminal and civil practice. One needs to know not only who the witness is, but also the type of witness the individual is, since the witness classification dictates the manner of evidentiary use. Generally speaking, witnesses are categorized by two major classifications: *lay* and *expert*.

How does one differentiate between lay and expert witnesses? Some legal scholars recount that any witness who is not an expert falls under the umbrella of "lay" witness. On this score, the comparison is undeniable. Expert witnesses are usually perceived as scientific, dispassionate third parties and outside observers to the ongoing litigation. The expert, whose subject matter will be covered extensively in the next chapter, is an individual possessing specialized knowledge, skills, or training and is granted wide testimonial latitude. The expert testifies broadly, subject to little hearsay restriction, while a lay witness testifies only to facts or conditions personally known to him or her. Lay witnesses testify to perceptions, facts, and data grounded in their own experience. Experts are accorded far more latitude.

The Federal Rules of Evidence, at Rule 701, lay out a general idea of what the lay witness is and the scope of his or her testimonial capacity:

> If the witness is not testifying as an expert, the witness' testimony in the form of opinions or inferences is limited to those opinions or inferences which are (a) rationally based on the perception of the witness and (b) helpful to a clear understanding of the witness' testimony or the determination of a fact in issue.[1]

In reality, lay witness testimony is the centerpiece of most cases. "A popular notion among most lay people is that expert testimony is the only form of evidence admissible in a criminal or civil action. This perception is a result of many factors, such as media coverage of flamboyant witnesses and other fringe litigation. However, the bulk of testimony given in any criminal or civil action is fundamentally 'lay' in nature."[2] Rules of admissibility regarding lay witnesses' testimonial evidence are discussed next.

## § 5.2 LAY WITNESS COMPETENCY

Before a lay witness's testimony can be introduced at trial, specific legal issues need attention, the first being the assurance of a witness's competency. Under most statutory schemes, courts are reticent to permit or accept the testimony of any witness who is not deemed competent. FRE Rule 601 outlines the theme of competence:

> Every person is competent to be a witness except as otherwise provided in these rules. However, in civil actions and proceedings, with respect to an element of a claim or defense as to which State law supplies the rule of decision, the competency of a witness shall be determined in accordance with State law.[3]

But what does competency mean? What measures dictate competency? Does competency mean the capacity not only to relate facts, but also to do so reliably and truthfully? The competency of a witness to testify regarding a particular matter requires the minimum capacity to observe, record, recollect, and recount, coupled with an understanding of the duty to tell the truth. This must be combined with evidence sufficient to support a finding of actual, personal knowledge of the matter.

But competency does not mean testimonial perfection. Perception and understanding are complex psychological and intellectual processes. Memory is essentially categorized by stages: "It is universally accepted that the memory process takes place in three stages: (1) perception of the event, (2) retention, and (3) retrieval of the stored information. Psychologists explain that information is transformed as it passes through each of these stages, and it can be distorted by internal and external factors that can eventually cause retrieval failure."[4] Even though this is a general formula, numerous mitigators influence the reliability of any witness's testimony and therefore affect one's level of competency.[5]

In determining competency, the court views the evidence in the light most favorable to the witness.[6] First, FRE Rule 602 demands that the witness possess personal knowledge, personal awareness, and understanding of the facts:

> A witness may not testify to a matter unless evidence is introduced sufficient to support a finding that the witness has personal knowledge of the matter. Evidence to prove personal knowledge may, but need not, consist of the witness' own testimony. This rule is subject to the provisions of rule 703, relating to opinion testimony by expert witnesses.[7]

Whether a potential witness has personal knowledge as it relates to the scope of his or her testimony is one of many critical questions:

1. Has this witness provided you with previously reliable information?

2. Does this witness have ulterior motives, such as economic or vengeful intentions or desires?

3. Does the witness possess personal knowledge of the event and portray the sequence and chronology in an assured and level-headed fashion?

4. Would a judge or jury believe the testimony of this witness?

5. Can this witness withstand a personal assault on character?

6. Can the witness withstand the impeachment of prior convictions, a reputation for dishonesty, a substantial record of criminal conduct, or prior bad habits or acts?[8]

The witness must be able to coherently relay a storyline and deliver a "rational, factual basis that supports the speaker's position."[9]

Weighing these criteria, competency determinations are physical and intellectual, but experiential, too. The witness needs to be capable of interpretation.

> To arrive at a determination of competency, several subjective and objective forms of evaluation are necessary.
>
> 1. The witness must have the capacity to actually perceive, record, and recollect impressions of fact (physical and mental capacity);
>
> 2. The witness in fact did perceive, record, and recollect impressions having a tendency to establish a fact or consequence in litigation (personal knowledge);
>
> 3. The witness must be capable of understanding the obligation to tell the truth (oath or affirmation);
>
> 4. The witness must possess the capacity to express himself understandably or if necessary with the aid of an interpreter.[10]

Nancy Schleifer has devised an incredibly useful *witness competency checklist*. See Form 5.1.[11]

A witness intent on providing falsehoods, in contempt of truth, will not be a competent witness either. Credibility promised by the witness's oath or affirmation signifies testimonial competency. FRE Rule 603 lends support to the interplay of competency and truthful testimony:

> Before testifying, every witness shall be required to declare that the witness will testify truthfully, by oath or affirmation administered in a form calculated to awaken the witness' conscience and impress the witness' mind with the duty to do so.[12]

A witness thoroughly lacking in credibility will negatively impact other witnesses or parties. In this event, the witness is incompetent and can be challenged.

_____ Duty to tell truth: witness must understand the duty to tell the truth.

    _____ Is witness too young or too mentally incompetent to understand the difference between the truth and a lie?

    _____ Does the witness have a prior conviction for perjury or criminal act based on dishonesty? (Federal Rules do not bar witness per se, but this factor can be used for impeachment.)

_____ Ability to perceive: witness must have the ability to perceive the incident which is the subject matter of her testimony.

    _____ Does witness have a handicap that would impair the ability to perceive, such as poor eyesight or lack of hearing?

    _____ Did conditions such as darkness, fog, distance, noise level prevent the witness from perceiving?

    _____ Was witness attentive or inattentive?

_____ Ability to remember: witness must be able to remember what she perceived.

    _____ Does witness have a medical or psychological handicap such as Alzheimer's disease, brain damage, schizophrenia, or other mental disorder that would prevent witness from remembering?

    _____ Does witness remember other events accurately? Test with questions about physical setting, time frame, or historical information.

    _____ Was witness distracted?

    _____ Does witness have a problem remembering other information such as schoolwork, names, faces?

_____ Ability to communicate: witness must be able to communicate to the jury.

_____ Personal knowledge: witness cannot testify unless she has personal knowledge of the subject of her testimony. Rule 602.

    _____ Was witness present during the event? Did witness actually see, hear, feel, smell or touch?

    _____ Is witness relying on perceptions or relying on hearsay?

    _____ An expert may testify on facts of which she has no personal knowledge but which have been disclosed to the expert at or before the hearing. Rule 703.

**FORM 5.1**   Witness competency checklist.

## § 5.3 THE SCOPE OF LAY TESTIMONY

Since lay witnesses lack scientific or specialized expertise, the scope of their testimony is more restrictive. Generally, personal knowledge serves as a guide to a lay witness's testimony. Minimally, witnesses can testify to facts or truths they have experienced. Lay witnesses can and do go beyond mechanical recitation of data and expand the scope of testimony by giving opinions on actually observed events. "Lay witnesses (regular witnesses who have not been shown to have any special expertise) can give opinions on subjects such as the speed of moving vehicles; the similarity in a person's voice or handwriting with which they are familiar; and whether or not a person is angry or intoxicated."[13] Against this backdrop, is it permissible to conclude that lay witnesses can give opinions as to a person's state of intoxication, a party's mental condition, or the identification of a smell, sound, or sight? FRE Rule 701 gives some guidance regarding this line of inquiry:

> If the witness is not testifying as an expert, the witness' testimony in the form of opinions or inferences is limited to those opinions or inferences which are (a) rationally based on the perception of the witness and (b) helpful to a clear understanding of the witness' testimony or the determination of a fact in issue.[14]

Part (a) of the above rule reaffirms the requirement of firsthand knowledge and personal observation; part (b) is a policy statement holding that even the subjective shortcomings of lay witness opinion are overcome when said opinion aids the trier of fact. To edify, some states, like Tennessee, are somewhat more restrictive and skeptical of lay witness opinion. Tennessee Rule 701 places additional burdens on the proponent of lay opinion, holding that if a witness is not testifying as an expert, the witness's testimony in the form of opinions or inferences is limited. The factors that Tennessee courts consider in the admissibility of lay opinion are these:

1. Whether the opinions or inferences do not require a special knowledge, skill, experience, or training;

2. Whether the witness cannot readily and with equal accuracy and adequacy communicate what the witness has perceived to the trier of fact without testifying in terms of opinions or inferences; and

3. Whether the opinions or inferences will not mislead the trier of fact to the prejudice of the objective party.[15]

Upon closer inspection, when Tennessee sets up these restrictions, it "expresses a preference for expert opinion testimony over lay opinion testimony."[16] But the world cannot, and does not, exclusively revolve around expert testimony, but earnestly looks forward to the explanation of the layperson.

When considering whether or not lay opinion will be admissible, review these issues:

1. Is the witness's testimony based upon his or her own unique perception?

2. Is the court convinced that the testimony of the lay witness is helpful in arriving at the truth, and does the witness, in actuality, have an opinion?

3. Is the witness capable and competent to testify as to that opinion?

4. Without the testimony, would the trier of fact, namely, the judge and the jury, not have the best case presented?

5. If the witness is giving lay testimony, rather than expert testimony, is an interpretation as to a rule of law being made?[17]

In modern litigation and legal interpretation, the preference is plainly toward a flexibility in the testimony of witnesses. Restricting witnesses' testimony because of technical rules and applications is frowned upon. The Federal Rules of Evidence liberate testimonial practice, a policy reaffirmed by the American Law Institute's Model Code of Evidence at Rule 101, which states:

> Every person is qualified to be a witness as to any material matter unless the judge finds that
>
> (a) the proposed witness is incapable of expressing himself concerning the matter so as to be understood by the judge and jury either directly or through interpretation by one who can understand him, or
>
> (b) the proposed witness is incapable of understanding the duty of a witness to tell the truth.[18]

## § 5.4 IDENTIFYING AND INTERVIEWING

### Identification and Screening

Witnesses and testimonial proof are always a core evidence concern. Witnesses provide, by testimonial evidence, a personalized view that breathes life into the evidence. At the outset of any case, witnesses need aggressive and creative preparation. A useful correspondence, which makes appropriate introductions and solicits the cooperation of the witness, is at Form 5.2.[19]

Assemble witnesses for every aspect of the case. Create a file system that catalogs witnesses. Verne Lawyer and the Association of Trial Lawyers of America (ATLA) publish a witness list that is simple and straightforward.[20] See Form 5.3.[21] Another tracking device for listing potential trial witnesses is shown in Form 5.4.[22]

On a more focused level, individual witnesses should be charted and tracked within a file. Emphasize the correlation between the witness and a particular evidentiary purpose. Gather "every document and item of tangible evidence relating to the matter the witness has seen or acted upon."[23] Coupling witnesses with exhibits, documentary evidence, or real evidence creates the necessary nexus for lay opinion. The attorney must be prepared to introduce those forms of evidence when the witness is on the stand. Furiously searching for documents and other evidence that relates to the witness's testimony during actual litigation presents less than an impressive picture to a jury.

NAME/ADDRESS

IN RE:   Witness Statement

Our Client:

Date of Accident:

Dear NAME-OF-ADDRESSEE:

I am writing to request your assistance in representing my client who was injured in an accident that you witnessed. I am attempting to recover my client's economic losses and damages as a result of this accident.

I have enclosed a form for information concerning the facts you observed on the day of the accident. I also have enclosed a self-addressed envelope for your use.

If, for any reason, filling out this form will be difficult or inconvenient, please feel free to call me, and my office will be glad to take your statement over the phone.

Thank you for taking the time to tell us the facts of this incident. Without your information, this matter may not be resolved justly.

If I can be of any assistance, please feel free to call.

Very truly yours,

_____

Name of Attorney/Investigator

**FORM 5.2**   Request for witness testimony.

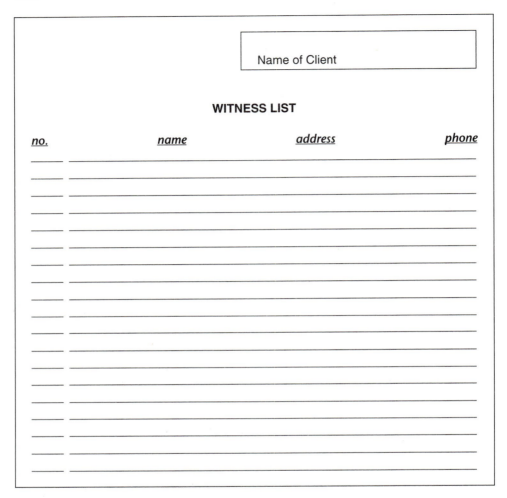

Name of Client

**WITNESS LIST**

| *no.* | *name* | *address* | *phone* |

**FORM 5.3**    Use a witness list for tracking purposes.

## Witness Interviews and Information Gathering

An invaluable investigative practice after witnesses are identified is to conduct preliminary witness interviews by using a witness questionnaire. When interviewing
witnesses, interviewers cannot simply rely on oral assertions. Formalize the assertions in a written document. For example, in a traffic violation case, a negligent auto
accident case, or a driving while under the influence case, "the witness is asked to
give his or her perceptions and understanding of the events that took place."[24] See
Form 5.5.[25]

Interviews can be conducted at various stages of the case, including at the initial meeting, during pretrial preparation, and during trial activity. Regardless of the

## PRELIMINARY WITNESS INDEX

| # | Name | Address | Phone | Capacity | Subpeona | Fee |
|---|------|---------|-------|----------|----------|-----|
| | | | | | | |
| | | | | | | |
| | | | | | | |
| | | | | | | |
| | | | | | | |
| | | | | | | |
| | | | | | | |
| | | | | | | |
| | | | | | | |
| | | | | | | |
| | | | | | | |
| | | | | | | |
| | | | | | | |
| | | | | | | |
| | | | | | | |
| | | | | | | |
| | | | | | | |

**FORM 5.4**   Witness lists are mandatory in complex litigation.

Your name has been given as a witness to the following described accident. It is only through the friendly cooperation of witnesses such as yourself that disinterested information can be obtained for the purpose of justly determining the rights of the parties involved. Therefore, it will be appreciated if you will answer each of the following questions and promptly return the completed statement in the enclosed envelope.

The accident referred to occurred on or about _____ at or near _____ between "A," which was a _____ owned by _____ and a _____, "B," owned by _____.

Hereafter the respective vehicles will be called A and B as indicated above.

Please state the following:

1. Your name _____

2. Your address _____

3. Your telephone number _____

4. Your occupation and employer _____

5. Location of accident _____

6. Date and time of accident _____

7. Did you see the accident occur? _____

   If not, how soon afterward did you arrive? _____

8. Where were you when you observed the accident or other events? _____

   _____

9. Where was A when you first saw it? _____

   Going what direction? _____

10. Where was B when you first saw it? _____

    Going what direction? _____

11. When you first saw the vehicles, what was the speed of A? _____

    The speed of B? _____

12. When the collision occurred, what was the speed of A? _____

    The speed of B? _____

13. Describe what you observed (use back of form if necessary)

    _____

    _____

    _____

    _____

    _____

**FORM 5.5** Witness questionnaire. Type of case: traffic, DUI, negligent auto.

stage, the interview form, checklist, or questionnaire confirms the facts, issues, and related evidentiary matters. In addition, these formats gauge the quality of the lay witness's memory, overall perception, integrity, credibility, and truthfulness. The Michigan Bar Association reminds practitioners that witness information will vary depending upon the witness's relationship to the examiner—that is, whether the witness is hostile, friendly, a defendant or co-defendant, a character witness, an alibi witness, or other type. "Each category requires a different approach."[26]

Interviews constructively corroborate tangible evidence and oral assertions by eyewitnesses and tend to eliminate testimonial inconsistencies. All in all, the tracking of witnesses by forms, checklists, or other suitable manner is an arduous task, but one that provides positive payoffs at trial. Other suggestions regarding the initial compilation of witness information are listed below:

1. Immediate contact, rather than delay, assures the accuracy of information.
2. Make personal appointments, rather than relying on phone consultations.
3. Represent truthfully your role and your corresponding functions.
4. Conduct the interview and at the same time assess the witness's demeanor and conduct, as well as appearance and personality.
5. Lead the witness into the testimonial direction you seek.
6. Search for other interested parties that result from the conversation and statement.
7. Record the witness's statement as is, rather than as you wish it to be.
8. Record all details of the conversation even if they seem incidental and irrelevant.
9. Relate events chronologically.
10. Record names, addresses, street locations, phone numbers, mail boxes, and other permanent reference points for location; make graphs, charts, or diagrams, if helpful.
11. Note the witness's conclusions.
12. Ask the witness for assessments of injuries.
13. Ask the witness to read the results of your recorded statement and then to sign it.
14. Witness reads own recorded statement to ensure veracity, credibility, and technical accuracy.
15. Keep notations and recorded statements available at trial.[27]

## § 5.5 PREPARING WITNESSES FOR LITIGATION

### The Human Elements

Not unexpectedly, some witnesses are fearful of litigation. For most of the populace, interaction with the judiciary, lawyers, and other justice officials is a vary rare occurrence. Therefore, there is a tendency to view legal players and processes with exaggerated seriousness. Witnesses called to testify often get the jitters and, at times, become emotionally overwhelmed. Justice personnel can experience these witness anxieties:

1.   Will I remember what I am supposed to say?
2.   Do I really know what I am going to say?
3.   Will I be embarrassed?
4.   Will I make a mistake?
5.   Will people like me?
6.   What is cross-examination going to be like?[28]

Needless to say, testifying in a formal judicial action causes marked apprehension. Investigators and other staff attend to and attempt to alleviate these natural fears. The National Institute of Trial Advocacy advises attorneys that witness trauma can be mitigated by being attentive to human needs.

> When preparing witnesses for trial, first try to make them as comfortable as possible about testifying. Focusing on the following matters may be helpful,
>
> • show an interest in witnesses as individuals,
> • be completely clear about what you want from the witness at trial,
> • try not to show any nervousness or anxiety about the case,
> • discuss courtroom procedure,
> • discuss what to expect from the judge and opposing lawyers,
> • discuss the importance of honesty,
> • discuss the importance of demeanor,
> • discuss courtesy,
> • discuss appearance,
> • discuss nervousness.[29]

Scrutiny of lay witnesses is not solely a pretrial affair. Watch as the lay witness testifies. Much can also be deduced from the witness's demeanor, body language, and behavior. Opposing counsel can learn a great deal from observing the following:

1.   Eye contact
2.   Body language
3.   Their intonation
4.   Nonverbal actions
5.   Looking in the eyes at the appropriate time, body position, fidgeting
6.   Relaxed, natural
7.   Lack of hesitation

Appearance and behavior of the witness:

8. Appearance
9. Demeanor
10. Naturalness, directness
11. If the witness act(s) normally
12. Sincerity, desire to help
13. Spontaneous testimony, responsive answers
14. He or she is responsive
15. Appearance of candor, objectivity, accurate, thoughtful, and reflective
16. Even nature of dealing with both direct and cross-examination
17. Firmness in opinion[30]

Prepare and educate the lay witness. No lay witness should be ignorant of the diverse procedural events that unfold in litigation. With important, trustworthy witnesses whose testimony will play a major part in the case, explain the case theory and theme, the planned closing argument, and the part that the witness's testimony plays in developing these elements.[31]

Mark Dombroff's *Dombroff on Unfair Tactics* proposes a preparatory witness checklist. See Form 5.6.[32]

The American Bar Association's Section on General Practice has devised a witness testimony profile, an outstanding tactical tool for use in the pretrial setting. See Form 5.7.[33]

Contained within this suggested format are not only the recommendations posed above, but also a special emphasis on mock trial preparation, employing real and hypothetical fact patterns, role-playing with lawyers on direct or cross-examination, and other staged exemplars. "Even the best witnesses need considerable preparation, good witnesses require a lot of it, and it is worth doing because they are often good learners and great contributors to your cause."[34]

Preparing a lay witness for all aspects of trial litigation is a demanding responsibility. Although the litigation team and investigating officers master the skills of witness interaction and the prediction of emotional reactions during testimony, foretelling all that a witness may experience on direct or cross-examination is an impossibility. The best remedy for unpredictability is preparation. A witness who is ignorant of the facts, unaware of his or her own correspondence, or unaccustomed to documents will be in considerable trouble soon after taking the stand. Review not only the plan or direction of testimony, but also the accompanying exhibits and demonstrative evidence. Review in detail the "elements of each claim or offense and map out, based on the case law of the jurisdiction, what proof is available for each claim. Then, craft questions for each witness designed to elicit relevant,

_____ 1. Find out exactly how the witness feels about testifying. Rarely do attorneys question a witness in this area. You must find out if the witness is scared.

        _____ Ask the witness what most concerns him or her, apart from the facts of the case or a general apprehension of the unknown.

        _____ Discuss these concerns, because they can overwhelm the ability of the witness to make a convincing presentation. (Remember, presumably opposing counsel is comfortable in the courtroom environment or, at the very least, more comfortable than the witness.)

        _____ Be sure to confront these apprehensions of the witness precisely and not in a peripheral or condescending manner.

_____ 2. Be sure that you tell the witness what your role will be during direct and cross-examination.

        _____ Explain how you will assist the witness during the direct examination to get over rough spots, remember areas that may be omitted, and generally shape the testimony as the witness delivers it.

        _____ Explain the objection process and how you will use it to control the flow of evidence during cross-examination.

_____ 3. Explain not only your themes but the themes of your opponent.

        _____ Tell the witness how his or her testimony fits into the overall case so that the witness cannot be blindsided or compartmentalized by your opponent on cross-examination. Good preparation in this area also will prevent the witness from delivering an answer or presenting a position, in the expectation that he or she will be helping you, which is inconsistent with your overall theme.

_____ 4. Take the witness to the courtroom.

        _____ Allow the witness to sit in the witness chair, the jury seats, counsel table, and, if possible, the judge's chair. This will allow the witness to see himself or herself as others will and will give him or her a better sense of perspective on the presentation.

_____ 5. When you rehearse the witness, use a videotape, if available.

        _____ This also permits the witness to see himself or herself as others do. It will inevitably be a humbling experience which will point up weaknesses in the witness's presentation that the witness never believed existed or was aware of in his or her personality.

_____ 6. Moot court the witness in the most aggressive, hostile fashion you can.

        _____ Don't tell the witness that you are doing this; rather, gauge the reaction and allow it to develop spontaneously.

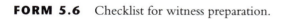

**FORM 5.6**   Checklist for witness preparation.

———— Coupled with this examination should be a physical placement of the witness, preferably either standing away from any table or chairs or sitting away from a table or chairs. This physical isolation will require the witness to, in effect, stand alone and will make him or her feel more vulnerable.

———— 7.  Be very careful about giving general advice to a witness.

———— A good example of this is telling the witness: "Answer only the question that is asked." As a practical matter, this is good advice. But remember that the witness has no frame of reference in which to place your advice.

———— Therefore, give examples of what you mean. For instance, say, "Answer only the question that is asked. What this means is that if you are asked your name, give the attorney your name but not your age or address."

———— 8.  Teach the witness to be an aggressive listener.

———— It is natural for a witness while being examined to want to have the examination over with. As a result, the witness generally will think ahead of the question being asked or answered, and will not be listening to the question because he or she is thinking about the answer or, perhaps, the next question.

———— Aggressive listening permits the witness to actively listen to and hear the question. Frequently, this will mean the difference between a correct answer and an incorrect or misleading answer.

**FORM 5.6**  *Continued*

admissible evidence that will help prove the client's case."[35] Witnesses need to review depositions, interrogatories, transcribed testimony, or other formal or informal statements. Charts, exhibits, diagrams, models, and other demonstrative and visual aids should be thoroughly scrutinized.

Suggestions on the extent and scope of the testimonial response, brevity being the ambition, should be regularly given. Witnesses should be cautioned not to volunteer information. Open, instructive recommendations for a witness about to be examined follow:

1.  Always tell the truth; don't guess at an answer.

2.  Avoid hearsay. Testify only about what you, yourself actually saw, heard, or felt.

3.  If you honestly can't remember something, it is o.k. to say so.

4.  Pause after each question is asked, and before you answer to make sure you understand the question, if you do not understand, say I don't understand,

Witness Name _____ Address _____

Telephones

   Home _____

   Work _____

   Fax _____

_____ Age

_____ Female    _____ Male

Race _____

Marital Status

   _____ Single    _____ Divorced

   _____ Married    _____ Other _____

Dependents _____

Special Honors, Achievements, etc. _____

Employer _____

Employment History _____

Witness for    _____ Plaintiff    _____ Defendant

Relationship to Pleadings

   _____ Complaint              _____ Affirmative Defenses

   _____ Counterclaim           _____ Crossclaim

Conflicts of Interest _____

Bases for Impeachment _____

**FORM 5.7**   Witness testimony profile. (Joan M. Brovins & Thomas Oehmkem, The Trial Practice Guide: Strategies, Systems and Procedures for the Attorney 24 (1992). Copyright the American Bar Association. All rights reserved. Reprinted by permission.)

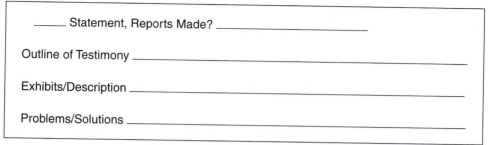

_____ Statement, Reports Made? _____

Outline of Testimony _____

Exhibits/Description _____

Problems/Solutions _____

**FORM 5.7** *Continued*

and ask for clarification by the questioner until you do understand the question.

5. If opposing counsel asks whether you discussed your testimony with your attorney, it is o.k. to tell them you did.

6. If a question can be answered yes or no give the appropriate answer then stop.

7. If a question cannot be answered with a simple yes or no, say so and ask for a chance to explain.

8. Never argue with opposing counsel even if it makes you angry and they say something you dislike.[36]

"Pre-try" the witness to determine strengths and weaknesses, and do not "ignore or gloss over flaws in witnesses who have something helpful to say."[37] Witness fees, travel, and other reimbursable expenses associated with testimony at trial need discussion.[38]

## Cross-Examination

Lay witnesses who testify directly will be cross-examined at trial. The experience of cross-examination is generally of first instance. Cross-examination bedevils even the best of lay witnesses. Cross-examination, while tough and relentless, is never so onerous that the lay witness cannot handle it. Truth-telling in lay witnesses is the great equalizer. When a witness is truthful, a genuineness comes forth, which positively affects both court and jury. A truthful person is usually attacked less on cross-examination than the party who is evasive, sleazy, or slippery in his or her responses. The primary purpose of lay witness cross in regard to the question of credibility is to demonstrate

- That the witness has lied, changed his or her story, or testified differently in the past;

- That the witness is biased or prejudiced due to relationships with a party or with one or more lawyers, or has a financial interest in the outcome;

- That the witness's testimony is improbable, contradictory, or unreliable due to the facts relied on;
- The witness's education or training; or
- The testimony of less biased, more competent witnesses.[39]

Since preparedness, knowledge and truth give comfort to a witness, the National Institute of Trial Advocacy has developed an unrivaled series of recommendations regarding a witness's reaction to cross-examination:

(A) Cross-examination can be as forthright as direct examination.

(B) Obvious weaknesses should be openly acknowledged.

(C) No information should be volunteered.

(D) Answers should be formulated only after questions have been completed.

(E) Explanation can be requested if a question is unclear.

(F) Answers should not include any speculation.

(G) Answers can be explained.

(H) Never argue with an opposing lawyer.

(I) Witnesses should not look over toward their own lawyer before answering questions.

(J) Prior discussions of testimony should be acknowledged.

(K) Witnesses should listen for objections.[40]

The opposition has every right to impeach the lay witness just like any other person that takes the stand. A frequently seen challenge in criminal litigation is reference to a lay defendant's silence upon police interrogation. Despite the 5th Amendment's rock-hard self-incrimination standard, crafty cross-examiners like to use silence as an indication of guilt.[41] Still, as a policy matter, avoid cross-tactics that usurp a constitutional protection.

Extensive preparation minimizes the potential for testimonial surprise, but cannot guarantee its nonappearance. Experienced trial attorneys are never surprised by witnesses who confidently relay facts in pretrial interviews and then confirm and memorialize these same facts in a witness memorandum, statement, or questionnaire, only to contradict these facts on the witness stand. Overpreparation can be just as devastating to the naturalness of witness testimony. Naturalness and spontaneity manifest candor and truth. In the end, a stellar lay witness is usually a person of simplicity, of truthfulness, of power in words and persuasive mannerisms. The key to effective testimony and presentation is in the "meticulous preparation of the potential sources of lay witness testimony, and thorough preparation of each witness who is selected to testify at trial."[42]

## § 5.6 SUMMARY

This chapter presented a series of recommendations regarding the identification interview and the tracking and preparation of lay witnesses. Special attention was given to the rules of admissibility regarding competency and the permissibility of opinion testimony under the Federal Rules of Evidence. Practical advice was provided regarding witness interview processes, the evaluation and screening of witnesses, preparatory steps in the pretrial and trial stages as they relate to testimonial evidence, and the important posture lay witnesses assume in civil and criminal litigation.

### Notes

1. Fed. R. Evid. 701.
2. CHARLES P. NEMETH, Litigation, Pleadings, and Arbitration 421 (1990).
3. Fed. R. Evid. 601. Rule 601, by its brevity, leads to the presumption that every individual, as a witness, is inherently competent.
4. Cindy J. O'Hagan, *When Seeing Is Not Believing: The Case for Eyewitness Expert Testimony,* 81 Geo. L. J. 741, 745 (1993).
5. CINDY O'HAGAN lists some of these factors. "During the perception stage 'event factors,' such as exposure time, frequency, detail salience, and the degree of violence, may affect the initial perception. Some of these factors may be familiar; for example, the more often a person observes the same event, the more accurate her recollection of that event. But 'witness factors,' such as stress, expectations, perceptual activity, and prior experiences also affect perception. A layperson may not realize that cultural expectations or expectations from past experiences can distort her initial perception of any event." *Id.*
6. MICHAEL GRAHAM, Evidence, Text, Rules, Illustrations and Problems 31 (1983).
7. Fed. R. Evid. 602.
8. NEMETH, *supra* note 2, at 420. For a quantitative study on how the age of the complainant impacts juror perceptions and subsequent judgment, review the research of Natalie J. Gabora, Nicholas P. Spanos, and Amanda Joab. Their conclusions as to age are intriguing. "Although there were no significant differences between the two age conditions for individual predeliberation votes, following deliberation guilty verdicts were returned significantly more often from jurors who saw the younger complainant than from those who viewed the older complainant. Jurors also rated the complainant as more credible when she was 13 years old than when she was 17. The age of the complainant had an opposite effect on jurors' perceptions of the defendant: when the complainant was 13, the defendant was rated as less credible than when the complainant was 17. In addition, jurors believed that the 13-year-old was more likely than the 17-year-old to lack the knowledge required to fabricate the sexual abuse allegation." Natalie J. Gabora, Nicholas P. Spanos, & Amanda Joab, *The Effects of Complainant Age and Expert Psychological Testimony in a Simulated Child Sexual Abuse Trial,* 17 Law & Hum. Behav. 103, 115–116 (1993).
9. Nancy J. Turbak, *Effective Direct Examination,* 34 Trial 68 (June 1998).
10. NEMETH, *supra* note 2, at 420.
11. NANCY SCHLEIFER, Litigation Forms and Checklists 13-25 (1991).

12. Fed. R. Evid. 603.

13. THOMAS EIMMERMANN, Fundamentals of Paralegalism 105 (1980).

14. Fed. R. Evid. 701.

15. *See* Tenn. R. Evid. § 701.

16. J. Huston, *The Admissibility of Lay and Expert Opinion,* 57 Tenn. L. Rev. 103, 105 (1989).

17. NEMETH, *supra* note 2, at 412.

18. Model Code of Evidence Rule 101 (1942).

19. CHARLES P. NEMETH, Paralegal Resource Manual 79 (2d ed. 1995).

20. The *Association of Trial Lawyers of America* also states that "the trial lawyer not only should be well organized prior to entering the courtroom, but then he should also give an obvious appearance of being well organized and well prepared in the presentation of his case to the jury . . . that all witnesses be listed and the undesirable witnesses, or the witnesses who may offer merely cumulative testimony be excluded." ASSOCIATION OF TRIAL LAWYERS OF AMERICA, Civil Practice Series 28 (1982).

21. VERNE LAWYER, Ass'n of Tr. Law. of Am., Trial by Notebook, A System of Trial Organization for the Modern Plaintiffs' Attorney 10 (1982).

22. BEVERLY HUTSON, Paralegal Trial Handbook 3-4 (1991).

23. Pamela B. Stuart, *The Basics of Direct and Cross-Examination of a Fact Witness,* 35 Trial (Jan. 1999).

24. NEMETH, *supra* note 19, at 20.

25. *Id.* at 83.

26. 2 Michigan Basic Practice Handbook § 15-12 (1985).

27. AMERICAN COLLEGE OF TRIAL LAWYERS, ALI-ABA, Committee on Continuing Professional Education Civil Trial Manual 55 (1976). Fred Lane's classic work, *Lane's Goldstein Trial Techniques,* insists that any real witness give full disclosure of all facts and conditions relating to the case. "When interviewing a personal injury client it is important to caution him against withholding any information. The client should be informed that the other side will investigate his life from the day of his birth and that his lawyer must be in possession of all the facts so that he can prepare for anything that is likely to develop." FRED LANE, Lane's Goldstein Trial Techniques §2.04 (3d ed. 1984).

28. MARK DOMBROFF, Dombroff on Unfair Tactics 399 (1988).

29. D. Lake Rumsey, *Selecting, Preparing and Presenting the Direct Testimony of Lay Witness, in* Master Advocate Handbook 84 (D. Lake Rumsey ed., 1986).

30. ROBERTO ARON, KEVIN T. DUFFY, & JONATHAN L. ROSNER, Impeachment of Witnesses: The Cross-Examiner's Art 175 (1990).

31. Rumsey, *supra* note 29.

32. DOMBROFF, *supra* note 28, at 400.

33. JOAN M. BROVINS & THOMAS OEHMKEM, The Trial Practice Guide: Strategies, Systems and Procedures for the Attorney 24 (1992).

34. Weyman Lundquist, *Selecting the Right Trial Witnesses,* 17 Litig. 25, 29 (1991).

35. Stuart, *supra* note 23, at 74.

36. HUTSON, *supra* note 22, at 3-12. Trial attorney David Berg, in his work *Preparing Witnesses,* hits the mark. There are countless other caveats about effective preparation of wit-

nesses: One is that the pretrial work never ends, even when the trial begins. For example, parties and those witnesses that are allowed to sit in a courtroom should profit from what they hear. During recesses and at night, go over the main areas of concern in light of the testimony elicited. Another caveat is to make the client aware of what is going to happen after you announce "ready," even to the point of outlining legal arguments you expect and their significance.

37. Chris Gair, *Problem Witnesses: Coping with Character Attacks* 32 Trial 64 (Sept. 1996).

38. *See* Demarest v. Manspeaker, 498 U.S. 184 (1991); Griffin v. Oceanic Contractors, Inc., 458 U.S. 564, 575 (1982).

39. Phillip I. Miller, *Planning the Cross-Examination,* 34 Trial 52 (Feb. 1998). Weyman Lundquist's *Selecting the Right Trial Witnesses* agrees with this profile: "My major instruction to a witness, which I repeat time and time again, is to tell the truth but to know the truth means to understand what the case is about and what the issues are." Lundquist, *supra* note 34, at 29.

40. D. Lake Rumsey, *supra* note 29, at 88–89 (D. Lake Rumsey ed., 1986).

41. The U.S. Supreme Court has considered such references to silent defendants and characterized the tactic as harmless error. In *Brecht v. Abrahamson,* 507 U.S. 619 (1993), the majority opinion so held: "The principal question before the jury, therefore, was whether the State met its burden in proving beyond a reasonable doubt that the shooting was intentional. Our inquiry here is whether, in light of the record as a whole, the State's improper use for impeachment purposes of petitioner's post-Miranda silence, 'had substantial and injurious effect or influence in determining the jury's verdict.' We think it clear that it did not." *Id.* at 638.

42. Frederick Overby, *Preparing Lay Witnesses* 27 Trials 88, 91 (1991).

CHAPTER 6

# Expert Evidence

## § 6.1 INTRODUCTION: THE NATURE OF AN EXPERT

Coming in contact with experts in criminal and civil litigation is an assured event during a career in the justice system. Experts, for better or worse, are increasingly relied upon in both pretrial and trial phases of a case. "Expert testimony has become almost indispensable in some areas of litigation. Psychiatrists and psychologists are testifying about the mental condition of criminal defendants and eye witnesses, while economists are establishing such tenuous claims as the hedonistic value of life in wrongful death actions."[1] To some, the legal system's heavy reliance on expert evidence has become an unbridled love affair. In sensationalized legal cases, expert testimony seems to be admitted without much resistance, from permitting the assertion that heavy metal music subliminally directs juveniles to commit suicide, to alleging as a defense that a criminal defendant murdered another because of an addiction to junk food—a premise commonly known as the "Twinkie defense." Think for a moment about other popular strategies in legal cases: the argument that criminal conduct is excusable because of PMS (premenstrual syndrome), the assertion that a drug such as Bendectin causes birth defects, the criminal defense of insanity, and the economic expert's valuation of a specific physical asset. From the very mundane matters to the avant garde, experts daily influence the course of civil and criminal litigation. "The role of expert witnesses in American litigation is a topic of considerable range and importance. In our complex society, judicial reliance on expert testimony as a form of explanation and understanding has steadily increased over the last five decades."[2]

173

Why is there a need for experts? From one perspective, it seems that "science," whether behavioral or physical, has garnered an almost unquestioned authority. Courts appear inclined not to second-guess the scientific premise. When experts testify in a planned, methodical format, testimony seems, at least on its face, impressively reliable. Unquestionably, the justice system gives extraordinary deference to scientific experts. Why else would so many courts admit, despite their inherent ignorance, the concept of DNA analysis? Why is there scant evidentiary resistance to the use of anatomical dolls as a form of testimonial aid in child abuse investigations? How is it that experts in recently established fields, like *sexual therapy, battered-woman syndrome,* and *postpartum pregnancy analysis,* are permitted to testify on unproven scientific novelties in some jurisdictions? Kathleen Herasimchuk, in her work *A Practical Guide to the Admissibility of Novel Expert Evidence in Criminal Trials Under Federal Rule 702,* characterizes the legal system as incredibly tolerant:

> Unfortunately, few judges or lawyers have the scientific training to weigh the merits of such testimony. Few are knowledgeable or even interested in the processes by which novel scientific theories are born and tested.[3]

> A faulty scientific premise will yield an incorrect legal conclusion. While faulty and absurd results may yield individual illicit benefits, these results are detrimental to the legal system and to society. . . .[4]

This ready, almost lemminglike, acceptance of newly discovered "science" is a dangerous phenomenon. Automatic acceptance of individuals claiming scientific, or even nonscientific, expertise does not foster evidentiary rigor. Be suspicious of trendy science, be constructively critical of a party who claims the status of an expert, and, most important, do not allow the case-in-chief to be overwhelmed or overly reliant on the evidence offered by experts. The debate is usually reduced to the question of whether the expert evidence is science or junk.

On the other hand, most litigators realize the inadequacy of juror preparation to fathom the expert's subject matter. "Consequently, the trial attorney must find ways to explain this technical evidence so that lay juries can process it intelligently when rendering a verdict. As a general matter, attorneys turn to experts when attempting to explain certain complex issues to a jury. Thus expert testimony becomes extremely important, for an average juror, when left to his or her own resources,"[5] is in dire need of someone qualified to relay testimony on complex issues.[6] Obviously, the ordinary layperson is incapable of relating testimony concerning environmental compliance, hydrogeological investigations, or the engineering aspects of facility construction. Experts serve an educational function in civil and criminal cases. "Expert testimony is beneficial to the trier of fact when experience and knowledge of lay persons does not generally extend to technical, scientific, medical, mathematic, or business areas."[7] From this analysis, the question is not whether the expertise of experts is helpful, but whether expert testimony has met the tests of admissibility and whether the employment of experts is a wise tactic.[8]

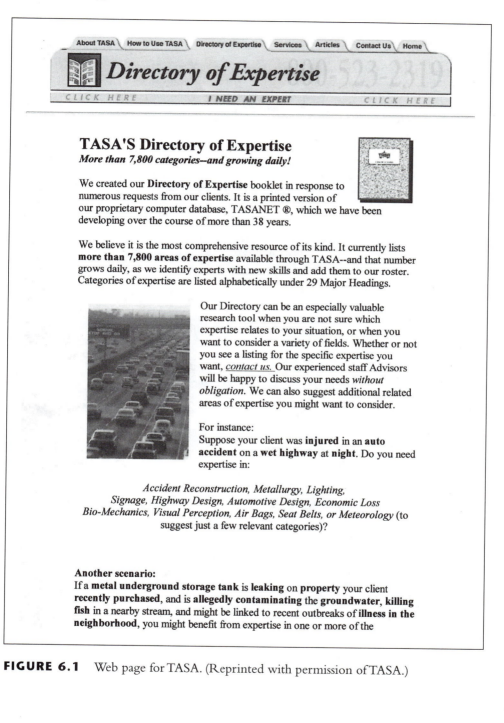

About TASA \ How to Use TASA \ Directory of Expertise \ Services \ Articles \ Contact Us \ Home

### *Directory of Expertise*

CLICK HERE | **I NEED AN EXPERT** | CLICK HERE

## TASA'S Directory of Expertise
*More than 7,800 categories--and growing daily!*

We created our **Directory of Expertise** booklet in response to numerous requests from our clients. It is a printed version of our proprietary computer database, TASANET ®, which we have been developing over the course of more than 38 years.

We believe it is the most comprehensive resource of its kind. It currently lists **more than 7,800 areas of expertise** available through TASA--and that number grows daily, as we identify experts with new skills and add them to our roster. Categories of expertise are listed alphabetically under 29 Major Headings.

Our Directory can be an especially valuable research tool when you are not sure which expertise relates to your situation, or when you want to consider a variety of fields. Whether or not you see a listing for the specific expertise you want, *contact us.* Our experienced staff Advisors will be happy to discuss your needs *without obligation*. We can also suggest additional related areas of expertise you might want to consider.

For instance:
Suppose your client was **injured** in an **auto accident** on a **wet highway** at **night**. Do you need expertise in:

*Accident Reconstruction, Metallurgy, Lighting, Signage, Highway Design, Automotive Design, Economic Loss Bio-Mechanics, Visual Perception, Air Bags, Seat Belts, or Meteorology* (to suggest just a few relevant categories)?

**Another scenario:**
If a **metal underground storage tank** is **leaking** on **property** your client **recently purchased**, and is **allegedly contaminating** the **groundwater**, **killing fish** in a nearby stream, and might be linked to recent outbreaks of **illness in the neighborhood**, you might benefit from expertise in one or more of the

**FIGURE 6.1**   Web page for TASA. (Reprinted with permission of TASA.)

following:

*Hydrogeology, Soil Contamination, Underground Storage, Environmental Engineering, Water Pollution, Metallurgy, Corrosion, Environmental Toxicology, Public Health, Environmental Medicine, Real Estate Appraisal, Environmental Impact Studies, Liability Insurance, Economic Damages, EPA Regulations, or Hazardous Spills Soil Cleansing.*

For expert assistance in virtually any area of expertise, or for a *free copy* of our **Directory of Expertise** booklet, <u>contact TASA</u>, *The Single Source for All Your Expert Needs.* ®

**NEW!!**
Now you can view a **representative sample** of fields in our Directory of Expertise by scrolling through the window below. Select a category and click the "GO" button to go to a sample list of areas of expertise.

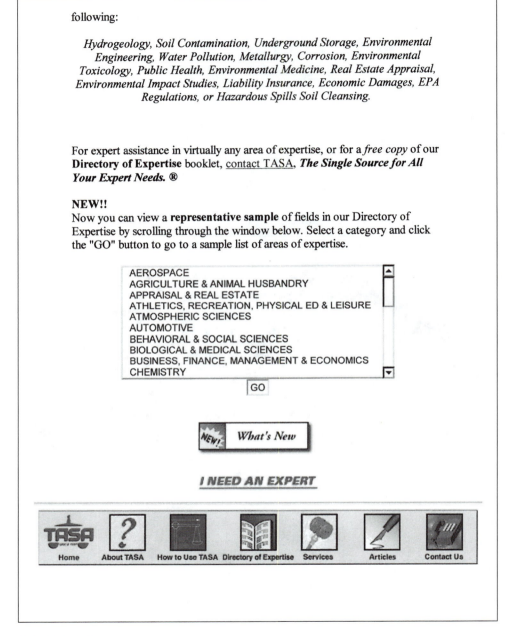

**FIGURE 6.1** *Continued*

The subject of an expert's testimony is hardly invented in a vacuum, and its purpose, usage, and meaning relate to the actual needs of the court. "What is regularly accepted is that an expert has a certain knowledge, understanding, and experience which exceeds that of the ordinary lay person. Standards of education, personal qualification, experiential activities, scholarly publication and production indicate whether a witness is properly qualified as an expert."[9] Technical Advisory Service for Attorneys (TASA), a service which refers expert witnesses, lists fields of expertise. See Figure 6.1.[10] Each of these scientific disciplines can be further refined into various subspecies and specialized classifications. At first glance, is engineering an exclusive scientific endeavor? A comprehensive review of evidentiary principles involving experts is next.

## § 6.2 THE ADMISSIBILITY OF EXPERT EVIDENCE

Whether or not the expert possesses the necessary knowledge to testify as an expert is a central factor, though not the exclusive basis in any admissibility determination. More is required. Whether the subject matter of the expert's testimony is reasonably reliable, has achieved scientific consensus, has generated a body of research and literature, and has been tested in the scientific marketplace are crucial considerations as well. Has the expert witness's subject matter, the scientific topic proffered, met with a generally favorable review in the scientific community, and, at the same time, do courts, either by current decision or by precedent, admit the same? Courts primarily consider whether or not the scientific field has generally gained acceptance in the scientific community or at least will be "helpful" to the trier of fact before admitting expert evidence. Both state and federal courts establish minimal legal thresholds for expert admission. That the law in this area of evidentiary analysis is evolutionary and unstable is a certainty.

### Crossing "the Barrier of Judicial Acceptability" or Being "Helpful"—The Threshold of Expert Evidence

In making any judgment on the admissibility of expert evidence, courts properly look to a long-standing precedent, *Frye v. United States,*[11] to determine whether or not a field has "crossed the barrier of judicial acceptability" or to the more recent *Daubert v. Merrell Dow Pharmaceuticals, Inc.,*[12] which provides a standard that is crudely known as the "helpfulness" test.

The *Frye* decision is much deliberated and oft-quoted. Its critical message conveys the following advice:

> Just when a scientific principle or discovery crosses the line between the experimental and demonstrable stages is difficult to define. Somewhere in this twilight zone, the evidential force of the principle must be recognized, and while the courts

will go a long way in admitting expert testimony deduced from a well recognized scientific principle or discovery, the thing from which the deduction is made must be sufficiently established to have gained general acceptance in the particular field in which it belongs.[13]

Determining whether evidence is reliable and has successfully engaged *Frye*'s barrier of judicial acceptability depends upon various factors, including

1. The validity of the underlying scientific principle,
2. The validity of the technique or process that applies the principle,
3. The condition of any instrumentation used in the process,
4. Adherence to proper procedures,
5. The qualifications of the person who performs the test, and
6. The qualifications of a person who interprets the results.[14]

Is it reasonable to assume that the PMS defense has crossed *Frye*'s barrier of judicial acceptability? What about the fields of astrology and parasensory perception? Will the Twinkie defense encompass the *Frye* criteria?

Initially, an expert's testimony must rest upon an acceptable subject matter, a field or intellectual endeavor that is generally credible and scientifically sound. Some legal interpreters extend these notions to nonscientific forms of expert testimony. While the field of ballistics depends on physics, a typically hard science, other fields have little or no scientific edge in the traditional sense (e.g., economics, accounting, and security law). Yet a scrutiny targeting acceptability and consensus will still occur in a *Frye* jurisdiction. With nonscientific evidence, the judicial test is one not of substance, but of method. *Frye*, as has already been shown, worries first about the field. "To evaluate the validity and accuracy of the expert's conclusions, *Frye* requires trial courts to survey relevant scholarship. Admission is predicated on a showing that the expert's conclusions command an independent, supporting consensus. Under *Frye*, trial courts therefore assess expert evidence in its native context, a process that does not discriminate against different nonscientific fields."[15]

Not all were happy with *Frye*'s restrictiveness. The federal courts, by and through a pivotal ruling, *Daubert v. Merrell Dow Pharmaceuticals, Inc.,*[16] have effectively made the *Frye* rule moot in their jurisdictions. *Daubert* has been the primary support of those hoping to achieve the admissibility of "sciences" once scorned. Strict reliance on the general consensus test of *Frye* is being replaced with a "more searching and flexible inquiry about the reliability and relevance of the offered evidence."[17] Under *Daubert*, judges are "gatekeepers" performing dual functions, screening "expert scientific testimony not merely to assure that the expert is qualified, but also to assure that the expert methodology is 'reliable.' "[18] Judges are to determine whether "the scientific evidence had sufficient testing, peer review and publication."[19] *Daubert*'s suggestions were toothless, and, as a result, unpredictability at the lower courts became normal. It is questionable whether judges are even capable of performing the latter function.[20] Like it or not, until *Daubert* is modified, judges can take on an increasing screening role with respect to scientific evidence.[21]

*Daubert's* lenient and inconsistent results have generated enormous criticism. The U.S. Supreme Court's 1999 ruling, in *Kumho Tire Co. v. Carmichael,*[22] increased the gatekeeping role of the judge when it comes to the quality and content of expert evidence. Not only are the questions of qualification and field pertinent, but also the methodology behind the results testified to must be considered.[23] *Kumho* is a valiant attempt to banish a burgeoning "junk science" industry from the courtroom. Expert evidence should be primarily rooted in a "real science"[24] that arises only from "careful and controlled experimentation."[25]

At the statutory level, some measures of scientific reliability are deemed essential. FRE Rule 702 calls for *scientific, technical,* and *specialized* knowledge as a prerequisite to expert evidence admissibility. The uniqueness of the knowledge being presented before the court—that is, knowledge above and beyond the normal competency of a lay witness—is what casts the evidence in an expert mode.[26] Succinctly stated, experts exist both because lay witnesses are incapable of giving testimony about technical subject matter and because such experts are necessary due to the practical benefits they bring to the judicial arena. Ordinary laypersons lack the intellectual, occupational, or educational background essential in the resolution of complex cases.

## Expert Opinion

While lay witnesses are prohibited from testifying as to their opinions, experts deliver opinions while on the witness stand. Because of experts' skill and qualifications, courts not only admit, but also expect such commentary. Even if an expert has particularized, specialized knowledge that would greatly aid the trier of fact, the expert's testimony must have a conceptual nexus with the case's subject matter. The expert's opinion must correlate with the issue before the court. FRE Rule 703 addresses this requirement:

> The facts or data in the particular case upon which an expert bases an opinion or inference may be those perceived by or made known to the expert at or before the hearing. If of a type reasonably relied upon by experts in the particular field, in forming opinions or inferences upon the subject, the facts or data need not be admissible in evidence.[27]

Keeping this rule in mind, the expert provides opinion testimony that is based on firsthand observation, or, on occasion, on hypothetical questions, or on an examination of data, test results, reports, documents, and other studies. In other words, the expert's testimony bases itself on a foundation of relevancy and materiality. Even at common law, the expert witness's opinion had to be based on reliable scientific, technical, or other specialized knowledge that formed the basis of the expertise—

firsthand observation of the facts, data, or opinions perceived by the expert before the trial, or facts, data, or opinions admitted in evidence in a trial—and elicited through either hypothetical or actual questions. Rule 703 also permits an expert witness to base his or her opinion or inference on facts, data, or opinions presented inside and outside of court other than by his or her own direct perception, without regard to whether such facts, data, or opinions have or will be admitted, or have or would be ruled inadmissible if offered into evidence. The facts, data, or opinions, however, must be of a type reasonably relied on by experts in the field for forming opinions or inferences on the subject.[28]

Witnesses with firsthand knowledge may be asked about the facts underlying their opinions because the facts themselves are needed to satisfy the burden of proof.[29] See Case Example 6.1.

Thus, while courts are flexible in their general approach to permitting expert testimony, testimony given without a proper foundation will be excluded. An expert's bare conclusions unsupported by factual evidence are simply inadmissible, and courts therefore require that an expert's testimony rest on some factual predicate.[30]

---

**CASE EXAMPLE 6.1**     *The Reliability of Expert Evidence*

**CASE:** *Ryan v. KDI Sylvan Pools,* 212 N.J. 276, 579 A.2d 1241 (1990).

**FACTS:** Plaintiff was a guest at a neighbor's home and suffered a spinal cord injury when diving into a swimming pool. A negligence action was brought against the neighbor and a product liability action against the manufacturer of the pool, KDI Sylvan Pools, Inc. The claim against KDI alleged a design defect and a lack of adequate warnings on the product. Plaintiff further alleged that the pool configuration and overall depth rendered the use of a diving board unsafe. Plaintiff offered expert testimony on pool depth standards as propagated by the National Spa and Pool Institute (NSPI), which found that the pool design of KDI was "totally inadequate to insure safe diving." In rebuttal, KDI presented the testimony of Joseph Schmerler, "an acknowledged expert in the propagation and revision of NSPI standards." Schmerler testified that residential swimming pools required no warning. Schmerler relied on reports from spinal injury centers and data he only generally identified.

**QUESTION AND ISSUE:** Is defendant's expert's testimony based upon personal knowledge or scientific reports that have been sufficiently identified in order to properly lay a foundation for the expert's testimony?

**RULING:** The Supreme Court of New Jersey ruled that the defendant's expert evidence should have been excluded because the data were unidentifiable, unreliable, and, at best, too vague. Who are the investigators? What are the spinal centers? Who and what are the authorities, data, and the findings the expert relied upon?

## Science or Junk

There is little question that the proliferation of experts and the proclaimed fields of expertise has caused concerns about quality and content. Those content with *Frye* are so because of its evidentiary rigor. *Daubert's* descent into "helpfulness" and judicial discretion is bound to propagate less than reliable evidence in some cases. The *Frye* camp desires limitation and strict interpretation. Others, affectionately known as judicial activists, want more. Such activists want as much admitted as possible. This has triggered the pejorative definition of "junk science."

Judicial activists emphasize the pervasive use of expert testimony by litigants to prove or disprove the cause of the alleged harm. They assert that judges must make a threshold determination of whether an expert's testimony will be more likely to aid or mislead the jury, rather than being tied to a stricter test of scientific reliability.[31]

A "junk science" witness is not hard to detect because the expert lacks the traditional prerequisites like the following:

1. He is qualified in his field, but the subject matter of his opinions is not quite in his field;
2. He has published, but not on the subject matter about which he is advancing opinions;
3. He has not offered his opinion in this case for publication in any peer-reviewed journal;
4. He is a member of numerous professional societies, but does not serve in any official capacity in any of them;
5. He can point to no literature in his field that supports or confirms his opinions;
6. His opinion is not shared by recognized authorities in his field;
7. His opinion relies upon unestablished facts, untenable inferences, and/or speculation;
8. His opinion is contrary to the facts, logic, and/or established science;
9. His opinion cannot be confirmed by collateral analysis; and
10. He sticks to his opinion even after his fallacies and inaccuracies have been exposed.[32]

On one side of the legal ocean are proponents of judicial restraint in the use of experts who perceive the role of judge and jury as nothing more than interpreters of evidence, rather than as people expertly qualified as to content. These same parties find that expert testimony is granted far too much weight in the judicial process.[33] This slavishness to expert advice reflects an overdependence on the expertise of others.[34] One does not simply "buy shoes" anymore. Instead, the customer seeks a "shoe consultant." "Experts" offer classes for every imaginable form of stress and give advice on things like parenting, heightened self-esteem, and enhanced assertiveness. Everyone is an expert, from the real estate sales agent to the pest inspector. This form of obsessive reliance upon expertise has irrefutably weakened the role of the jury and the judge in the processes of litigation. If the expert says something, it is perceived *ex cathedra*. The judicial system is vanquished by the same cultural tendency. "The expanding array of scientific (as well as some not-so-scientific) specialties available for testimony raises hard questions. Will courts require that the witness' opinions be reasonably based upon trustworthy data? How far must judges inquire into the practice of other experts in the same field prior to allowing a trial witness to proffer an expert opinion?"[35] While some courts admit "junk" science because they believe that the trier of fact cannot be harmed by the most vacuous of fields, others are comfortable only in admitting hard, concrete, and well-established sciences like physics, chemistry, and pathology and its academic counterparts. On a more liberal front, some judges hold that the legal sufficiency of evidence does not necessarily translate into or equate to scientific certainty, and, thus, if a field is not fully developed, its admission should be permitted regardless. Then again, nonscientific expertise (e.g., police use of excessive force, real estate valuation) is more attuned to methodology than field. Although courts are leery of expert testimony when the basis and scientific foundation for the testimony have not been rigorously scrutinized, this shortcoming does not preclude admission.

To be sure, most science commences its intellectual life with a minority of scientific support, and only by subsequent research and experience is the general scientific community eventually persuaded. The legal system and law enforcement community should avoid the use of "junk" science, the stuff popularized by tabloid television and magazines. Beware of fashionable consulting groups whose services win cases at any cost. Of recent interest has been the blurred acceptance of experts who testify to the injuries inflicted on sexual abuse victims. Sensationalized trials, such as the McMartin Pre-school case in California and the Kelley trial in North Carolina, have highlighted the inordinate influence of so-called sexual abuse experts.[36] Emotionally reaching out to child victims of sexual abuse is a commendable response, but such empathy must be tempered by evidentiary discipline.[37]

Let's illustrate the debate. A few courts have affirmed the use of expert testimony regarding child sexual abuse syndrome,[38] while others resist. What science defines the syndrome? Sexual abuse experts deduce abuse because the child suffers from sleep disruptions, nightmares, and sexual dysfunction; abuses other children; "acts out" or exhibits pseudomature seductive behavior, anxiety, and guilt; runs away; experiences isolation from peers; suffers bed-wetting; or faces other habitual reactions. These characteristics and traits are presented as being a typical personality profile of a sexual abuse victim. Are these traits dependable predictors of a syndrome? Nightmares, anxiety, and bed-wetting are not conclusive of sexual abuse, but are reliable indicators only of something emotional in scope.[39]

At the same time, litigators should think creatively about experts and be on the lookout for experts not used before. Uncannily, some junk evolves into substance and worth. "An open mind is also helpful in keeping up with the rapidly evolving 'technology of expert testimony.'"[40]

## § 6.3 THE ULTIMATE ISSUE DOCTRINE

Aside from quality questions, expert evidence has other restrictions. Granted, the scope of expert testimony is generally liberal, with opinions permissibly given, few restrictions in the presentation of hearsay, and little objection to the expert's reliance on secondary sources of information and reports in making analytical judgments. Truly, experts are granted preferential latitude. However, some states attempt to put constraints on the scope of expert testimony. These limitations are largely the result of a suspicion that experts exert too much evidentiary authority, which inevitably undermines the jury function. An expert is placed on a testimonial and evidentiary pedestal, with each and every word enunciated given greater weight than the normal lay witness. By elevating expert testimony, it is both probable and realistic that experts' testimonial portrayal overly influences the court. In order to deflate the expert's role, some states—and in a de minimis fashion, the federal system—hold that testimony about the "ultimate issue" is off-limits. What is the ultimate issue?[41]

Consider a psychiatrist testifying as to the mental condition of a defendant and then being asked by the prosecutor:

Q. In your opinion is the defendant mentally insane?

A. Yes.

Q. Therefore, Doctor, if we hold true to your finding that the defendant is mentally insane, would you say that this condition existed at the time that the defendant committed the crime?

A. Yes.

Q. Accordingly, Doctor, would you find, since the defendant was mentally ill at the time that he committed this offense and that he could not substantially appreciate the conduct of his acts, the defendant to be guilty or innocent?

A. Innocent.

Within this construction, one finds the ultimate issue, *innocence* or *guilt*. Traditionally, findings on guilt or innocence are in the jury's province. Should experts supplant these determinations? In selected jurisdictions, the *ultimate issue doctrine* restricts such expert testimony. In the federal courts, under FRE Rule 704, opinions on ultimate issues are restricted:

(a) Except as provided in subdivision (b), testimony in the form of an opinion or inference otherwise admissible is not objectionable because it embraces an ultimate issue to be decided by the trier of fact.

(b) No expert witness testifying with respect to the mental state or condition of a defendant in a criminal case may state an opinion or inference as to whether the defendant did or did not have the mental state or condition constituting an element of the crime charged or of a defense thereto. Such issues are matters for the trier of fact alone.[42]

Under this statutory scheme, in the fact pattern above, the psychiatrist would have breached the ultimate issue doctrine within this limited exception at FRE Rule 704. However, the rule does not restrict other ultimate decision-making.

In some cases, the expert's ultimate determination is admissible. "Thus, the expert may express the opinion that 'the fire was not accidental but was deliberately set' but not that the defendant is guilty of arson."[43] In this sense, the ultimate issue is whether or not arson has occurred, and the expert will testify as such. Being liberal about this form of testimony is dangerous policy.[44]

The challenges to the ultimate issue doctrine are sensibly grounded. First, permitting an expert to reach a conclusion and then to educate a jury as to its correctness is minimally undue evidentiary influence. Second, scientific and other experts may possess the greatest intellectual skill in their subject matter, but transferring those intellectual traits to the legal arena is a quantum leap. A stark contrast between legal and scientific methodology is obvious in insanity hearings. Richard Rogers and Charles Ewing, in their study *Ultimate Opinion Prescriptions,* state:

> The corpus of law on insanity clearly contains implicit moral judgments. Indeed, the very decision of the law-makers to create and maintain an insanity defense is, itself, a moral judgment. Clinicians attempting to apply the legal standards of insanity to disordered defendants are not creating or even answering moral questions. Those questions have already been raised and answered by the legal authorities.[45]

Placing constraints on an expert's ultimate issue testimony has been criticized in some legal circles. Christopher Slobogin, in his article *The "Ultimate Issue" Issue,* portrays such evidence in a positive light:

> The more "ultimate" such testimony becomes, the more energetic we should be in subjecting it to adversarial testing. Conversely, if such testing—including cross-examination of the expert's data and the submission of rebuttal evidence—is present, opinion testimony that is based on specialized knowledge should be not only accepted but welcomed as helpful to the fact finder.[46]

For years, as a sort of compromise position, state and federal courts have toyed with the charade of hypothetical questions. Testimony concerning ultimate issues—ultimate facts—was permissible as long as it was posed in a hypothetical scenario. The fact patterns posed under the hypothetical scheme were nothing but amorphous, phony replacements for the real facts. Jurors with the densest of mental faculties could easily discern the lack of distinction. Even so, "such a hypothetical question need only include facts sufficient to form a reliable basis for an opinion as opposed to all the potential relevant facts. On the other hand, if the question assumes facts so clearly exaggerated or unsupported by inferences for the evidence as to be misleading or confusing, the question should be properly disallowed."[47]

## § 6.4 QUALIFICATIONS OF THE EXPERT

### Experience

Once the determination has been made that the subject matter of the witness's testimony has "crossed the barrier of judicial acceptability" and is a discipline that passes credible review with respected scientific researchers or that assists the tribunal, the next issue is the qualification and character of the proposed expert witness. Under FRE Rule 702, an expert should be "qualified as an expert by knowledge, skill, and experience."[48] A finding of suitable qualification can depend on the following criteria:

- The witness has specialized training in the field of his or her expertise.
- The witness has acquired advanced degrees from educational institutions.
- The witness has practiced in the field for a substantial period of time.
- The witness has taught courses in the particular field.
- The witness has published books or articles in the particular field.
- The witness belongs to professional societies or organizations in the particular field.
- The witness has previously testified and has been qualified as an expert before a court or administrative body on the particular subject on which he or she has been asked to render an opinion.[49]

Degreed and intellectually advanced persons do not automatically qualify as experts. Qualifications bear a foundational relationship to the evidence being proffered. For example, in *Will v. Richardson-Merrell, Inc.,*[50] a plastic surgeon's testimony regarding the influence and effects of a drug called Bendectin was declared improper, since the expertise of the plastic surgeon was not pharmacological. While knowledge is an a priori expert qualification, the extent of an expert's knowledge is demonstrated under these lines of inquiry:

- How many times has the expert acted as a consultant?
- In how many cases has the expert actually testified?
- Were the issues in previous cases similar to the issues in the case before the bar?
- Has the expert ever been employed by the opposing counsel?
- What percentage of the expert's previous trial work was done on behalf of plaintiff's cases and what percentage was on behalf of defendant's cases?
- What record-keeping method does the expert use to insure against conflict of interest problems?
- Has the expert written or published any articles, papers, or treatises concerning the subject matter involved in your case?[51]

Witnesses without a remarkable experiential history can hardly be taken seriously as experts. Weight given the expert evidence largely depends on the credibility of the expert's testimony. An expert with no experiential base is less believable than one with a substantial history.

## Education and Training

Experience is merely one aspect of qualification. Another facet is the academic background of the proposed expert. Does the proposed expert have advanced degrees from a college or university? Aside from a baccalaureate degree, most experts possess a minimum of a master's degree. In many scientific fields, a doctorate is required. Psychiatric evaluations call for an M.D. with postdoctoral training in psychiatry. Certain other fields, such as ballistics and fingerprint analysis, do not necessarily call for postbaccalaureate study and are usually manned by law enforcement forensic experts. Plainly though, more degrees lead to the proposition, rightly or wrongly, that the witness's education makes the witness's testimony more credible. Degrees are in some ways merely pieces of paper. Look to the grantor of the degree, since some institutions are suspect. Less-than-honorable degree-granting institutions of higher learning that commonly advertise in periodicals, magazines, and newspapers need to be avoided.

Unfortunately, a negative stereotype is often applied to certain degree-granting state and religiously affiliated schools. This author has been a long-term critic of the legal profession's heavy and unwarranted emphasis on Ivy League degrees. Being a graduate of an Ivy League institution is no assurance of expertise or superior intelligence. In selecting experts, extreme positions at either end of the educational spectrum are to be shunned. An expert whose educational preparedness is based on a "matchbook" university will be given very little weight, if admitted at all. On the other hand, a jury and the court alike should resist dogmatic acceptance of the testimony of expert witnesses from historically prestigious institutions. There is an amazing diversity of expertise in the modern world based on both experience and academic training, from graduates of the smallest of religiously affiliated institutions, of the largest of state universities, and of the Ivy-covered halls.

## Professional Associations and Other Memberships

Memberships in professional groups or organizations are a supposed sign that the expert is currently maintaining the expertise espoused. Membership in professional organizations and scientific groups keeps the expert on the cutting edge of his or her developing discipline.

In discerning the utility of an expert witness, careful consideration is given to memberships. An impressive membership history will shape jurors' perceptions.

"[T]he jurors will form their initial impressions regarding the expert's demeanor and credibility, and those impressions will determine their overall empathy and identification with the expert then testifying."[52]

Pay significant attention to whether or not the proposed expert has all required licenses and certifications in a proclaimed specialization, and is in receipt of a certificate of training or other documentation or has been admitted to any professional associations or groups that attest to the specialized nature of the expertise.

## Publications, Conferences, and Presentations

Expert witnesses become even more compelling when their publications—whether books, studies, or periodical articles—are highlighted during qualification questioning. Whether correct or not, the layperson perceives a publication record as evidence of an enlightened professional. Publications, especially those that are found in refereed or edited journals, manifest the general academic community's acceptance of the expert's theoretical posturing. The expert who frames theoretical problems in publicly published forums is more persuasive than the one with only practical experience in his or her field. The true expert, the more believable one, is that witness who has written and researched in his or her field as a complement to pure experience. Not to be forgotten are textbook publications, authored participation in legal materials, and editorial contributions to legal advisory committee reports and documents. The formality and permanency of writing indelibly impress the fact finder.

Indicative of expertise is the expert's record of attendance at continuing education seminars, conferences, and conventions. These actions impress upon the jury the expert's commitment to excellence, willingness to be in the scientific forefront, and recognition that his or her field of study is constantly changing, maturing, and intellectually developing. In medical and scientific fields, this approach is mandatory.

What the attorney wants in all cases is the most technically competent expert, with the most exemplary credentials obtainable in the field. In general, credentials should show that the expert has devoted a substantial part of his or her professional experiences to his or her fields of specialization. Among the matters to investigate are education; licensure or board certification, if applicable; and practical experience. Experience should be evaluated in terms of quality, as well as quantity. Factors affecting quality include exposure to authorities in the field or recognition by peers through awards or honors or membership in professional societies. Authorship of articles in applicable trade or professional publications is also impressive, and any articles should be reviewed for content to determine what positions the expert has gone on record as taking. The more education or practical experience the expert has, the better the expert is, from the standpoint both of evaluating the case and of testifying at trial.[53]

Undoubtedly, certain experts will be stronger with respect to some of these criteria than others. In a perfect world, all of these qualifications would be met. Generally, keep in mind the following in determining as to whether or not an expert is worthy of hire:

1. Previous experience with the witness, if any.
2. Reputation amongst other experts.
3. Degree of specialization and technical areas.
4. Publications.
5. Previous testimony recorded in transcripts, newspaper articles or other information about the witness.
6. Catalogs or other types of university or college literature where the witness is on faculty.
7. Professional advertising literature that is published by the expert.
8. The expert's resume.
9. Previous depositions of the expert.[54]

Employ the checklist at Form 6.1 as a screening and qualification device.

Name: _____

Address: _____

_____

Home Phone: _____ Work Phone: _____

Fax Number: _____ E-mail address: _____

Business or Occupation: _____

Name of Organization: _____

Length of Time in Business: _____

Position Held in Organization: _____

Prior Positions: _____

Education:

Undergraduate Degree: _____ Institution: _____

**FORM 6.1** Expert witness questionnaire.

Graduate Degree: _____ Institution: _____

Postgraduate: _____ Institution: _____

Specialized Training:

Courses: _____

Licenses and Certifications: _____

Professional Associations and Organizations: _____

_____

Academic Background: _____

_____

Expert Witness Experience: _____

_____

Specializations: _____

_____

**FORM 6.1**  *Continued*

## Human Traits and Characteristics of the Expert

The term "technically qualified" means that the expert is educated enough, is competent in the field being testified to, and has an enviable record of publication and professional development. If technical proficiency was the only concern in the selection of experts, selection would never be a burden. Humanity, personality, and personal demeanor are the crucial criteria in expert selection. Attorney William Mulligan, in his superb work *Expert Witnesses: Direct and Cross-Examination,* cogently states:

> A good expert witness needs more than grounding in his or her specialty. An expert witness needs the flexibility to accept trial counsel's suggestions, the courage to defy intimidating tactics, the street smartness to survive courtroom give and take while retaining composure, and a dignified but not arrogant mien. It is a tall order.[55]

This author has suggested that sometimes experts have personalities that exude intellectual superiority. This aura patronizes or condescends to the jury. "Bearing, stature, and demeanor of an expert are often very important."[56] At all costs, experts must be advised to descend from the ivory tower. Their fundamental purpose before the tribunal is to translate complex technical information into easily discerned facts. Repeatedly emphasize the need to speak in simple, elementary terms. Advise the prospective witness that giving trial testimony is a most serious matter. "Joking and flippant answers should be avoided at all costs. Exaggeration, underestimation, or overestimation are all enemies of unwary and ill-advised witnesses."[57]

Hair, clothing, and physical appearance, while essentially superficial, are additional major public relations concerns. Though often trite, these human touches make a dramatic difference in the presentation of expert testimony. Expert witnesses who are exquisitely capable and prepared, at least on paper, are sometimes incapable of translating and communicating their expertise to the listener. Experts, first and foremost, must be educators, teachers of the information presented. Experts must tell juries what they need to know, not esoterically relay the full depository of their training and experience. Combining good personal traits with the substantive qualifications discussed above assures a potent and reliable expert witness. See Qualification Exercises 6.1 and 6.2.

---

## QUALIFICATION EXERCISE 6.1

Using the resume of James M. Green, a professional engineer and author of *Bicycle Accident Reconstruction for the Forensic Engineer* (1991), prepare a series of questions to prove his qualification as an expert.

**James M. Green, P.E.**

James M. Green, P.E., is President of Resource Engineering, a general civil engineering firm with a specialty in bicycle accident reconstruction. Mr. Green is a member of the *National Society of Professional Engineers, American Society of Civil Engineers,* and *National Academy of Forensic Engineers* and is a Diplomate in the *American Academy of Environmental Engineers*. He is a registered Professional Engineer in 18 states. He is two-time USCF District Road Champion and is a bicycle builder and tester. He has investigated over 300 bicycle accidents in his professional career.

## QUALIFICATION EXERCISE 6.2

Respond to the following series of questions with hypothetical information that would satisfy the court as to the qualification of an expert witness.

1. What is your educational background?

2. At the completion of your medical studies, where did you serve your medical internship?

3. After completing your internship, did you engage in any postdoctoral studies or postgraduate training leading to a specialization?

4. Upon completion of your medical studies and internship, where did you serve out your residency?

5. Have you had any postgraduate studies or continuing education?

6. Do you have a private practice?

7. In what states are you currently licensed and/or certified?

8. What hospitals do you have an affiliation with?

9. What professional organizations do you belong to?

10. Have you ever held an office in professional organizations?

11. Have you ever received any honors as a result of your practice and profession?

12. Have you ever written any periodical articles, studies, or textbooks in your field?

13. Have you ever held an academic appointment or done any college or university teaching?

14. Have you been found qualified to testify as an expert in court prior to this case?

15. Have you ever served as an expert in your field in a state, federal, local, or private agency?

16. Have you ever been appointed an expert by any one of the judges in this jurisdiction?

## § 6.5 LOCATING EXPERTS

Expert witnesses are not in short supply and aggressively market services to the legal and justice communities. Advertising in publications dedicated to trial lawyers, such as *Trial For the Defense, The American Bar Association Journal,* and others of similar bent, is extensively witnessed. The more important question is not whether there are experts, but whether or not they are qualified, competent, and economical. Briefly stated, experts can be found through these types of resources:

- Professional organizations
- State or federal agencies
- Private consulting firms
- Law enforcement agencies
- Colleges and universities
- Business and industrial centers

## Advertisements

Consult local bar publications and other legal periodicals for appropriate listings. Also, practitioner magazines and periodicals are an excellent source of experts and consulting services. Look to their extensive classified ad sections listing expert services.

Often overlooked, in terms of classified advertising, is the Yellow Pages. Look under topics such as engineers, medical specialists, doctors, and consulting services. Local, national, international, and professional associations frequently publish information about expert services in the area, and checking into that resource is sound planning.[58]

## Academic Experts

Another source in the expert search is the local college or university. As discussed previously, since expertise is largely a qualification of education, training, and experience, faculty members at colleges and universities often possess the special knowledge and skill necessary to be qualified as an expert. Such witnesses can be identified by contacts at an institution, with alumni of an institution, or with people involved in a particular industry who are aware of research and other activities conducted at an institution.[59]

## Directories

Seen regularly in the legal community are published directories that compile listings of experts and their intellectual endeavors. Some examples follow:

- *The Directory of Medical Specialists,* A. N. Marquis Co., 200 East Ohio Street, Chicago, IL 60611;
- *Consultants and Consulting Organization Directory,* Consultant's Project, Box 428, College Park, MD 20740;
- *Locating Scientific and Technical Experts,* in 2 Am. Jur. Trials 302–356 (1987);

- *Locating Medical Experts,* in 2 Am. Jur. Trials 112–133 (1987); and

- *The Lawyer's Guide to Legal Consultants, Expert Witnesses, Services, Books and Products,* Attorney's Profiles International, 30700 Bainbridge Road, Suite H, Solon, OH 44139-2291.

Consult *Who's Who* directories for specific fields from the law, engineering, bio-chemistry, geology, and mathematics, to psychology, psychiatry, and related fields. Most reference librarians will be happy to assist in sorting out and discovering these rich forms of source material.

## Private Consulting Services

No area of expert consulting services is more dynamic than that provided by private entities. Expert consulting services are structured for two major purposes: first, to act as a resource directory, a referral network for attorneys searching for a specific expert and a corresponding topic; and second, to provide evaluative and research services. As to the former, a fee of some type is usually charged, say, between $50 and $200 for that referral. Two of the most often seen and well known of these private consulting services are

- Technical Advisory Service for Attorneys (TASA), 1166 DeKalb Pike, Blue Bell, PA 19422-1853, 1-800-523-2319; and

- Professional Safety, Inc. (PSI), 100 Euston, Royal Palm Beach, FL 33411, 1-800-562-7233.

Another influential player in providing references to experts and litigation support in general is the Association of Trial Lawyers of America (ATLA), 1050 31st Street, NW, Washington, DC 20007.

The second major function of private consulting services is to evaluate and an-alyze certain aspects of an attorney's case. Whether it be economic or wage losses, future earnings, medical expenses, trauma, or outpatient or acute care standards, pri-vate consulting services are major players in litigation analysis.

The representations of any expert consulting service should be closely scruti-nized. Insist on comprehensive resumes, and discuss the expertise of the recom-mended person as to education, training, and previous experience in the litigation forum. The reality of private consulting is its hard and fast profit orientation, and in this business climate, the best interests of the law firm's client may be secondary to the balance sheet of the private consulting firm. Be wary of private entities that stretch the qualifications and expertise of recommended individuals. Experts are not jacks-of-all-trades, but, more likely, narrow specialists. Be persistent in your evalua-tion, and act as if you are a consumer critiquing a product or service.

In the end, the choice of an expert depends on many variables, none of which is more important than the economic cost. The charges of private consulting firms can be quite prohibitive, and there are many public-sector alternatives that can accomplish the same end. Remember that the opposition, during the impeachment process of this expert witness, will repeatedly emphasize the fee paid as evidence of bias. Undeniably, a juror views an expert who is being paid a sum of a thousand, two thousand, or three thousand dollars a day for his or her testimony more skeptically than the learned university expert giving testimony because the court has so ordered or because it is the expert's personal wish to participate in the dynamics of the litigation. The expert chosen must not garner the juror's cynical reaction and must not be the expert who will attest to anything, swinging like a weather vane, blown to the direction in which the checkbook opens. It is common knowledge that for every five defense psychiatrists holding a defendant insane, five prosecution experts will claim the reverse. In a sad sense, facts and the law are open for hire in the private sector. Given the vacillation exhibited on supposed "science," it is almost wondrous that experts have achieved their current level of credibility.

One final source of expertise from the private sector provides case analysis and evaluation. The merits of a case can be submitted to a private firm, such as LRP Publications, Department 460, 747 Dresser Road, Horsham, PA 19044. Case evaluation, settlement analysis, and database research dealing with potential verdict amounts, liability situations, past and future medical expenses, wage losses, similar cases and precedents, and a mind-boggling array of other variables are offered.

## § 6.6 EXPERT SERVICE CONTRACTS

Expert consulting services charge litigation teams in various ways, including a set fee, an hourly rate, and, in some circles, a fee based upon whether or not the case is won or lost. Profit motive is the driving force of private consulting firms. Expert service contracts are initiated either by the consulting firm or by the law firm; an example of the latter is at Form 6.2.

Be certain that the contract covers accurately the costs and fees of usage. Surprises are avoided by clear contracts. Experts can become an extraordinary liability.[60]

[Date]
[Name]
[Address]
RE: Matt Helms v. Christine White

_____ County Common Pleas Court Case No. _____

Dear Dr._____ :

This letter will confirm our conference of April 4, 2000, in connection with retaining your services as an accident reconstruction expert. As discussed, please evaluate this case to determine the following:

1. The pre-skid speed of the Helms vehicle;

2. The time comparison from Mr. Helms's first reaction to the White vehicle as a hazard to the interval of time that the White vehicle was on Route 79 before impact; and

3. Whether the presence of a guardrail on the south edge of Route 79 could have lessened the severity of the impact and resulting injuries.

I am enclosing a check for $1,000.00 representing your retainer for work on this case. It is my understanding that, should the work be completed or stopped for any reason before using up the amount of the retainer, the balance will be refunded. It is my further understanding that your normal fee schedule for this type of work is as follows:

• Preparation Time........................$75.00/hour
(Includes background review, site visit, fieldwork, engineering analysis, reports, meetings, depositions, travel time)

• Court Time.....$500.00/eight-hour day or part thereof

• All Expenses
(Includes airfare, tolls, lodging, meals, mileage, film, prints, aerial photography, etc.)

Under separate cover, I am forwarding a packet of background materials on this case for your review. You may feel free to contact my client, Mr. Stephen Helms, at (216) 555-2432 if you need any information directly from him. I would ask that you not prepare a written report of your findings until I request it at a later date. Please note that the trial of this case has been scheduled for September 10, 2000.

Mr. Bart Brizee is the paralegal in my office who will be assisting me on this case. Please feel free to contact either of us if you have questions. If the terms outlined above comport with your understanding of your engagement on this case, please so indicate by signing the enclosed copy of this letter and return it to me in the envelope provided.

Very truly yours,

_____

Attorney

**FORM 6.2**   Expert witness engagement letter.

## § 6.7 PREPARING AN EXPERT FOR TRIAL

Once an expert has been retained from whatever source, the initiation, training, and preparation of that expert for trial begin. Of critical importance to an expert's level of preparedness is the level of knowledge he or she possesses about the case in which his or her testimony is solicited. Share all available information. The entire case file—all documentation, other expert reports and analyses, depositions, interrogatories, and pleadings documents—and the work product of the attorney that is relevant to the expert's testimony should be made available. When the expert witness understands the reason for being called in, his or her testimony will be more meaningful. Professor Tom Hagen reminds the practitioner that experts cannot cooperate fully and to their maximum extent unless the general aims of their use are fully elaborated:

> There are a number of general aims of such preparation. Four primary ones are:
>
> 1.  To familiarize each witness with the objectives to be obtained through his testimony;
> 2.  To familiarize each witness with specific subject matter of his testimony;
> 3.  To discuss the appropriate demeanor the witness should exhibit during direct and cross-examination;
> 4.  To instruct the witnesses concerning some of the pitfalls that may arise while testifying on cross-examination.[61]

Sit down with the expert and explain the content of the file and the case, and outline a list of questions for the expert's use in reviewing the documentation. Merely assaulting the expert with the file results is intellectual chaos and personal intimidation. "The best way to have expert difficulties is not to know what you want your expert to do. Ill-defined projects and general instructions are licenses for experts to run off, cogitate, and produce big fees and small results."[62]

### Testimonial Suggestions

Preliminary matters abound when preparing the expert for trial. The scope, range, and content of testimony must be controlled by diligent preparation. Emphasize the importance of giving careful testimony and avoiding inconsistent testimony between the deposition and trial; repeatedly admonish the expert to tell the truth at all costs. Some sound bits of advice regarding testimony can be summarized in the following commandments:

*   Be objective.
*   Remain within the expert's field of expertise.
*   Stay out of the clouds, remain on firm ground.
*   Be prepared.

- Do not confuse the legal distinction between possibilities and probabilities.
- Do not answer questions not fully understood.
- Do not guess at answers.
- Do not volunteer information.
- Do not lose one's temper.
- Distinguish between testimony as an expert witness and witness as to facts.
- Define complex terms so a layman can understand.[63]

Above all, tell your expert witness to tell the truth, to not stretch the facts, and to look confident. Expert witnesses who think stretching the facts while on the witness stand will help your case are *wrong*. Juries watch a witness carefully, and even when a witness is giving damaging testimony, it will not likely have as severe an impact on your case if he or she looks confident.[64] Litigator Mark Dombroff provides general insight on how all experts should testify. See Appendix B.

The *American College of Trial Advocacy* entreats attorneys to have a face-to-face conference of some notable duration before trial with the expert, coupling the use of a file, examination by witness checklist, and mock direct examination or other simulation. "Preparation of the expert testimony should begin immediately after his selection. Close cooperation between attorney and expert is necessary. Too many attorneys conduct their preparation in complete isolation from their expert and then try to achieve a unity of approach by a ten-minute conference in the courthouse shortly before the expert is scheduled to testify."[65]

To summarize, many obligations exist in the selection and preparation of experts in civil and criminal litigation. If recommendations and suggestions have been forthcoming, common sense should guide the use of the expert. Common sense decrees that the expert at least accomplish the following:

- Never talk down to your audience.
- Be simple and precise.
- If ignorant of certain facts, just admit it.
- If paid for services admit that too.
- Expect cross-examination.
- Expect impeachment.[66]

## Personality and Demeanor

Don't ever assume that individuals who have obtained the highest levels of educational training and experience will perform impressively during litigation. During pretrial strategy sessions and other mock testimonial preparation, experts must be prepared, informed of all issues, and afforded the opportunity to thoroughly scrutinize the case. Remember that, in this setting, experts need "coaching."[67] Arthur Moore, in his discerning commentary *Expert Opinion Testimony: Experts, Where Do They Come from and Why Are They Here,* insists that an expert without a personal aura, a convincing, pleasant personality that relays well to jurors, is a weak witness. Labeling this condition as a *dynamism,* he states:

> Dynamism refers to the witness' demeanor on the stand and the manner in which he delivers his testimony. Although this component is, unlike expertise, an intangible, it would seem the faultiest indicator for credibility. It is arguably the most influential of the three.[68]

On a vigilant note, do not attempt to clone personality types, for there is room for diverse approaches and different emotional structures. Professor James Jean's classic treatise, *Trial Advocacy,* reminds us to be open to different approaches and to latch onto an expert who is empathic and credible: "Admittedly the guidelines for ascertaining the proper personality are rather vague. When in doubt fall back on the old reliable, 'would you buy a used car from him.' "[69]

## § 6.8 CROSS-EXAMINATION AND IMPEACHMENT

Nothing stirs fear in the heart of an expert more than potent cross-examination. If an expert is not nervous about the consequence of cross-examination, remind him or her that no matter what level of educational attainment has been acquired, no matter how many publications or treatises have been authored, and no matter how many other trials or trial experiences have occurred, a sharp cross-examiner can belittle and denigrate an expert. The anxiety involved in cross-examination can be alleviated by heeding these hints:

- Listen carefully to all questions, and think about the answer before giving it.
- If a question is not understood, indicate this.
- If a mistake is made while answering, correct it immediately.
- If an answer needs to be explained or clarified, indicate so.
- Do not give answers quickly.
- Do not look toward counsel when the opponent asks questions.
- Strive to remain calm and polite.
- Never argue with the cross-examiner.
- Avoid appearing flippant or cocky or acting like a wise-guy.
- Stop speaking immediately if the judge or counsel states or rules on an objection.[70]

Furthermore, remind the expert that much of what takes place on cross-examination, if damaging, can be reshaped and rehabilitated on redirect and rebuttal examination. In cases where the cross-examiner begins to badger and be belligerent toward the expert, remind the expert that retaining a courteous and polite posture impresses a jury more than the conduct of the cross-examiner. "Also tell the expert to bear in mind that he has been found qualified and that a good last resort answer to any cross-examiner is 'that is my opinion, Sir.' "[71]

Provide simulation opportunities for the expert subject to cross-examination. Make the expert aware that contradictions, confrontations, and attacks on the position offered are natural.[72] Relay to the expert how cross-examinations mirror the ebb and flow of trial process. Upon completion of direct examination, any party, plaintiff or defendant, is viewed favorably. Cross-examination takes the luster off this positive appearance. If a plaintiff presents an expert witness unreservedly qualified and authoritative in approach, the jury or judge is naturally impressed. However, that initial infallible impression becomes diluted by the effects of cross-examination. "The defense counsel must be prepared to cross-examine the expert, to destroy the bases of the expert opinion, thereby destroying the expert's credibility and taking away the initial advantage given by the court in qualifying the expert to testify."[73]

Of course, the scope of cross-examination lies within the contents of direct examination. In general, the cross-examiner attacks the foundational aspects of an expert's testimony—"those bases for which the expert raises his voice, those data, facts, reports, experiences whether first-hand or secondary, which support the expert's testimony. Counsel may probe weakness in the bases of the expert's opinion, the sufficiency of his assumptions, and the soundness of his opinion."[74]

Effective cross-examination causes the expert consternation and mental challenge. As David Lewis says in *Cross-Examination:*

> The result in the courtroom is that the witness looks like he is frantically trying to find a way out while the examiner merely proceeds inexorably forward. Because of the witness' mental flight towards some avenue of escape, the jury sees the witness is rattled and will assume that a rattled witness is not a truthful witness. This sociological conclusion emerges from the psychological clues transmitted to the jury.[75]

"Surprise" undermines the expert.[76] Surprises come in all shapes and sizes—from previous testimony to contradictory depositions, from inconsistent intellectual opinion to demonstrations of economic bias. Impeachment of the expert is to be expected. See Cross-Examination Exercise 6.1.

Whether counsel cross-examines a physician in a case of medical malpractice or a real estate appraiser in a valuation conflict, a myriad of impeachment strategies are available. No one method is necessarily superior to another, but the tactic minimally puts the witness on the defensive. Some view the technique of cross-examination in a warlike fashion. "Some people insist that proper cross-examination consists of a rolling ball of butcher knives directed toward and upon the witness. Some people

# CROSS-EXAMINATION EXERCISE 6.1

**FACTS:** Assume you are assigned to prepare initial questions in the cross-examination of a psychiatrist who is prepared to testify that the state should take custody of a child of a mentally disturbed mother. The mother who is the subject of the inquiry, while obviously strange and bizarre, is being defended on the theory that "strangeness" is not indicative of a mother's incompetency or insanity. While on the stand, the psychiatrist testified to the following issues: that psychiatry and psychology are reputable fields, that every individual suffers uniform reactions to stress and trauma, that certain individuals have a more noticeable predisposition to mental instability than others, and that the mother was suffering from severe mental illness, which made her unfit as a mother, and was diagnosed as having *cracked egg shell syndrome.*

## ISSUES FOR CROSS-EXAMINATION:

- Whether psychiatry is an acceptable scientific discipline that has crossed the barrier of judicial acceptability.
- Whether the expert is qualified in forensic or clinical psychiatry.
- Whether the expert has a foundational basis for the testimony relevant to the mother.
- Whether the expert has an economic bias, since he is being paid for his services.
- Whether *cracked egg shell syndrome* is a scientifically reliable diagnosis.
- Whether the mental examination conducted was done properly.
- Whether the diagnostic conclusions are within the *Diagnostic and Statistical Manual of Mental Disorders.*
- Whether psychological testing that was conducted was reliable.
- Whether the opinions were based on facts, data, reports, firsthand observation, or secondary authority.
- Whether there are differences of opinion or a majoritarian academic position opposite the expert's opinion.

Prepare a series of questions utilizing these cross-examination issues.

---

believe that the butcher knife strategy is always appropriate. Others would ask the padre about adultery just in case. One lawyer inexplicably began a cross-examination by asking whether the cooperating witness had a hair piece and if so, whether he was allowed to wear it in jail (he was not). Some lawyers prove that cross-examination is, in fact, more often suicidal than homicidal."[77] From whatever perspective, the cross-examiner makes the witness insecure, sheds negative light on the witness's account, and makes the jury see doubt in the witness's recitation.

## Bias or Conflict of Interest

Attacking the expert's objectivity and credibility based on allegations of favoritism is a cherished cross-examination technique. Bias can be demonstrated by economic interest, level of income, and intellectual integrity—that is, whether or not the expert is comfortable advocating either side of the argument. In the latter case, the inference drawn is that an expert is an expert for hire, rather than an honest purveyor of the subject matter. Experts willing to reside in either the defense or the prosecution camp are, in a sense, mercenary. Questions courting the issue of bias can be directed as follows:

1. Has the expert ever testified for the opposing party or the opposing attorney before? Was such testimony favorable to the party or the party represented by that attorney?
2. Is the expert paid by the opposing party or the attorney for the opposing party?
3. What is the expert's hourly fee for this case? Does the expert have a higher rate for testifying at trial?
4. How much money has the expert made so far in this case?
5. What is the ratio between the number of times the expert has testified for plaintiff firms and the number of times the expert has testified for defense firms?
6. How many times does the expert testify each year? How many times this year?
7. What is the amount of money or percentage of income the expert makes for testifying in an average year?
8. Has the expert himself or herself used the services or products of opposing party? If not, why not?
9. Has the medical expert examined or treated the opposing party? For how long? How many times? For what purpose?

An expert with a substantial track record of testifying will often prompt juror skepticism. A significant testimonial history "opens them to charges of bias or financial interest."[78]

## Qualifications

As previously enunciated, experts must be qualified to relate testimony on a specialized topic. On cross-examination, the background, education, scholarship, professional associations and groups, and experiential level are critiqued. Remember that attacking the qualifications of an expert largely depends on the jurors' perception of the education, training, memberships, and record of scholarship of that expert. These are the very criteria that make the expert serve the cross-examiner. "The issue here is not just whether the expert is qualified, but whether he is honest about his qualifications."[79] A sensible questioning scheme would involve the following:

1. Whether or not the educational institution was accredited.
2. Whether the institution was foreign or domestic.
3. Whether or not advanced degrees had been obtained.
4. Whether or not the degrees were the result of correspondence or other nontraditional means.
5. Whether the institutions of higher learning have decent reputations or are suspect in the public eye.
6. Whether or not the expert has passed all licensure and certification exams.
7. Whether or not the expert is board certified.

## Experience and Employment

Another avenue of attack on the credibility and veracity of an expert sheds light on experience and employment. In the employment sector, being fired from any position negatively reflects on an expert's reputation, especially if the termination involved a position that had a high level of responsibility or was a career track with extraordinary technical proficiency, such as a surgeon or neurologist. Questions in this area may encompass the following:

- How many positions of employment has the expert held over the last few years?
- Has the expert ever been disciplined for unprofessional conduct?
- Has the expert ever been discharged from employment?
- Has the expert ever been sued in the area in which they claim expertise?
- Has the expert ever been disciplined, sanctioned, suspended or terminated from a particular position?
- For how many years has the expert conducted activities in the subject matter before the court?
- How many cases has the expert dealt with which are similar to the facts before the bar?
- How much time did the expert spend with the party about which the testimony is being solicited?
- Did the expert have actual, first-hand experience and knowledge involving the injury, the accident, the product or the location?
- What secondary information does the expert rely upon?[80]

     Review the questioning sequence below:

Lawyer:  You hold a doctoral degree in medicine, not a doctoral degree in psychology, is that right Doctor?

Doctor: Yes, that is correct.

Lawyer: Would it be fair to say that you have had fewer formal courses in psychology than an individual with a Ph.D. in psychology?

Doctor: Although I have had fewer psychology courses, many of my psychiatric seminars cover the same material.

Lawyer: You didn't take any courses in learning, memory, and perception, did you?

Doctor: No, I did not.

Lawyer: Then you don't really have the same background as a psychologist, do you?

Doctor: No, not in all areas of psychology.

Lawyer: The fact that you have seen a lot of patients doesn't mean that you are more accurate, does it?

Doctor: Not the experience alone, but the extensive supervision and consultation that comes with years of experience should improve the quality of my work.

Lawyer: But Doctor, isn't it possible that you or others might simply reinforce each other's mistakes?

Doctor: I guess anything is possible.[81]

## Contrary Authority

Cross-examination that plays into the egos of experts frequently deals with contrary authority. When using contrary authority, the expert's position and testimony are challenged by reputable intellectual authority that reaches an opposite conclusion or judgment—a position, article, textbook, or treatise contrary to the testimonial position being offered by the opposition's expert. Understanding the nature of an expert's self-perception is critical to this technique of cross-examination. Since most expects are intelligent, well educated, and intellectually "a cut above" the masses, there is a certain nonmalicious (in most cases) arrogance, a form of absolutism in their bearing, their projection—a feeling of singular righteousness in their testimony and position. Nothing deflates the expert's ego, once so unassailable, more than a prestigious contrary authority. James McElhaney warns that the tactic is not effective when technical or peripheral differences of opinion emanate. Instead, the contrast and comparison between the expert witness's testimony and another learned treatise or work must be graphic. McElhaney urges that, in using contrasting texts or treatises, the cross-examiner directly undermines credibility. He notes:

> Just what does that mean, reputation for truth is at issue, and if the author is in bad professional repute, that is admissible. Bias and prejudice are relevant and if the article was written by someone who had an ax to grind, it is admissible too.[82]

## Attacking the Expert's Opinion

As FRE Rules 702 and 703 make plain, the expert's opinion must rest on a solid foundation. There must be facts, data, experiences (whether firsthand or secondary), reports upon which the expert relies, and a reasonable, credible, and acceptable scientific discipline in which the expert testifies. Only then can opinions be formulated. "The possibilities for attacking, narrowing, and destroying such opinions are limited only by the facts of the particular case and the imagination and preparation"[83] of the supervising attorney. The advocate's function in this form of cross-examination is to poke holes in the groundwork upon which the expert bases his or her opinion. Lines of inquiry such as these are on target:

- How much information does the expert have?
- How many reports, documents, studies, and research findings is the expert relying upon?
- How much time has the expert spent with the injured party at the accident site or at another location, or in assessing and analyzing a product?
- How much primary information did the expert rely upon?
- How many secondary authorities did the expert rely upon?
- Does the expert have any information beyond a hypothetical examination?
- How many other cases has this expert handled that are similarly situated?

Using other experts to challenge the expert's method or to lead to a differing opinion is another viable tactic on cross-examination.[84]

## Character

In selected cases, the character of an expert witness is a permissible avenue of cross-examination. While character generally applies in the lay witness setting, there are instances in which the credibility of the expert is dubious, based upon his or her personal attributes. FRE Rule 608 opens up this avenue:

> The credibility of a witness may be attacked or supported by evidence in the form of opinion or reputation, but subject to these limitations: (1) the evidence may refer only to character for truthfulness or untruthfulness, and (2) evidence of truthful character is admissible only after the character of the witness for untruthfulness has been attacked by opinion or reputation evidence or otherwise.[85]

Similarly, FRE Rule 608 permits a discussion of specific instances of conduct involving a witness that attacks his or her credibility. Using extrinsic evidence involving fraud and collusion, disbarment, loss of licensure or certification, and other matters, including a potential discussion of drug and alcohol addiction, may be a permissible approach in impeaching the expert witness. FRE Rule 609 permits in selected circumstances the evidence of conviction of a crime if any witness has been convicted of a crime that involves dishonesty or false statement or that is punishable by imprisonment in excess of one year. Under FRE Rule 609 analysis, the court weighs the probative and prejudicial impact of such admission. Fraudulent behavior crosses all economic, professional, and occupational territory, and there are certainly examples of experts who have been less than ethical in their academic and intellectual inquiry and less than scientific in their methodology and findings. "The testimony of experts cannot be viewed as dogma, but instead must be critically evaluated in light of all the evidence posed before the trier of fact. Gauge with caution the testimonial and evidentiary results of experts."[86]

## § 6.9 SUMMARY

The use of experts in civil and criminal litigation is commonplace. The role of experts in all forms of litigation has evolved to the delight of some and the consternation of others. This chapter viewed first the rules covering admissibility, including expert subject matter, crossing the barrier of judicial acceptability, and the "expertise" required to testify. Full-scale review was provided regarding expert qualifications, particularly looking at the education, training, experience, and previous trial participation of the proposed expert.

In addition, practice pointers regarding the finding, selection, and preparation of experts for case evaluation and trial were outlined. Finally, special attention was given to the use of impeachment in cross-examination and various defensive measures to counteract its effects.

## *Notes*

1. William Pipkin, *Expert Opinion Testimony: Experts, Where Do They Come from and Why Are They Here,* 13 Law & Psychol. Rev. 103 (1989).

2. CHARLES P. NEMETH, Paralegal Resource Manual 20 (2d ed. 1995).

3. Kathleen C. Herasimchuk, *A Practical Guide to the Admissibility of Novel Expert Evidence in Criminal Trials Under Federal Rule 702,* 22 St. Mary's L. J. 181, 183 (1990).

4. Sam A. LeBlanc III, *Scientific Truth in Toxic Tort Litigation,* 35 For the Def. 2 (1993).

5. James S. Schutz, *Symposium: Juries: Arbiters or Arbitrary?: Redefining the Role of the Jury: The Expert Witness and Jury Comprehension: An Expert's Perspective,* 6 Cornell J.L. & Pub. Pol'y 107 (1997).

6. The decision of the U.S. Court of Appeals for the 5th Circuit in *In re the Air Crash Disaster* is instructive. When assigning the label "expert trial judges must be sensitive to the qualifications of persons claiming to be expert because the universe of an expert is defined only by the virtually infinite variety of fact questions in the trial courts. The signals of competence cannot be cataloged. Nonetheless, there are almost always signs both

of competence and of the contributions such experts can make in a clear presentation of the dispute. While we leave their detection to the good sense and instincts of the trial judges, we point by way of example to two. First, many experts are members of the academic community who supplement their teaching salaries with consulting work. We know from our judicial experience that many such able persons present studies and express opinions that they might not be willing to express in an article submitted to a refereed journal of their discipline or in other contents subject to peer review. . . . Second, the professional expert is now commonplace. That a person spends substantially all of his time consulting with attorneys and testifying is not a disqualification." *In re* the Air Crash Disaster, 795 F.2d 1230, 1233–1234 (5th Cir. 1986).

7. Harold A. Feder, *The Care and Feeding of Experts,* 21 Trial 49 (1985).

8. As Judge Hand cautions, "No one will deny that the law should in some way effectively use expert knowledge wherever it will aid in settling disputes. The only question is to how it can do so best." Learned Hand, *Historical and Practical Considerations Regarding Expert Testimony,* 15 Harv. L. Rev. 40 (1901).

9. NEMETH, *supra* note 2, at 20.

10. Technical Advisory Service for Attorneys (TASA), 1166 DeKalb Pike, Blue Bell, PA 19422-1853, <http://www.tasanet.com/directory.html>, visited January 19, 2000.

11. 293 F. 1013 (D.C. Cir. 1923).

12. 509 U.S. 579 (1993).

13. *Frye,* 293 F. at 1014.

14. MICHAEL GRAHAM, Evidence, Text, Rules, Illustrations and Problems 305–306 (1983).

15. Peter B. Oh, *Assessing Admissibility of Nonscientific Expert Evidence Under Federal Evidence Rule 702* 64 Def. Couns. J. 556–567 (Oct. 1997).

16. 509 U.S. 579 (1993).

17. Ellen Moskkowitz, *Junk Science,* 47 Hastings L.J. 48 (1996).

18. Michael H. Gottesman, *Should State Courts Impose a "Reliability" Threshold?* 33 Trial 20–23 (Sept. 1997).

19. Edward R. Cavanagh, *Decision Extends Daubert Approach to All Expert Testimony,* N.Y. St. B.J. 9 (July/Aug. 1999).

20. Paul Reidinger, *They Blinded Me with Science,* 82 A.B.A.J. 58–62 (Sept. 1996).

21. In fact, the Federal Judicial Center has formally recognized the need for judicial involvement by increasing science training for district court judges and by publishing a handbook on scientific evidence, which includes detailed "reference guides" on scientific and technical specialties frequently encountered in the courtroom. Paul S. Miller & Bert W. Rein, *Whither Daubert? Reliable Resolution of Scientifically-Based Causality Issues in Toxic Tort Cases,* 50 Rutgers L. Rev. 563 (1998).

22. 119 S. Ct. 1167 (1999).

23. Robert W. Littleton, *Supreme Court Dramatically Changes the Rules on Experts,* 71 N.Y. St. B.J. 8, 12 (July/Aug. 1999).

24. *Id.*

25. *Id.*

26. Jason Ladd states, "There is no more certain test that works for determining when experts may be used than the common sense inquiry where the untrained lay witness

would be unqualified to determine intelligently, and to the best possible degree, the particular issue without enlightenment from those having a specialized understanding of the subject involved in the dispute." Jason Ladd, *Expert Testimony*, 5 Vand. L. Rev. 414, 418 (1952).

27. Fed. R. Evid. 703.

28. Michael Graham, *Evidence and Trial Advocacy Workshop*, 40 Crim. L. Bull. 360, 362 (1984). Professor Ronald Carlson, in his outstanding study *Policing the Bases of Modern Expert Testimony*, relates in part, "The litmus test of admission or exclusion of an expert's opinion based upon the reports of others is the reasonableness of the testifying expert's reliance on such reports. If the underlying facts or data that help the expert reach conclusions are of a type on which other experts in the field customarily rely, most courts will permit the expert to testify." Ronald Carlson, *Policing the Bases of Modern Expert Testimony*, 39 Vand. L. Rev. 577, 578 (1986).

29. DEAN WEINSTEIN, in his text *Evidence*, states, "A witness' acquaintance with certain data may have to be shown in qualifying him as an expert pursuant to Rule 702. And the necessity of making the evidence understandable to the jury will often result in the posing of some foundational questions before the opinion is requested." 3 Weinstein, Evidence 705 (1981).

30. Brian Simon, *The Basis of Expert Testimony: Ryan v. KDI Sylvan Pools Lets the Experts Have Their Ways*, 43 Rutgers L. Rev. 1235, 1240 (1991).

31. Moore, *Exploring the Inconsistencies of Scrutinizing of Expert Testimony Under the Federal Rules of Evidence*, 22 Texas Tech L. Rev. 885, 891 (1991).

32. George M. Walker, *What to Do When It Happens to You*, 17 Ala. Law. 117, 118 (1993).

33. Moore, *supra* note 31, at 891.

34. The judicial use of psychometric data measuring racist or sexist tendencies is another clear example of the *Daubert* influence. How does one really measure, at least scientifically, one's racial inclination? Better said, who has the expertise to formulate such findings? In Price Waterhouse v. Hopkins, 490 U.S. 228 (1988), the U.S. Supreme Court addressed this issue. In weighing the viability of psychological research on sexual stereotypes by Dr. Lisa Luke, the Court rejected defendant's characterization of her testimony as "Gossamer evidence" based only on "intuitive hunches" and of her detection of sex stereotyping as "intuitively divined." "Nor are we disposed to adopt the dissent's dismissive attitude toward Dr. Fiske's field of study and toward her own professional integrity. . . . Indeed, we are tempted to say that Dr. Fiske's expert testimony was merely icing on Hopkins' cake." *Id.* at 255–256. *See* Jane Goodman, *Evaluating Psychological Expertise on Questions of Social Fact: The Case of Price Waterhouse v. Hopkins*, 17 Law & Hum. Behav. 249, 253 (1993).

35. Carlson, *supra* note 28, at 578.

36. There is a passionate, ongoing debate about the "helpfulness" of child advocates in sexual abuse cases. "Child advocates say that such expert testimony is necessary because legal proof of sexual abuse is often unavailable, especially when a parent or family member is the alleged abuser. Defense attorneys say that there is no documentable profile of the sexual abuse victim and that juries can understand the manifestations of abuse without expert help." Note, *The Unreliability of Expert Testimony on the Typical Characteristics of Sexual Abuse Victims*, 74 Geo. L. J. 429, 431 (1985).

37. In a wide-ranging study conducted by Andrew Cohen for the *Georgetown Law Journal*, expert testimony in child abuse cases, while well intentioned, was found to be suspect.

"However strong are the policies of protecting victims of child abuse and of liberally allowing expert testimony, most expert testimony on the typical characteristics of sexual abuse victims has not been helpful for juries and presents serious dangers of prejudice." *Id*. at 429.

38. State v. Floody, 481 N.W.2d 242 (S.D. 1992).

39. Note, *supra* note 36, at 449.

40. Nancy Hollander & Lauren M. Baldwin, *Winning with Experts,* 29 Trial 16, 23–24 (1993).

41. Christopher Slobogin gives a cogent example of an *ultimate issue.* "Take as an example the issue of whether a criminal defendant is competent to stand trial. Even if a mental health professional finds, and no one disputes, that the defendant's ability to interact with an attorney and understand the courtroom processes is significantly compromised, a finding of incompetence may not be appreciated," but said finding is not germane to the case's ultimate aim—innocence or guilt. Instead, competence is about procedure, not substance, and therefore violates no ultimate issue. Christopher Slobogin, *The "Ultimate Issue" Issue,* 7 Behav. Sci. & L. 259, 260 (1989).

42. Fed. R. Evid. 704.

43. Dennis R. Suplee & Margaret S. Woodruff, *Direct Examination of Experts,* 33 Prac. Law. 53, 60 (1983).

44. The Federal Rules of Evidence also represent a clear repudiation of the ultimate issue rule, a common law evidentiary doctrine developed in the nineteenth century that forbade witnesses to give an opinion on ultimate issues to be decided by the jury. Deon J. Nossel, *The Admissibility of Ultimate Issue Expert Testimony by Law Enforcement Officers in Criminal Trials,* 93 Colum. L. Rev. 231, 235 (1993).

45. Richard Rogers & Charles P. Ewing, *Ultimate Opinion Prescriptions,* 13 Law & Hum. Behav. 357, 363 (1989).

46. Slobogin, *supra* note 41, at 265–266.

47. JAMES MCCARTHY, Making Trial Objections 5-28 (1988).

48. Fed. R. Evid. 702.

49. *See* CHARLES P. NEMETH, Litigation, Pleadings and Arbitration 421 (1990). *See also* JOHN TARANTINO, Trial Evidence Foundations 4-5 (1987).

50. 647 F. Supp. 544, 547 (S.D. Ga. 1986).

51. BEVERLY HUTSON, Paralegal Trial Handbook 3-15 (1991).

52. MARK DOMBROFF, Dombroff On Unfair Tactics 415 (1988).

53. LAWRENCE S. CHARFOOS & DAVID W. CHRISTENSEN, Personal Injury Practice: Technique and Technology (1986).

54. DOMBROFF, *supra* note 52, at 417.

55. WILLIAM MULLIGAN, Expert Witnesses: Direct and Cross-Examination 2 (1987).

56. CHARLES P. NEMETH, Paralegal Resource Manual 200 (1989).

57. Harold A. Feder, *The Care and Feeding of Experts,* 21 Trial 51, 52 (1985).

58. MULLIGAN, *supra* note 55, at 4.

59. Abraham Ordover, *Cross Examination of Expert Witness,* in Master Advocate Handbook 209 (D. Lake Rumsey ed., 1986).

60. Michael Wagner, in his keenly authored work *Expert Problems,* manifests a brilliant recognition of expert fees out of control. "Perhaps more than any other professionals, lawyers know what hourly rate billing can mean. Hours are deposited on billing sheets, bit by bit, day by day. They do not look like much while they accrete, but before long the bill is a mountain. The gradual deposits of time are continuous; with hourly billing there is less incentive *not* to do something. If you are paid for every hour, you think less about the need for what fills up that hour's time. If you want to be stuck by your expert like some clients are stuck by their attorneys, insist on an hourly billing." Michael J. Wagner, *Expert Problems,* 15 Litig. 35, 36 (1989).

61. Thomas Hagel, *Defending Against Claim of Ineffective Assistance of Counsel,* 30 Am. Jur. Trials 607, 677 (1983).

62. Wagner, *supra* note 60, at 35.

63. DOMBROFF, *supra* note 52, at 450.

64. P. Arley Harrel, *A New Lawyer's Guide to Expert Use,* 39 Prac. Law. 55, 63 (1993).

65. ALI–ABA COMMITTEE ON CONTINUING PROFESSIONAL EDUCATION, Civil Trial Manual 249 (1974).

66. CHARLES P. NEMETH, Paralegal Handbook: Theory, Practice and Materials 106 (1986).

67. NEMETH, *supra* note 56, at 200.

68. Pipkin, *supra* note 1. This enlightened position has other supporters, including forensic expert Professor Andre Moessens, who holds that personality often weighs greater in the mind of a jury than pure substance. "The juror is more easily persuaded to a desired line of thinking by a personable or friendly expert who is able to reduce the jargon of his expertise to the common terms of the juror-layman. This is true whether or not what he says is technically or medically truthful. Thus, a pleasant demeanor may mean more to a juror than an expert's knowledge." Andre Moessens, *The "Impartial" Medical Expert: A New Look at an Old Issue,* 25 Med. Trial Tech. Q. 63, 65 (1979).

69. JAMES JEAN, Trial Advocacy 271 (1975).

70. *See* CAROLE BRUNO, Paralegal Litigation Handbook 345 (1980).

71. MULLIGAN, *supra* note 55, at 9.

72. As Charfoos and Christensen so poignantly argue, "Although raising doubts about the expert's credentials or motivations serves an important purpose, the main objective of cross-examination is to undermine the substance of the expert's direct testimony. . . . The objective is to raise questions about the validity of the conclusions reached." CHARFOOS & CHRISTENSEN, *supra* note 53, at 924.

73. Glenn G. Goodier, *The Defense Perspective on Expert Witnesses,* Brief, Fall 1988, at 48.

74. GRAHAM, *supra* note 14, at 337. In *Cross-Examination: End Game,* Steven Lubet states that effective cross-examination must elicit a last point, an end result that is unadulteratedly undeniable. "It is crucial that you plan carefully the last point that you intend to make on cross-examination. It must be a certain winner, the proposition on which you are willing to make your exit. Indeed you should write the last few questions at the bottom of your notepad, underlined and in bold letters. Your final point should stand alone, with nothing to obscure it or distract from it. Then, if disaster strikes, you can skip to the bottom of the page, deliver your fail-safe zinger, proudly announce, 'Your witness, Counsel,' and sit down." Steven Lubet, *Cross-Examination: End Game,* 17 Litig. 40, 42 (1991).

75. David L. Lewis, *Cross-Examination,* 42 Mercer L. Rev. 627, 637 (1991).

76. Scott M. Seaman & James F. Martin, *Using Surprise to Capture the Expert Witness,* 35 For The Def. 19, 23–24 (Ap. 1993).

77. David L. Lewis, *Cross-Examination,* 42 Mercer L. Rev. 627 (1991).

78. Note, *Finding the Right Expert Witness for Your Case,* 81 Ill. B. J. 51, 52 (1993).

79. Richard S. Cornfeld, *Help Stamp Out Junk Science: A Practical Approach,* 35 For The Def. 27, 29 (1993).

80. NANCY SCHLEIFER, Litigation Forms and Checklists 13-31 (1987).

81. Richard Rogers, R. Michael Bagby, & Cheryl Perera, *Can Ziskin Withstand His Own Criticisms? Problems with His Model of Cross-Examination,* 11 Behav. Sci. & L. 223, 232 (1993).

82. JAMES MCELHANEY, McElhaney's Trial Notebook 39, 55 (3d ed. 1994). To illustrate, consider the heartfelt attacks on psychiatry and psychology by theorist J. Ziskin. "A major emphasis of Ziskin is to challenge the science and credibility of psychology through general principles of cross-examination; these principles are composed of basic strategies to discredit experts that may be applied across a wide range of criminal and civil cases. Such principles include: (a) the scientific status of psychology and psychiatry, (b) training and background of experts, (c) inadequacies in diagnosis, (d) frailties of clinical judgment, and (e) uncontrolled situational influences on assessment." Rogers et al., *supra* note 81, at 223.

83. Kenneth L. Harrigan, *Deposing the Plaintiff's Expert Witness,* 27 For The Def. 12 (1986).

84. Environmental law specialist George Krafcisin urges, in cases where toxic exposure is alleged, a sequential challenge to the toxic samples. He poses the following questions:
    * Has medical evidence matched the injury to the effects of a specific agent?
    * Does exposure data for the agent exist? Check safety inspection reports, insurance files, OSHA records.
    * Can sampling be done under simulated conditions?
    * Were samples taken for an adequate time? Peaks captured for fast-acting agents, full shift for others?
    * Was sampling done by or under the direction of a certified industrial hygienist?
    * Was standard methodology used?
    * Are results being compared to appropriate exposure standards?
    * Was the analytical laboratory accredited?

    George Krafcisin, *Air Sampling Data in Toxic Exposure Cases,* 35 For The Def. 26, 29 (1993).

85. Fed. R. Evid. 608.

86. NEMETH, *supra* note 56, at 210.

# CHAPTER 7

# *Admissions and Stipulations*

## § 7.1 INTRODUCTION: PRETRIAL EVIDENTIARY REQUESTS

To ensure efficient litigation in the justice system, prosecution and defense teams, prior to trial, should seek agreement on issues of fact and potential evidentiary disputes. When the parties resolve issues before trial, time and expense are saved. Stipulations and requests for admissions play a major role in this judicial economy.

In state and federal courts, both practices are common. Once obtained, trial evidence may be offered without formal proof, provided that the supporting documents are filed and recorded.[1]

*Requests for admissions* seek the opposition's agreement on certain facts and/or legal issues. The said evidence is agreed to and can be offered without challenge or dispute. Such requests attempt to frame issues involved in the litigation and to eliminate needless contention. "Unlike other discovery devices, such requests are not usually used to obtain a detailed knowledge of the evidence. Instead [requests for admissions are] often used to determine whether or not other parties will concede the accuracy of facts already known to the discovering party."[2] A request's content may solicit agreement on documentary evidence, real or physical evidence, forensic expertise, or other evidentiary questions. The party propounding the request desires to remove any potential for legal debate. "Requests for admission are the least used discovery method, yet one of the most valuable. Through a request for admission the other party might admit unequivocally to an issue relevant to your case."[3]

Requests for admissions compact the legal dilemmas and anticipate needless arguments or support pretrial motions for summary judgment or evidence exclusion. Other examples where the request is appropriate are as follows:

- Admission of genuineness of documents, e.g., insurance policy, deed, confession or other operative legal document.
- Admission of facts showing no insurance coverage for varying reasons.
- Admission of facts establishing tort immunity, privilege or other status.
- Admission of facts showing plaintiff's status on defendant's land, or ownership or other interest.
- Admission of facts showing plaintiff to be guest, invitee or trespasser.
- Admission of facts showing availability of defenses.
- Admission of facts as to ownership of an automobile.
- Admission of facts that may deprive the court of jurisdiction.[4]

Admissions force the issue and make it difficult for an opposing party to object during trial. Thus, requests for admissions are tools of preliminary discovery that promote agreement on issues of fact, legal opinions, conclusions, legal relationships and the quality and content of evidence.

*Stipulations* are just as efficient, if not more so, in assuring that opposing parties concur on specific facts, issues, exhibits, evidence, or any imaginable issue in dispute. Stipulations eliminate the contentiousness between parties in pretrial activities and foster a more efficient and economical use of tactical resources. Stipulations are either oral or written agreements representing the lack of dispute on an issue, and, by said stipulation, the parties to the agreement forego usual challenges to the evidence's admissibility.

## § 7.2 ADMISSIONS: PURPOSE AND EFFECT

Statutory codifications usually guide admission practice. Rule 36 of the Federal Rules of Civil Procedure gives instruction:

> A party may serve upon any other party a written request for the admission . . . of the truth of any matters within the scope of Rule 26(b) (1) set forth in the request that relate to statements or opinions of fact or of the application of law to fact, including the genuineness of any documents described in the request. Copies of documents shall be served with the request unless they have been or are otherwise furnished or made available for inspection and copying. Without leave of court or written stipulation, requests for admission may not be served before the time specified in Rule 26(d).[5]

The content and thrust of Rule 36 are multifaceted, from the gentle urging that opposing counsel attempt to seek admission and recognition of documents, to the more subtle suggestion that issues of fact and matters of law should be agreed to. Requests to admit tend to focus on narrow issues before the court, forcing the litigants into defined, factual positions and determining legal postures based on admitted matter. The American College of Trial Lawyers characterizes the admission's request as a tool that is "helpful in both clarifying and sharpening issues, Rule 36 [being] tailor-made to perform this function."[6]

Administratively, Federal Rule of Civil Procedure 36 also serves a vital function in the reduction and minimization of trial time. "Admissions are sought, first to facilitate proof with respect to issues that cannot be eliminated from the case, and secondly, to narrow the issues by eliminating those that can be."[7] Hence, requests for admissions have the tendency to weed out issues on both nonsubstantive and substantive grounds. "The simplification of the points in controversy has a 'ripple effect,' simplifying many of the other matters involved in the suit."[8]

Historically, at least under the Federal Rules, as well as many states' codifications, the primary rationale for making requests for admissions is to settle factual issues, such as whether the parties admit to names, addresses, dates, and locations of particular events or circumstances. Other matters might include whether or not an agency relationship existed between an employer and employee, whether a contract existed, and whether a deed of trust was signed and attested to by a certain party. In sum, the primary purpose is the reduction of controversy between the parties.

Requests for admissions are tools that, if used effectively, can help simplify a complex case. They ease the burden of proving items that are necessary for a case, but that are not subject to real dispute.[9] Some practitioners have argued that admissions requests, when coupled with the original complaint, put the defendant on notice of the plaintiff's seriousness in bringing the action. Serving requests for admissions with a complaint establishes an aggressive attitude at the outset of the litigation and encourages the defense to treat the lawsuit seriously. Requests for admissions by themselves may not be very onerous to answer, but in combination with a complaint and with other discovery requests, they give the impression of a plaintiff determined to win.[10]

## Procedural Aspects of Requests for Admissions

Procedural rules provide specific timetables and deadlines for response to these preliminary requests, and the effects of failure to adhere or respond are severe. Those who fail to respond or object will be deemed to have consented to the request. Under Federal Rule of Civil Procedure 36, the consequence of nonresponse is precisely addressed:

> Each matter of which an admission is requested shall be separately set forth. The matter is admitted unless, within thirty days after service of the request, or within such shorter or longer time as the court may allow or as the parties may agree to in writing, subject to Rule 29, the party to whom the request is directed serves upon

the party requesting the admission a written answer or objection addressed to the matter, signed by the party or by the party's attorney.[11]

A response to the request signifies a bona fide attempt to cooperate. Refusal to respond or a bad-faith denial may trigger sanctions or other judicial penalty. Federal Rule of Civil Procedure 37(c) grants the court authority to take actions in a case in which the respondent refuses to admit to something that is thoroughly noncontroversial and should not be the subject of dispute. The rule states in part:

> If a party fails to admit the genuineness of any document or the truth of any matter requested under Rule 36, and if the party requesting the admissions thereafter proves the genuineness of the document or the truth of the matter, the requesting party may apply to the court for an order requiring the other party to pay the reasonable expenses incurred in making that proof, including reasonable attorney's fees.[12]

In determining a failure of good faith, the court will review the following criteria:

1. Whether the request for admission was objectionable as provided under Rule 36(a).
2. Whether the admission sought was integral to the issues before the court or of secondary, non-substantive importance.
3. Whether the party failing to admit had a reasonable basis or ground to believe that the party might prevail in the matter.
4. There was other good reason for the failure to admit.[13]

## Responding to Requests for Admissions

Genuine issues of dispute and factual argument need not be admitted. Respondents have every right to object to a request for admission when content, structure, and format are burdensome and unwieldy or so voluminous and indiscernible that an admission cannot be formulated. On the other hand, respondents cannot purposely be ignorant. Under Rule 36 of the Federal Rules of Civil Procedure, the respondent is required to make a reasonable effort to discern and decipher the question, or to conduct a viable investigation in order to respond. Once admitted, the fact or issue is conclusively established in the evidentiary record. Withdrawal or amendment of the admission is possible in exceptional circumstances.[14] Any well-founded grounds for disagreement should cause the respondent to not admit the evidence or facts. "Any statement that is not truthful should be denied. However, you should resist the temptation to deny a statement on a technicality, such as a misspelled word or an obvious typographical error. On the other hand, should the error actually alter the substance of the statement you may consider denying it."[15]

A request for admission, under Rule 36, is presumed admitted if not responded to within 30 days after the service of the request. Objection to the request's content can rest on a variety of theories, including the following:

1. The information, documents, or factual subject matter, if responded to, would breach the attorney–client privilege.
2. The information, documents, or factual subject matter, if responded to, would breach the attorney work product rule or the privilege or confidentiality principles.
3. The request for admission as so posed is unduly burdensome.
4. The request for admissions seeks evidence that is irrelevant or is inadmissible.
5. The request is repetitious or duplicative.
6. The request as drafted is in need of partition, since the rules require singular issues in each request.

Requests and responses should be well thought out and not spontaneous. Once the evidence is admitted in the record, it is tough to resurrect a challenge to its admissibility. If additional time is needed to evaluate the request, a request for a continuance or an extension of time to respond is appropriate. See Form 7.1.[16]

---

_____, defendant in the above-entitled action, moves this court to allow it additional time to answer _____ [plaintiff's] request for admissions for the reason that _____ [specify, such as: the request for admissions did not come to the attention of defendant's attorney _____, until _____, [20]_____, at which time defendant's attorney was, and still is, engaged in the trial of cases in the _____ [court], State of _____, and has not had sufficient opportunity to ascertain the information with which to make answer to the request for admissions as filed].

This motion is based on _____ [cite statute], the records and files in this cause, and on the affidavit of _____, attorney for defendant in this cause.

Dated _____, [20]_____.

---

**FORM 7.1** Motion—For extension of time to respond to request for admissions. (Reprinted by permission of West Group.)

## § 7.3 DRAFTING REQUESTS FOR ADMISSIONS

In framing admissions requests, precision in language is crucial, since it "traps" the opposition into dealing with an issue honestly. Requests for admissions should be crafted only after mastery of the case file. Without a complete understanding of the case file, requests for admissions cannot be intelligently composed. Discovery documents, complaints, answers, counterclaims, interrogatories, responses to interrogatories, depositions, witnesses' statements, and subpoenas all provide the essential data for admissions requests. "If your requests are drafted properly and the responding party denies them, but your attorney can later prove that the admissions set forth in the request are true, then your client may be awarded the cost of proving the facts set out in the request."[17]

Requests for admissions are subject to the same technical pleading rules of construction and formatting as most other legal documents. Caption heading, title, introductory paragraph, and specifically enumerated requests are the usual document components. See Form 7.2 for the body of the motion.[18]

In the example at Form 7.3, a document request could potentially be a contract originally attached as Exhibit "A" to plaintiff's complaint. At paragraph 1, the request deals with the genuineness; at paragraph 2, the request attempts to document the employer–employee relationship and to prove a failure to pay plaintiff for services rendered and the outstanding credit balance. The proposed language

---

Plaintiff A.B. requests defendant C.D. within _____ days after service of this request to make the following admissions for the purpose of this action only and subject to all pertinent objections to admissibility which may be interposed at the trial.

1. That each of the following documents, exhibited with this request, is genuine. (Here list the documents and describe each document.)

2. That each of the following statements is true. (Here list the statements.)

[Signature and address]

---

**FORM 7.2**   Request for admission under Rule 36.

UNITED STATES DISTRICT COURT
FOR THE EASTERN DISTRICT OF PENNSYLVANIA

Plaintiff                    )

     v.                    )     Civil Action _____

Defendant                    )

REQUEST FOR ADMISSION TO PLAINTIFF

    Plaintiff, _____, respectfully requests that defendant, within thirty days after service of this request, make the following admissions for the purpose of this action only.

1. As to the following documents, copies of which are attached to this request, that each is genuine.

    Document A.   a bill of sale

    Document B.   a credit exchange form

    Document C.   letters between consumer and retailer

2. Each of the following statements is true:

    a. That retailer stated to consumer that a "full refund" would be made.

    b. Such statement was made on June 1, 1991, at retailer's office.

**FORM 7.3**   Request for admission to plaintiff.

should be unambiguous, clear, and concise and ultimately force the opposing party to respond.

The request for admission at Form 7.4 is more perfunctory. Place of residence, age, ownership, and vehicle agency are evidentiary matters that will not be subject to proof if agreed to. Auto accident, product liability, and other tort-based cases benefit greatly from using these requests in litigation strategy.[19]

Make requests for admissions an even more potent evidentiary tool by attaching a cover letter that directs the responding party. The letter at Form 7.5, which essentially mirrors the content of Federal Rule of Civil Procedure 36, lays out a responding party's obligations. Family law cases, like divorce and support cases, benefit from this litigation tactic. See Form 7.6.

United States District Court for the _____
District of _____

_____
                                                                        Plaintiff,

v.                                                    Civil Action No.

_____
                                                                        Defendant.


First Request of Plaintiff for Admissions of Fact

COMES NOW, Plaintiff, _____, through his under-signed attorney, and requests that Defendant, _____, hereby respond to the following Admissions of Fact within thirty (30) days of the date of this filing:


REQUEST NO. 1:

Admit that Defendant _____ is, and was, as of August 1, 2000, a resident of _____.


REQUEST NO. 2:

Admit that Defendant _____ is over the age of eighteen years.


REQUEST NO. 3:

Admit that Defendant _____ is a licensed automobile driver in the State of _____.


REQUEST NO. 4:

Admit that on or about August 1, 2000, at approximately 2:30 a.m., Defendant _____ was driving a car northbound on Delaware Avenue, at or near its intersection with Pennsylvania Avenue, _____ [city, state].

**FORM 7.4**   Pleading format for admissions.

REQUEST NO. 5:

Admit that on or about August 1, 2000, at approximately 2:30 a.m., Plaintiff _____ was driving a car northbound on Pennsylvania Avenue, at or near its intersection with Delaware Avenue, _____ [city, state].

REQUEST NO. 6:

Admit that Defendant _____ owned the vehicle she was operating on or about August 1, 2000, at approximately 2:30 a.m.

REQUEST NO. 7:

Admit that on or about August 1, 2000, at approximately 2:30 a.m., as Defendant _____ reached the intersection of Delaware Avenue and Pennsylvania Avenue, the traffic light for northbound Delaware Avenue changed to red.

REQUEST NO. 8:

Admit that on or about August 1, 2000, at approximately 2:30 a.m., the traffic light for northbound Pennsylvania Avenue, at the intersection of Delaware Avenue and Pennsylvania Avenue, changed from red to green, thereby granting northbound Pennsylvania Avenue traffic the right-of-way into the intersection.

REQUEST NO. 9:

Admit that as a result of the accident occurring on or about August 1, 2000, at approximately 2:30 a.m., caused directly by the action of Defendant _____, Plaintiff _____ was severely and permanently physically injured.

Respectfully submitted,

_____

Charles P. Nemeth, Esquire
15761 Knapp Shores Road
Kent, New York 14477
(412) 555-2740
Attorney for Plaintiff

DATED: September 30, 2000

**FORM 7.4** *Continued*

Dear _____ ,

Enclosed is a Request for Admissions regarding certain facts, legal relationships, documents, and other evidence. As you respond to this pleading, you are expected to act in good faith, using all information that is readily available to you, including information that is in the possession of your firm or other attorneys or staff. As the Rules of Civil Procedure require, you are to personally respond to the following requests.

If you cannot fully admit to a specific request, state which part of the request you must deny and which part is acceptable to you. If you deny the request, give a rationale, stating specific facts and conditions that prompt the denial. If you are simply unable to respond due to a lack of knowledge, indicate insufficient knowledge.

If there is some way we can clarify the question or aid you as you interpret our request, please call. You have thirty days to respond.

Sincerely,

_____
Attorney

**FORM 7.5**   Cover letter.

Practitioners should institute a system that tracks the history of the admissions requests posed. A timetable for requests for admissions is provided at Form 7.7.[20]

## § 7.4 DRAFTING RESPONSIVE PLEADINGS TO THE REQUESTS

As noted previously, responses are guided by the principle of legal "good faith." Contextually, responses vary, from the simple term "admit" or "deny," to a more verbose response, such as

> The request is denied because the request fails to state what is meant by the term "escrow" and such a term is open to interpretation.

Or the response may raise an objection based on multiple theories:

> Objection to the request since the request violates the work product doctrine and the protections afforded under the attorney/client privilege.

To _____, defendant:

Pursuant to the provisions of _____ [cite statute], plaintiff requests defendant within _____ days from receipt of this demand to make the following admissions for the purpose of this action only and subject to all pertinent objections to admissibility.

1. _____, plaintiff, and _____, defendant, were married on _____, 19_____, in the City of_____, County of _____, State of _____.

2. _____ children were born of this marriage, namely _____, born _____, 19_____, and _____, born _____, 19_____.

3. The plaintiff and defendant are wife and husband respectively.

4. The plaintiff and defendant separated on _____, 20_____, and have been living separate and apart.

5. The plaintiff did, on or about _____, 20_____, request the defendant to return and live with her at the family home of the parties.

6. The defendant is the owner of a _____ business located at _____ [address], City of _____, County of _____, State of _____.

7. For the month of _____, 20_____, and each month prior thereto, the defendant obtained from the operation of such business either as a salary or account the sum of $_____.

**FORM 7.6** Request for admissions.

| Discovery | Days | Court/ Calendar | Authority | Serve/File |
|---|---|---|---|---|
| After complaint | _____ | _____ | _____ | _____ |
| Response due | _____ | _____ | _____ | _____ |
| Before trial | _____ | _____ | _____ | _____ |
| Response due: discovery cut-off | _____ | _____ | _____ | _____ |
| Extra if mailed out of state | _____ | _____ | _____ | _____ |
| Demand if not adequate | _____ | _____ | _____ | _____ |
| Notice that requests have been deemed admitted | _____ | _____ | _____ | _____ |
| Motion for Protective Orders | _____ | _____ | _____ | _____ |
| Notice of Motion | _____ | _____ | _____ | _____ |
| Extra if mailed | _____ | _____ | _____ | _____ |
| Extra if mailed out of state | _____ | _____ | _____ | _____ |
| Extra if mailed out of country | _____ | _____ | _____ | _____ |
| Opposition to Motion | _____ | _____ | _____ | _____ |
| Reply to Opposition | _____ | _____ | _____ | _____ |
| Proof of Service | _____ | _____ | _____ | _____ |
| Meet and Confer Statement | _____ | _____ | _____ | _____ |
| Motions cut-off before trial | _____ | _____ | _____ | _____ |
| Other: | _____ | _____ | _____ | _____ |
| _____ | _____ | _____ | _____ | _____ |
| _____ | _____ | _____ | _____ | _____ |

**FORM 7.7** Timetable for request for admissions.

_____ [name], _____ [defendant or plaintiff], objects to the request for admissions served on him by _____ [plaintiff or defendant] in the above-named case because each of the admissions sought in the request is irrelevant, is immaterial, and has been answered previously in _____ [defendant's or plaintiff's response to _____ [plaintiff's or defendant's] interrogatories propounded to _____ [defendant or plaintiff] filed previously in this case].

Dated _____, 2000

_____
[Signature]

**FORM 7.8**   Response to admissions.

The respondent may also find the request's content "irrelevant" or "immaterial." Answers or responses may have already been provided in another legal setting, like a deposition or a written interrogatory. The responding party has the right to formally object on these grounds. See Form 7.8.

The scope and content of a reply continue the admission's evolution. Those items that are admitted will no longer be in contention; those items that are denied will form the core controversy in an upcoming trial.

The form of a reply to a request for admission is similar to the format for an answer to a complaint. Each request for admission is repeated verbatim in the response, mirroring the request and constantly referring to the original request. The pleadings format—just as in the request—consists of a caption, an introductory paragraph, and _ad seriatim_ responses with signature and verification provisions. Two examples of replies, the first being a response to the admission of facts and the second regarding the genuineness of documents, are reproduced in Forms 7.9[21] and 7.10.[22]

In conclusion, plaintiff and defense counsel, in conjunction with their support staff, should make enlightened use of the admissions tactic. The process is designed "to simplify and clarify the issues of a case rather than to unearth large quantities of new information."[23] Used wisely, the request forces the advocates to cogently evaluate the quality and content of a client's assertions, the party's defenses and

_____ [Defendant or Plaintiff] in the above-entitled action makes the following admissions denials on the request for admissions served on him on _____, [20]_____, by_____ [plaintiff or defendant]:

1. _____ [Defendant or Plaintiff], in answer to request No. _____, _____ [denies or admits] the matter stated herein.

2. _____ [Defendant or Plaintiff], in answer to request No. _____, cannot truthfully admit or deny such request because he is not in possession of sufficient facts and cannot reasonably obtain such facts as would enable him to admit or deny such request.

3. _____ [Defendant or Plaintiff], in response to request No._____, cannot truthfully admit or deny such statement because he does not know by whom _____ was employed, but as to _____, the matters stated therein are denied.

4. [Set out each request by number and reply in a manner similar to the foregoing.]

_____
[Signature]

**FORM 7.9**   Answer to admissions. (Reprinted by permission of West Group.)

---

Responding to the demand dated _____, [20]_____, defendant admits, for the purpose of this action only, the genuineness of the following documents mentioned in demand No. _____: _____ [give details].

You are further notified that on your failure to admit the facts above set forth within _____ days after service of this notice on you or within such further time as the court may allow, the expenses incurred in proving such facts will be ascertained at the trial or immediately thereafter and payment thereof by you will be demanded, including reasonable counsel fees.

Dated _____, [20_____].

_____
[Signature]

**FORM 7.10**   Admission response. (Reprinted by permission of West Group.)

224

mitigating factors, and the overall evidence. The ALI–ABA Committee on Continuing Professional Education asserts:

> When attorneys use the Rule [Rule 36] with this goal in mind, request for admission can often drastically cut trial preparation time, streamline the trial process and encourage settlement.[24]

In essence, requests force the litigants to see the raw state of their cases. Litigants can also benefit from the results of these queries, in that the responses can be used as a basis for summary judgment, in other motions that weigh substantive aspects of a case, in trial memoranda or briefs, or as a "carrot" in settlement negotiations.

## § 7.5 STIPULATIONS

Some conceptual coverage of *stipulations* and their usage is sprinkled throughout various chapters of this text. Compared to admissions, stipulations are joint understandings between parties. Requests for admissions are items propounded by one party to another in hopes of confirming understandings or agreements. Stipulations are documents, memoranda, or other confirmations that indicate that both plaintiff and defendant agree on central facts or items, evidence, exhibits, documents, or other matters.

Stipulations encourage litigation efficiency on various fronts. First, the stipulation may address the admissibility of demonstrative evidence. Second, parties may agree that certain evidentiary questions—whether constitutional claims of exclusion in a criminal case, findings of falsehood in a paternity claim, or agency relationships in a contract case—are accepted without dispute.

In the federal courts, stipulations are promoted in the pretrial conference setting. The court, in its discretion, can direct the attorneys for the parties to appear before it for the purposes of

1. expediting the disposition of the action;
2. establishing early and continuing control so that the case will not be protracted because of lack of management;
3. discouraging wasteful pre-trial activities;
4. improving the quality of trial through more thorough preparation; and
5. facilitating the settlement of the case.[25]

Stipulations as to essential facts and evidence assist the parties to accomplish these ends. The court, if satisfied with the preparation and presentation of trial counsel, will eventually ask counsel to submit a pretrial order outlining those issues and evidence that are stipulated to. Stipulated evidence listing and marking often in-cludes trial exhibits, which, if not agreed to prior to trial, will be subject to needless challenges as to authenticity. At the pretrial conference, the stipulation streamlines proof as to exhibits and other evidence forms.

Further support for stipulation actions is evident in Federal Rule of Civil Pro-cedure 16(c), which states:

> At any conference under this rule consideration may be given, and the court may take appropriate action, with respect to
>
> (1)   the formulation and simplification of the issues, including the elimination of frivolous claims or defenses;
>
> (2)   the necessity or desirability of amendments to the pleadings;
>
> (3)   the possibility of obtaining admissions of fact and of documents which will avoid unnecessary proof, stipulations regarding the authenticity of documents and advance rulings from the court on the admissibility of evidence;
>
> (4)   the avoidance of unnecessary proof and of cumulative evidence and lim-itations or restrictions on the use of testimony under Rule 702 of the Federal Rules of Evidence; . . .
>
> (7)   the identification of witnesses and documents, the need and schedule for filing and exchanging pretrial briefs, and the date or dates for further con-ferences and for trial; . . .[26]

Tactically, certain types of evidence and essential facts may or may not be stipu-lated to. Stipulations may take the "oomph" out of the evidence during its delivery and presentation in the trial setting. Jurors may be less impressed with the quality and power of evidence admitted under a stipulation. Stipulations may corner the advocate and prevent examination of a host of other issues that emanate from the agreed evidence. An expert's testimony may be severely limited regarding his or her expertise. On the other hand, it "is frequently desirable to stipulate to matters that can easily be proved by the adverse side because a stipulation tends to reduce the importance of the matter in the eyes of the jury. The stipulation usually takes less time than the testimony does."[27]

## § 7.6  STIPULATION PLEADINGS

A stipulation is as varied as the factual and legal issues in the case it serves, from the simple agreement between opposing counsel that copies are acceptable in lieu of original documents, to a confirmation of the admissibility of duplicate documents despite the best evidence rule. The stipulation format is fairly straightforward. See Form 7.11[28] for a standard pleading in a case of medical malpractice.

A stipulation pleading can simplify the technical requirements in the admit-tance of documentary evidence. The parties can stipulate that the documentary,

The parties to the above-numbered and entitled action, through their respective undersigned attorneys, stipulate as follows:

1. _____ [name], a _____ [identify expertise of witness] of_____ [address], is appointed as an independent expert to examine_____ [specify item to be submitted], which _____ [item] shall be delivered to _____ [expert] within _____ days of this date. _____ [expert] is authorized to make such tests, examinations, photographs, and chemical analysis, and to perform such other investigative procedures as in his judgment are appropriate to determine the following: _____ [specify matters to be determined].

2. Each party shall be entitled to submit to _____ [expert] such questions as may be desired pertaining to the foregoing, and _____ [expert] shall submit a written report of his findings to all parties.

3. It is understood that _____ [expert] shall act as the court's witness and shall not in any way be obligated to any party. The reasonable charges of _____ [expert] shall be fixed by the court. The same shall be taxed as an item of costs; however, pending final determination of this action, such charges shall be advanced by _____ [identify advancing party].

4. After the examination has been made, the _____ [specify item examined] shall be preserved and shall either remain in the custody of _____ [expert], or such other disposition shall be made of it as the court may order.

5. _____ [expert] shall photograph _____ [specify item] when it comes into his possession and shall deliver such photographs to _____, attorney for _____ [identify party]. Upon such delivery, _____ [expert] shall be relieved of any future responsibility for custody thereof.

Dated _____, [20_____].

_____

[Signatures and Addresses]

**FORM 7.11** Stipulation. (Reprinted by permission of West Group.)

It is hereby stipulated by and between _____ and
_____ [identify parties] that copies of the
_____ [specify documents] involved in this litigation or rele-
vant hereto, when properly certified as true and correct copies of the originals thereof
by _____ [custodian of originals], may be introduced in evi-
dence by _____ [identify party] and may be used as primary
evidence with like force and effect as though the originals were introduced, subject,
however, to all objections to their introduction that might be made to the originals.

Dated _____, [20____].

_____
[Signatures and Addresses]

**FORM 7.12** Document stipulation. (Reprinted by permission of West Group.)

photographic, or other demonstrative evidence will be admitted without foundational testimony or authentication. By doing so, the court accepts the documents
"as is" without concern for the foundational practices outlined in previous discussion. See Form 7.12[29] for representative language in a document stipulation.

When physical evidence is to be examined by a court-appointed expert, the
parties may stipulate as to various matters involving its usage, like the recognition of
a witness as expert; agreement the evidence is accurate, to scale, and credible; acceptance of the integrity in the chain of custody; and agreement that sufficient time
for the evaluation of the evidence has been afforded. A stipulation that no liens exist
or are outstanding in a construction project is at Form 7.13.

Stipulations are a major means for the opposing parties to efficiently narrow the
factual and evidentiary issues. Stipulations are by no means a sign of weakness or the
"caving in" of a vulnerable advocate. Stipulations do an admirable job of minimiz-
ing strife and contentiousness in legal advocacy.

Application No. _____

THIS AGREEMENT Made and concluded this _____ day of _____ A. D. [20]\_\_\_\_\_, between _____
of _____, party of the first part (hereinafter called Owner),
AND _____,
party of the second part (hereinafter called Contractor).

WHEREAS, the said parties have by a duly executed Agreement under seal, bearing even date herewith, entered into a written contract for the erection and completion of _____

to be erected on

in which Agreement the Contractor covenanted, promised and agreed that no mechanics' claims or liens should be entered and filed against the said building or buildings or any part thereof, or the curtilage or curtilages appurtenant thereto,

NOW THIS AGREEMENT WITNESSETH: That Contractor for and in consideration of the awarding to him by Owner of said contract as aforesaid, as well as the further consideration of One ($1.00) Dollar to him paid at or before the ensealing and delivery of these presents, the receipt whereof is hereby acknowledged, does hereby covenant, promise and agree that no mechanics' lien or claim or other lien or claim of any kind whatsoever shall be filed against the said building or buildings or the curtilage or curtilages appurtenant thereto, by Contractor or by any sub-contractor, materialmen or laborers for work done or materials furnished under said contract for and about said building or buildings or any part thereof, or on credit thereof, and that all sub-contractors, materialmen, and laborers on said work shall look to and hold Contractor personally liable for all sub-contracts, materials furnished and work and labor done, so that there shall not be any legal or lawful claim of any kind whatever against Owner for any work done or labor or materials furnished under said contract for and about the erection, construction and completion of said buildings as aforesaid, or under any contracts for extra work, or for work supplemental thereto, or otherwise.

AND, in order to give the Owner full power and authority to protect himself and the lot or lots of ground against any and all claims filed by the Contractor or anyone acting under or through him or it in violation of the foregoing covenant, the said Contractor for himself, themselves, itself, hereby irrevocably authorizes and empowers any Attorney of any Court of Common Pleas of the Commonwealth of Pennsylvania, to appear for him, them, it, or any of them, in any of the said Courts of Common Pleas as Attorney for him, them or it and in his, their, its, name, mark satisfied of record at the cost and expense of the Contractor or of any Sub-Contractor or Materialman, or Materialmen, any and all claims or claim, lien or liens, filed by or for the Contractor, or any Sub-Contractor or Materialman, or in his or their name against said building or buildings, lot or lots of ground or any part thereof and for such act or acts this shall be good and sufficient warrant and authority, and a reference to the Court, Term and Number in which and where this Agreement shall have been filed shall be a sufficient exhibit of the authority herein contained to warrant such action, and the Contractor for himself, themselves, itself, do hereby remise, and quit-claim all rights and all manner of errors, defects and imperfections whatsoever in entering such satisfaction or in anywise touching or concerning the same.

IN WITNESS WHEREOF the said parties have hereunto set their hands and seals dated the day and year first above written.

Witnesses Present:

_____

_____

**FORM 7.13**   Stipulation against liens, property of Charles P. Nemeth.

## § 7.7  SUMMARY

Both the request for admission and the stipulation focus on factual and legal issues
before trial, urging the opposing parties to frame the litigation amongst those issues
that remain in contention, rather than those preliminary and self-evident matters
that the parties can readily agree to. Requests for admissions and stipulations are as
varied as the facts and legal issues involved. Pleading formats and advocacy suggestions were covered in depth.

### Notes

1. MILFORD MEYER, Pennsylvania Trial Advocacy Handbook 207 (1976).
2. ALI-ABA COMMITTEE ON CONTINUING PROFESSIONAL EDUCATION, Civil Trial Manual 227 (1974).
3. DIANE D. ZALEWSKI, Paralegal Discovery 5-2 (1988).
4. Herbert Greenstone, *Request for Admissions by Plaintiff,* 4 Am. Jur. Trials 185, 213 (1966).
5. Fed. R. Civ. P. 36.
6. ALI-ABA Committee on Continuing Professional Education, *Supra* Note 2, at 227.
7. Fed. R. Civ. P. 36, advisory committee's note.
8. PEGGY N. KERLEY ET AL., Civil Litigation for the Paralegal 297 (1992).
9. 2 MICHIGAN BASIC PRACTICE HANDBOOK 769 (1985).
10. ROY D. SIMON, JR., A Complete Course In Pretrial Litigation 188 (1987).
11. Fed. R. Civ. P. 36.
12. Fed. R. Civ. P. 37.
13. ALI–ABA COMMITTEE ON CONTINUING PROFESSIONAL EDUCATION, *supra* note 2, at 231.
14. Fed. R. Civ. P. 36.
15. KERLEY ET AL., *supra* note 8, at 306.
16. 8 AM. JUR. PL. & PRAC. FORMS 821 (1986).
17. CAROLE BRUNO, Paralegal Litigation Handbook 213 (1980).
18. Fed. R. Civ. P. Form 25.
19. A recent case involving the General Motors Corporation witnessed the aggressive use
    of admissions. See the series of requests at Appendix C.
20. ZALEWSKI, *supra* note 3, at 5-4.
21. 8 AM. JUR. PL. & PRAC. FORMS 819 (1984).
22. *Id.*
23. ALI–ABA COMMITTEE ON CONTINUING PROFESSIONAL EDUCATION, *supra* note 2, at 234.
24. *Id.*
25. Fed. R. Civ. P. 16.
26. Fed. R. Civ. P. 16(c).
27. ALI–ABA COMMITTEE ON CONTINUING PROFESSIONAL EDUCATION, *supra* note 2, at 313.
28. 1 FED. PROC. FORMS 518 (1975).
29. *Id.* at 515.

CHAPTER 8

# *Motion Practice and Evidence*

§ 8.1 Introduction: Motions and Evidence Law

§ 8.2 Motions on the Production of Evidence

§ 8.3 Motions in Limine

§ 8.4 Motions to Exclude on Constitutional Theories

§ 8.5 Summary

## § 8.1 INTRODUCTION: MOTIONS AND EVIDENCE LAW

From the advocate's perspective, the study and application of evidence are more than a theoretical exercise. The evidence's proponent or advocate deals not only with its collection and analysis, but also with the technical rules regarding its admissibility in the tribunal. No matter how compelling and seductive the evidence might be, it is an utterly useless artifact if it cannot be admitted. Defense counsel hopes to exclude, strike, suppress, or prohibit the introduction of the plaintiff's evidence in general. The defense undermines the theory of any plaintiff's case by the ruination of evidence. For technical, procedural, or substantive reasons, defense advocates will challenge the admissibility of evidence. Prosecutors and public defenders daily contend with admissibility problems, but from differing hilltops. The implication for police practice and procedure is almost impossible to gauge. The police task is, much like that of prosecutors, to garner evidence necessary to convict the guilty.

In the former role, evidence, and as much of it as possible, seeks admission. The plaintiff's evidentiary approach is geared to the widest field of evidence admission, whether by direct introduction or motion. Defense counsel is driven primarily to challenge the quality and content of evidence. *Motions* are the chief means to launch the evidentiary challenge.

Motions request a judicial authority to review a given aspect of a case or controversy. Motions cover evidentiary questions as much as any other legal area. "Motion practice exists at all stages of the legal process including pre-trial, trial, and numerous post-conviction and post-judgement processes. A motion seeks a specific resolution of a singular aspect of a claim, controversy, or cause of action."[1] To be effective, a motion must have an end, an objective, in mind. Thoughtful scrutiny is crucial to motion practice success. Each motion should be designed with the general parameters set out at Figure 8.1.[2]

**I.** Objectives

    **1.** What objectives can you accomplish with a motion?

    **2.** Which of these objectives apply to your case?

    **3.** How does your motion objective further your representational strategy?

**II.** Preparation

    **1.** What preparation will you do when planning to make motions in your case?

    **2.** What information will you look at? Who will you talk to?

    **3.** How will you obtain the information?

**III.** Content Planning

    **A.** Obtaining Information

        **1.** Looking at the various "situations" in your case, which motions are indicated?

        **2.** What are the typical motions that arise in a case such as yours?

            **a.** Are any indicated in this case?

            **b.** Which ones?

        **3.** Do you have any needs (e.g., problems) that a court order could assist?

            **a.** Which needs?

            **b.** What specific type of court order would help?

        **4.** Think of your motion legal theory (MLT):

            **a.** Which theories are available to support the motion you have chosen?

            **b.** Which ones appear viable in the present case?

                **(1)** What are the elements of such theories?

                **(2)** Are there any problems with your legal theories?

                **(3)** How do you propose to deal with such problems if raised by your opponent or the court?

        **5.** Think of your motion factual theory (MFT):

            **a.** What is your "story"?

**FIGURE 8.1** Motion strategy sheet. (MARILYN J. BERGER, JOHN B. MITCHELL, & RONALD H. CLARK, Trial Advocacy: Planning, Analysis and Strategies 112-13 (1989), Little, Brown and Company. Reprinted with permission of Aspen Publishers, Inc.)

**b.** What is the information upon which you intend to base this story?

    **(1)** Where did (will) you obtain this information?

    **(2)** How will you present it to the court (e.g., declaration, testimony)?

    **(3)** Do you anticipate any admissibility problems?

**6.** Specify the information that you possess so as to meet "sufficiency" concerns as to each element of your legal theory.

**7.** How will you make your story persuasive?

    **a.** Will you tie your story to the policy rationale that underlies your legal theory?

    **b.** Will you try something else or something additional (e.g., vivid imagery)?

**8.** How do you expect your opponent to respond to your factual theory?

    **a.** Do you anticipate your opponent putting forth any information of his or her own?

    **b.** How will you respond?

**9.** Thinking of your case theory:

    **a.** What effect will winning your motion have on your case theory?

    **b.** What effect if you lose?

    **c.** What will you do if you lose?

    **d.** Does your motion risk putting you in a position that is inconsistent with your case theory?

    **e.** If so, can you avoid this consequence and still bring the motion?

**B.** Reassessment and Reevaluation

    **1.** Whether you won or lost:

        **a.** How did the result of the motion affect your case theory?

        **b.** What information did you obtain in the motion process?

        **c.** What bearing (if any) does this information have on your case theory? Your representational strategy?

**FIGURE 8.1** *Continued*

**2.** If you lost:

    **a.** Will you seek some form of appeal or reconsideration?

    **b.** Will you try to "clean up" the record?

    **c.** Did the court's decision give you room to renew the motion?

    **d.** If so, will you renew it? When?

**IV.** Performance Planning

  **A.** Technical Skills

    **1.** How (generally) do you make a "record"?

      **a.** What record would you make to preserve the issue in your motion for appeal?

      **b.** What kind of record would you make to "win"?

    **2.** What points will you emphasize in argument?

      **a.** Which are the strengths of your argument? Weaknesses?

      **b.** How will you deal with the weaknesses?

      **c.** What practical concerns might the court have?

      **d.** How will you address these concerns?

      **e.** What is the key point on which you must persuade the court in order to win?

  **B.** Nut-and-Bolts Matters

    **1.** What are the local rules, procedures, etc., for bringing motions?

    **2.** Who (if anyone) will you subpoena?

    **3.** What procedure must you follow to serve such subpoenas?

    **4.** Will you calendar all your motions for one hearing?

  **C.** Ethical Considerations

    **1.** Do you think it proper to bring a motion to gain some tactical advantage unrelated to the object of the motion itself? For example:

      **a.** Does it seem proper to bring a suppression motion (with a plausible legal basis) solely to get discovery?

      **b.** Is this the same problem as seeking the name of a police informant, not because you want the name, but because you hope the prosecution will dismiss the case rather than turn over the name if the court orders it to be revealed?

**FIGURE 8.1** *Continued*

> **c.** What about bringing a motion to gain leverage for dismissal or settlement because you know the motion will embarrass your adversary?
>
> **2.** Assuming that you believe the above conduct improper, how would you have the courts control attorneys' use of motions for purposes other than those explicitly stated in the motion if the motion were otherwise based on reasonable legal grounds? Does your method for control jeopardize other interests?

**FIGURE 8.1** *Continued*

## § 8.2 MOTIONS ON THE PRODUCTION OF EVIDENCE

Since the forms of evidence are highly differentiated, the types, contents and purposes, of motions reflect these variations. Confronted with an inability to collect evidence—whether the testimonial response to an interrogatory; a doctor, physician, or other expert report; or an opportunity to examine a tangible object—the litigator moves the court for access. Before formally moving, counsel should informally

> Dear Counselor,
>
> As you know, I represent _____ in the above-captioned matter. The discovery process we are about to engage in should hopefully be courteous and adherent to the Rules. In light of the informal emphasis in the Rules, advise when my office could review the following files:
>
> [insert desired information]
>
> Sincerely,
>
> _____
> Charles P. Nemeth
> Attorney for _____
> 415 Kings Highway
> Rosslyn Farms, PA 15106
> (412) 555-1111

**FORM 8.1**    Informal request for evidence.

request access. See the letter to opposing counsel at Form 8.1. Unfortunately, the informal route does not always work. A *motion for production* is the next appropriate step. See Form 8.2.[3]

## Motion for a Physical or Mental Examination

Courts are empowered to order the physical or mental examination of a person. "The order may be made only on motion for good cause shown and upon notice to the person to be examined and to all parties and shall specify the time, place, manner, conditions, and scope of the examination and the person or persons by whom it is to be made."[4] Requests for examinations frequently occur in medical insurance disputes where the opposing party challenges the severity of injuries. For example, if an insurance company wishes to verify the nature of injuries, it will informally request that the plaintiff see its company physician or other expert. If rejected, a *motion for physical examination* is a legitimate strategy. See Form 8.3.[5]

In the criminal context, the mental or psychological condition of a plaintiff-victim is raised as part of the defense strategy. In rape allegations, the defendant sometimes counters by claiming the delusional, inventive tendencies of the victim. Unfortunately, many legitimately based claims of sexual assault and sexual harassment go unreported because of a victim's fear of this form of mental examination.

## Motion to Compel Production

In the preliminary discovery and disclosure stages of civil and criminal litigation, requests are made through interrogatories, subpoenas duces tecum, and other means, whereby opposing counsel seeks information, tangible objects, documents, and other evidence. The permissible nature of production requests is clearly profiled in the Federal Rules of Civil Procedure at Rule 34:

> Any party may serve on any other party a request (1) to produce and permit the party making the request, or someone acting on the requester's behalf, to inspect and copy, any designated documents (including writings, drawings, graphs, charts, photographs, phonorecords, and other data compilations) from which information can be obtained. . . .[6]

On some occasions, the request for material is objected to as violating the doctrine of privilege, work product, or confidentiality or as irrelevant or overly burdensome. While nonresponse can be based on these good-faith reasons, it is a frustrating reality for some practitioners that opposing counsel can be noncooperative for unprofessional motives. Noncooperation is increasingly the result of mean-spiritedness and unethical behavior. In any event, if a party wishes to examine the evidence over the objection of the opposing party a *motion to compel production* of said evidence is in order. See Form 8.4.[7]

UNITED STATES DISTRICT COURT FOR THE DISTRICT OF COLUMBIA

|  |  |  |
|---|---|---|
| JOHN DOE, | ) | |
| Plaintiff, | ) | |
| v. | ) | Civil Action No. 87-0071 |
| | ) | |
| JANE SMITH, | ) | |
| Defendant, | ) | |

### FIRST REQUEST OF PLAINTIFF, JOHN DOE FOR PRODUCTION OF DOCUMENTS AND THINGS

Pursuant to Rule 34 of the Federal Rules of Civil Procedure, Plaintiff JOHN DOE (hereinafter "Plaintiff") hereby requests that Defendant JANE SMITH (hereinafter "Defendant") produce and permit Plaintiff to inspect and copy the following items, or in lieu thereof, that she furnish to Plaintiff copies of the following, within forty-five (45) days of this Request.

The materials as to which production is sought are all documents and things referenced in the First Set of Interrogatories of Plaintiff to Defendant: 5, 7, 8, 10, 12, 13, 14, and 26.

It is requested that the inspection and copying take place in the office of Plaintiff's undersigned counsel, Charles P. Nemeth, Esquire, 513 Lydia Street, Carnegie, Pennsylvania 15106, at such time as may be convenient to the parties, but not later than November 15, [2000].

Respectfully submitted,

_____

Charles P. Nemeth, Esquire
415 Kings Highway
Rosslyn Farms, PA 15106
(412) 555-1111
Attorney for Plaintiff
DATED: September 23, [2000]

**FORM 8.2** Request for production of documents.

Plaintiff/Defendant _____

[name of plaintiff/defendant], pursuant to Fed. R. Civ. P. 35(a), requests an Order requiring Defendant/Plaintiff _____

[name of defendant/plaintiff], to appear at the offices of _____

[name of doctor], located at _____

[address], and to submit to a _____

[physical/mental] examination of the following injuries which are at issue in the present litigation. The examination shall consist of _____

[manner, conditions, and scope of examination].

Plaintiff/Defendant submits that there is good cause for the issuance of such order for the reason that [good cause, e.g., such party alleges that he suffered severe spinal injuries but has been treated by a chiropractor or general practitioner, thus requiring the need for examination by a specialist; subsequent medical reports are inconsistent with the injuries complained of; defendant asserts that a pre-existing condition has caused the current complaints; etc.].

WHEREFORE, Plaintiff/Defendant requests that an Order be issued as prayed herein.

_____

PLAINTIFF/DEFENDANT

By its Attorney,

_____

[Name of Attorney]

**FORM 8.3** Motion for physical/mental examination.


Defendant moves the court for an order compelling inspection and copying of documents in accordance with his request served on plaintiff on _____,
[20]_____. _____ days were designated in the request for time to respond thereto. More than _____ days have elapsed and plaintiff has failed to respond.

Defendant further requests that the court order plaintiff to pay defendant reasonable expenses incurred in obtaining this order including attorney fees. A copy of said expenses and attorney fees is attached hereto, marked "Exhibit A."

[Closing]

**FORM 8.4** Motion to compel production of documents.

## Motion to Compel Discovery

Attorneys who do not cooperate during the discovery process, especially the interrogatory and deposition stage, are now subject to Federal Rule of Civil Procedure 37 sanctions for such noncompliance. Under Federal Rule of Civil Procedure 37, a party who does not cooperate can be sanctioned and ordered by the court to provide answers:

> If a party or an officer, director, or managing agent of a party or a person designated . . . fails to obey an order to provide or permit discovery, including an order made under subdivision (a) of this rule or Rule 35, or if a party fails to obey an order entered under Rule 26(f), the court in which the action is pending may make such orders in regard to the failure as are just, and among others the following:
>
> (A) An order that the matters regarding which the order was made or any other designated facts shall be taken to be established for the purposes of the action in accordance with the claim of the party obtaining the order;
>
> (B) An order refusing to allow the disobedient party to support or oppose designated claims or defenses, or prohibiting that party from introducing designated matters in evidence;
>
> (C) An order striking out pleadings or parts thereof, or staying further proceedings until the order is obeyed, or dismissing the action or proceeding or any part thereof, or rendering a judgement by default against the disobedient party;
>
> (D) In lieu of any of the foregoing orders or in addition thereto, an order treating as a contempt of court the failure to obey any orders except an order to submit to a physical or mental examination . . . [8]

Judges prefer the informal resolution of discovery and disclosure problems and the courteous exchange and examination of the opposing party's evidence. If informal overtures do not produce a remedy, the attorney advocate and his or her cooperating staff have little choice but to seek judicial intervention. A *motion to compel* must be particular, short, and simple.

Form 8.5 narrowly turns its attention to the opposing party's refusal to answer interrogatories.

Parties who object to the compulsion of any evidence may seek a protective order. There may be solid legal reasons why evidence is not forthcoming—for example, privilege, confidentiality, or Fifth Amendment self-incrimination protection. Other grounds or justifications for a *motion for a protective order* may be embarrassment, annoyance, oppression, or undue burden or expense. A motion for a protective order is at Form 8.6.

In criminal cases, defense counsel often seek the disclosure of sensitive information regarding informants. Prosecutors wish to protect their sources, while defense attorneys want names. See the motion to compel at Form 8.7.[9]

State of _____, _____ COUNTY CIRCUIT COURT

_____,

   Plaintiff(s),                                    [assigned judge]

     v.                                             Civil Action No.

_____,                                [Year-file-code]

   Defendant(s).

MOTION TO COMPEL ANSWERS TO INTERROGATORIES

     Pursuant to _____, Plaintiff moves for an order compelling Defendant to answer Plaintiff's interrogatories and to award Plaintiff costs, expenses, and attorneys' fees of _____. In support of this motion Plaintiff states:

1. Plaintiff served interrogatories on Defendant on _____ [date]. Proof of service of the interrogatories is attached.
2. As of the date of this motion, Defendant has failed to make adequate or complete answers to these interrogatories.
3. Defendant's refusal to answer is without substantial justification and Plaintiff is entitled to costs, expenses, and attorneys' fees in accordance with _____.

_____

[firm name]

By _____/s/_____

[typed name of attorney]
[address]
[phone number]

Dated: _____, 20____

**FORM 8.5**   Motion to compel answers to interrogatories.

_____ [party], by the undersigned, his/her attorney, moves the _____ [Administrative Law Judge] of the above-entitled _____ [Commission] for an order directing that _____ the deposition of _____, noticed by _____ [party] to be taken herein on _____, 20_____, to be taken on oral examination instead of written interrogatories, to be taken at a designated place other than that stated in the notice of taking such deposition, within the City of _____, State of _____ on the ground that _____ [specify].

   This motion is based on the records of this proceeding and on the affidavit of _____, attached hereto as Exhibit "_____."

Dated _____, 20_____.

[Signature and address of attorney]

**FORM 8.6**   Motion for protective order.

## Motion to Inspect or View a Premises

Certain cases call for an on-site view. A particular location may contain physical and tangible evidence relevant to the resolution of a civil or criminal case. Under Federal Rule of Civil Procedure 34, a party may informally or formally request the right to inspect or view a premises, location, piece of land, or other place. The rule states specifically that any party may serve on any other party a request

> to permit entry upon designated land or other property in the possession or control of the party upon whom the request is served for the purpose of inspection and measuring, surveying, photographing, testing, or sampling the property or any designated object or operation thereon, within the scope of Rule 26(b).[10]

This rule has also been construed to include any scientific examination of a designated object, such as dirt, rocks, cloth, fiber, or other forensic evidence, that is part of a claimant's evidentiary record. A sample *motion to inspect* a specific location is at Form 8.8.[11]

> The defendant by his/her attorney, upon all the files, records and proceedings in this case, moves the court for an order compelling the State to disclose the identity and location of any and all unnamed and/or confidential informants relied upon or otherwise employed by the State or any of its agents in this case.
>
> AS GROUNDS THE DEFENDANT ASSERTS:
>
> 1. The informant used by the State in this case can give testimony necessary to a fair determination of the issue of guilt or innocence of the defendant.
> 2. The informant played an active role in events leading up to and including the alleged unlawful transaction(s), including among other actions:
>    a. (Prior discussions, entreaties and arrangements leading up to the alleged unlawful transaction(s) in this case;)
>    b. (Prior deliveries of controlled substances to the defendant or other persons in the presence of, or with the knowledge of, the defendant;)
>    c. (Prior use of controlled substances with, or in the presence of the defendant;)
> 3. The informant was present at the time of the transaction(s) alleged in this case.
>
>
> [Jurisdictional Reservation]
>
>
> Dated _____, 20_____
>
>
> [Closing]

**FORM 8.7**    Motion to compel disclosure of confidential informant.


## § 8.3 MOTIONS IN LIMINE

When filing a *motion in limine,* the proponent stands at the threshold, the doorway, the entrance, to the courthouse. The Latin term *in limine* means "at the gateway or threshold." Strategically, motions in limine are preliminary, pretrial requests to consider the admissibility of certain types of evidence. When the evidence to be proffered is controversial, highly scientific or technical, or so inordinately relied upon by its proponents, the in limine motion is highly advisable.

The motion is perfectly suitable for controversial evidence or evidence that is so risky that its content would shed an unfavorable light on a specific party. "A motion *in limine* allows a party to obtain a ruling admitting or excluding evidence without exposing the jury to such evidence. Thus, use of the motion *in limine* prevents possible delays and limits the potential for embarrassment. An opponent of proffered evidence can avoid public disclosure of such evidence through usual

Plaintiff/Defendant _____ (name) pursuant to Fed. R. Civ. P. 34, requests an Order permitting it to enter upon the premises of Plaintiff/Defendant _____ (name) for the purpose of examining and/or photographing _____ (entering items to be inspected or photographed) involved in the incident which is the subject of the complaint filed in this action and which is located at such premises. Plaintiff/Defendant requests permission to be accompanied by his expert, _____ (name of expert), and other agents associated with the prosecution/defense of this action _____ (name of other agents) during the inspection.

WHEREFORE, Plaintiff/Defendant requests that an Order issue as prayed herein.

Plaintiff/Defendant

By its Attorneys,

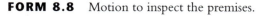

(Name of attorney)

**FORM 8.8**   Motion to inspect the premises.

means, objections at trial, by questioning its admissibility out of the jury's presence. The proponent of the evidence avoids offering evidence that may be excluded and thereby appearing to seek admission of improper evidence."[12]

Motions in limine can be used either offensively or defensively. Offensively, the advocate seeks an advance ruling on admissibility. Defensively, the antagonist to the evidence forces the court to preliminarily consider the limited value of such evidence and call for its exclusion. At the same time, the antagonist may wish to show that the evidence being introduced is so prejudicial that its probative value is limited.

Some of the topical concerns for motions in limine might be the following:

- Witnesses, expert or lay;
- Prior bad acts;
- Criminal convictions;
- Driving records;
- Police reports; and
- Collateral sources of benefits in civil actions.

Motions in limine serve a filtering function by eliminating excessive argumentation before the jury. Too much argumentation and objection over the evidence leaves an imprint in the jurors' minds that may not be favorable to the
proponents.[13]

Under Federal Rule of Civil Procedure 16, a motion in limine is granted preferential status during the pretrial conference. At subsection (c), participants are en-
couraged to take action at pretrial conferences with respect to

(3)  the possibility of obtaining admissions of fact and of documents which
     will avoid unnecessary proof, stipulations regarding the authenticity of
     documents, and advance rulings from the court on the admissibility of ev-
     idence;

(4)  the avoidance of unnecessary proof and of cumulative evidence, and lim-
     itations or restrictions on the use of testimony under Rule 702 of the
     Federal Rules of Evidence.[14]

Rulings on in limine motions are left primarily to the court's discretion. "In
ruling on a motion in limine, the court must be satisfied it has enough information
to make an informed ruling. It is up to the movant to provide the court with an adequate basis to make an informed ruling. However, a court should not require a
party to try a case twice, once outside the presence of the jury to satisfy the trial
court of the motion's sufficiency and a second time before the jury. Furthermore, a
motion in limine should not be a mere substitute or continuation of discovery.
Preferably, the facts needed for the motion should be developed during discovery
for use in the motion."[15]

Whether used offensively or defensively, the tactical advantages to a motion in
limine are self-evident. Novel scientific evidence and highly charged and potentially
prejudicial and controversial evidence are suitable subject matter of this motion. See
Form 8.9.[16]

Counsel and cooperating staff are firmly reminded that in limine argumentation generally calls for external support in the form of memoranda, points and authorities, and other briefings.

## Motion as to the Quality and Content of Evidence

Challenges to the quality and content of evidence depend heavily on FRE Rule
403, stating that even if evidence is substantively relevant, it can be excluded "if its
probative value is substantially outweighed by the danger of unfair prejudice, confusion of the issues, or misleading the jury, or by considerations of undue delay, waste
of time, or needless presentation of cumulative evidence."[17] The American Law Institute's Model Code of Evidence grants judicial authority far-reaching discretion in

To _____ and _____ [parties in the action] and to _____ and _____ [the attorneys of record for each party in the action]:

Notice is hereby given that on _____, [20] _____, at _____ [time] _____.m., or as soon thereafter as the matter can be heard, _____ [at the courtroom of _____ [presiding judge], or in Department No. _____, or in the Law and Motion Department], of the above-entitled Court at _____ [address], _____ [moving party] will move the court for an order _____ [specify order, such as: instructing defense and counsel not to refer to, comment on, examine regarding, or suggest to the jury in any way the fact that the plaintiff, who was widowed and unmarried at the time of her son's death, has since remarried].

This motion is made on the grounds that _____ [specify grounds, such as: the fact of remarriage is not relevant to any issue in this cause and any attempt to expose the jury to such information would be highly prejudicial; to plaintiff, even if the jury was instructed to disregard it]. The motion is based upon this notice, the pleadings, records, and papers on file in this action, the attached memorandum of points and authorities, or on documentary evidence, that may be presented at the hearing of the motion.

Dated _____, [20] _____


[Signature]

**FORM 8.9**   Motion in limine.

the exclusion of evidence that has relevant content and quality, but is prejudicial in effect. Rule 303(e) of the Model Code of Evidence states:

(1)   The judge may in his discretion exclude evidence if he finds that its probative value is outweighed by the risk that its admission will

   (a)   necessitate undue consumption of time, or
   (b)   create substantial danger of undue prejudice or confusing the issues or misleading the jury, or
   (c)   unfairly surprise a party who has not had reasonable grounds to anticipate that such evidence would be offered.[18]

Case by case, the court considers whether generally admissible evidence should nonetheless be excluded. Examples illuminating this principle include out-of-scale demonstrative models, gruesome photographs, unreliable statistical presentations, overly edited works, unreliable summaries of voluminous documents, misleading films or videotapes, excessive hearsay, and evidence lending to unfair surprise. Photographic exhibitions provide the best illustration of these principles. Review the list of objections to photographic content:

- Exaggeration,
- Minimization,
- Elaboration,
- Omission,
- Reversal of left and right,
- Optical illusions,
- Single viewpoint and compression of time,
- Color of photograph, and
- Correct viewing distance.

## Motion to Strike

If the advocate wishes that a certain statement be stricken from the record, he or she should object first orally; if overruled, he or she should preserve the record for an appeal and then immediately file a *motion to strike* the evidence.

Even though lawful, the motion to strike is sometimes strategically unjustified because the jurors will then be told to disregard what they have heard. This draws attention to evidence jurors may have paid little attention to. Following is other advice to keep in mind:

- Determine when and where to strike consistent with your strategy.
- Seek a mistrial.
- Press your point. Make sure your grounds are set forth on the record to support the request for a mistrial.
- Ask for a brief recess to supply the judge with a short memorandum of law on the issues involved.
- Take your time to ensure that you have protected the record.

As to the matter of pure prejudice, the courts are not hesitant to restrict the admissibility of evidence that inflames or prompts bias in jurors' decision-making. Unfair prejudice means an undue influence on improper grounds—commonly, though not necessarily, an emotional one. As such, the admission of a decapitated head from a murder victim, while extraordinarily relevant, incites decision making in a highly charged, prejudicial atmosphere.

The Notes of the Advisory Committee on the Federal Rules of Evidence recognize that the exclusion of unquestionably relevant evidence will "entail risks which range all the way from inducing decision on a purely emotional basis, at one extreme, to nothing more harmful than merely wasting time, at the other extreme."[19] A judgment about admissibility based on relevancy and prejudice is not a mathematical equation, but instead a balancing of interests, an evaluation of numerous factors and variables on a case-by-case basis. "If the probative value is not outweighed by countervailing considerations, the evidence should be admitted, even if there are identifiable dangers."[20]

## Motion for Summary Judgment

If the evidence proffered by the expert is insubstantial and the party's case-in-chief heavily rests upon a questionable legal claim, a *motion for summary judgment* is in order. In the federal court system, the award of a summary judgment is determined according to the existence and substantiality of legal or factual issues. Federal Rule of Civil Procedure 56, for example, lays out the standards for meeting the summary judgment threshold.

> (c) Motion and Proceedings Thereon. . . . The adverse party prior to the day of hearing may serve opposing affidavits. The judgment sought shall be rendered forthwith if the pleadings, depositions, answers to interrogatories, and admissions on file, together with the affidavits, if any, show that there is no genuine issue as to any material fact and that the moving party is entitled to a judgment as a matter of law. A summary judgment, interlocutory in character, may be rendered on the issue of liability alone although there is a genuine issue as to the amount of damages.

> (e) Form of Affidavits; Further Testimony; Defense Required. . . . When a motion for summary judgment is made and supported as provided in this rule, an adverse party may not rest upon the mere allegations or denials of the adverse party's pleasing, but the adverse party's response, by affidavits or as otherwise provided in this rule, must set forth specific facts showing that there is a genuine issue for trial. If the adverse party does not so respond, summary judgment, if appropriate, shall be entered against the adverse party.[21]

## § 8.4 MOTIONS TO EXCLUDE ON CONSTITUTIONAL THEORIES

Under the Fourth, Fifth, Sixth, and Fourteenth Amendments of the U. S. Constitution, relevant, material, probative, and nonprejudicial evidence may still be excluded. Criminal litigators experience constitutional challenges far more often than their civil colleagues do. Defense counsel usually pokes holes in police practice—for example, violations of *Miranda,* coerced confessions, and tainted sources. A *motion to suppress or exclude* evidence asks that the evidence be excluded for constitutional faults like these:

1. Warrant's application or affidavit was defective
2. Warrant's lack of specificity and particularity in description

3. Warrant was not supported by facts or other corroborative evidence

4. Defendant was stopped and frisked without reasonable suspicion

5. Incriminating evidence was seized by an illegal random stop or road block of an automobile

6. Police lacked a warrantless exception such as for public safety reasons, exigent circumstances, the item was in plain view, the property was abandoned, the search was consensual

7. Police conducted an inventory or automobile search without legal justification for impoundment

8. Evidence was acquired from the person in a shocking manner or by an extremely invasive procedure

9. Police exceeded the scope and parameter of their search area

10. The incident-to-arrest search went beyond the arm's length of the individual's possessions

11. Police lacked probable cause

12. Police searched more than the personal, portable effects of a defendant

13. Confession was coerced

14. Confession was acquired without Miranda rights

15. Confession was acquired even though defendant asked for counsel.[22]

Motion practice thrives on the evidentiary challenges made possible by the *exclusionary rule*. The exclusionary rule disallows evidence procured in breach of constitutional rights. "Counsel in criminal defense litigation continually analyze the legality of police conduct. If an argument can be posed or made regarding constitutional violations of rights based on the 4th, 5th, 6th, and 14th Amendments of the United States Constitution, then a motion to suppress or other exclusionary request can be, and has been regularly upheld. While public furor and clamor over these technical rights is growing, defense lawyers have an obligation to proceed with such argumentation."[23] A motion to suppress based on illegal arrest, search, and seizure processes is at Form 8.10.[24] A confession that is coerced, rooted out by undue force and intimidation, or acquired in violation of the *Miranda* doctrine is the proper object of the motion to suppress at Form 8.11.[25]

Other motions to suppress zero in on particular physical evidence, such as an improper seizure from an automobile (Form 8.12). See Case Example 8.1.

## Motions for Post-trial Relief

In extraordinary circumstances, post-trial relief may be appropriate when it involves an evidentiary matter. Generally speaking, post-trial relief is granted when one or more of the following conditions exist:

• General showing of injustice.

NOW COMES the defendant herein, through undersigned counsel, and moves this Court for an order suppressing the introduction of evidence. As reasons for this Motion, the Court is respectfully shown:

1. The defendant is charged with the offense of _____ ;

2. During the course of the investigation of this case certain property belonging to the defendant was seized by law enforcement officers in violation of the defendant's right to be free from unreasonable searches and seizures as guaranteed to him by the Fourth and Fourteenth Amendments of the United States Constitution. The evidence seized consisted of:

   A. _____ ;
   B. _____ ;
   C. _____ ;

3. The evidence seized by the police officers was in violation of the defendant's rights for the following reasons:

   A. _____ ;
   B. _____ ;
   C. _____ ;

   WHEREFORE, it is respectfully prayed that this Court will order the evidence in question suppressed.

This the _____ day of _____ , [20] _____ .

Respectfully submitted,

_____

Attorney for Defendant

**FORM 8.10**   Motion to suppress evidence. (NORTH CAROLINA BAR FOUNDATION, Practical Skills Course, 1988, vol 3, Criminal and Juvenile Law. Reprinted with permission.)

- Fraud, accident or mistake preventing fairness of the trial, with no negligence or inattentiveness on the part of the moving party.
- Surprise resulting from some circumstance which was unforeseen and where a party or his counsel were not negligent or guilty of laches. The surprise must have prejudiced the moving party.
- Illness of counsel or sudden illness of a witness.
- Absence of a party for a very compelling reason.
- Absence of counsel, but only where it can be clearly shown that a different result would have been reached if said counsel had been present.
- Lack of notice.
- Defect in proof.

NOW COMES the defendant herein, by and through undersigned counsel, and moves this Court that the confession alleged to have been made by the defendant be suppressed for the following reasons:

1. The defendant is charged with the offense of _____;

2. The law enforcement officers in this case took a confession from the defendant under the following circumstances:

   A. _____;
   B. _____;

3. The defendant alleges upon information and belief that the statements attributed to him were illegally obtained in violation of the Fourth, Fifth, Sixth and Fourteenth Amendments to the United State Constitution.

This the _____ day of _____, [20] _____.

Respectfully submitted,

_____

Attorney for Defendant

**FORM 8.11**   Motion for suppression of defendant's alleged confession. (NORTH CAROLINA BAR FOUNDATION, Practical Skills Course, 1988, vol 3, Criminal and Juvenile Law. Reprinted with permission.)

The defendant by [his/her] attorney, upon all the records, files and proceedings in this case moves the court, pursuant to the provision of sec. _____, for an order suppressing for use as evidence any and all articles seized by the law enforcement officers from the motor vehicle of the defendant, on or about [month] [day], 20 _____, in [city and county], State of _____.

AS GROUNDS the defendant asserts that the taking of the articles from [his/her] automobile was without a lawful warrant and violated rights guaranteed [him/her] by the provisions of Article _____, Section _____ of the _____, the 4th and 14th Amendments to the United States Constitution, and the provisions of the Statutes.

Dated _____, 20 _____

[Closing]

**FORM 8.12**   Motion to suppress physical evidence.

---

**CASE EXAMPLE 8.1**  *Motion to Exclude*

**FACTS:** In a trial for first-degree murder, prosecutor made certain references about the defendant that were the subject of an appellate review. Even though defendant was found guilty of murder in the first degree and sentenced to the death penalty, the defendant's appeal rested on certain remarks made by the prosecutor that concerned the defendant's associations with the Aryan Brotherhood, Inc. This membership was cast as evidence of character and a propensity for violent conduct. Upon appeal, defendant's counsel argued that the sentence of the death penalty could not be upheld because undue prejudice and bias were exhibited by references to his membership in the Aryan Brotherhood. Prosecution argued that statements and testimony relevant to his membership exhibited a factual trait in defendant and were relevant to the trier of fact regarding his capacity to be a first-degree murderer (United States v. Williams, 504 U.S. 36 (1992)).

**QUESTIONS AND ISSUES:**

1. Is membership in the Aryan Brotherhood, an avowed racist organization, relevant in the case of a first-degree murder?

2. Is the same evidence relevant in a sentencing hearing?

3. Is the same evidence relevant, yet so highly prejudicial and inflammatory that its probative value is overruled by the prejudicial impact of such evidence?

**HOLDING:** As to the first two issues, one could soundly argue that the evidence is relevant. In fact, the U.S. Supreme Court held that the evidence may have been relevant, but that its mention was so prejudicial and inflammatory that the death penalty determination had to be reversed in exchange for a life sentence. By an 8–1 margin, the Court so held. Justice Clarence Thomas was the lone dissenter.

---

- Misconduct of any person connected with the trial during its progress which might affect the result, whether such conduct is fraudulent or not.
  (a) Misconduct of judge, such as improper comments in charge.
  (b) Misconduct of court officers, witnesses or others.
  (c) Misconduct of any party.
  (d) Conversing with or any contact with juror(s).
  (e) Misconduct of counsel.
  (f) Misconduct of juror(s).
- Departures from proper practices and procedure in the conduct of the trial, resulting in prejudicing or adversely affecting substantial rights of a party.
  (a) Admission of improper evidence.
  (b) Exclusion of proper evidence.
- Misdirection or error in charge to jury
  (a) Complaining party must show that he was prejudiced.

- Matters relating to the verdict
  - (a) Where verdict is contrary to law, the weight of the evidence is either inadequate or excessive.
  - (b) Where jury rendered verdict by failing to follow instructions of law or properly appraising the evidence.
  - (c) Where verdict is the product of prejudice or sympathy.
    - (i) Court will usually grant new trial when jury has disregarded the measure of damages laid down by the court in favor of one of their own, especially where it is the product of prejudice, sympathy, passion or corruption.
- Newly discovered evidence, if it meets certain judicial requirements. Ordinarily, a granting of a new trial by the trial judge on this ground will not be reversed. There are several tests which must be met to entitle an applicant to a new trial on this ground.
  - (a) the testimony must have been discovered since the former trial.
  - (b) the testimony could not have been obtained at the former trial with due diligence.
  - (c) it must be new and different testimony, not merely cumulative or corroborative of other testimony.
  - (d) the testimony must go to the merits of the case, not merely to the credibility of a witness and must tend to show that an injustice has been done by the verdict.
  - (e) the testimony must be such as will probably produce a different verdict in the event a new trial is granted.
- False testimony
  - (a) the testimony must have been material.
  - (b) the moving party must have exercised due diligence and must be free from negligence and laches.[26]

The subsequent discovery that the evidence on which the lower court's decision rested was tainted, polluted, or questionable, or that the testimonial evidence that the court relied upon was biased, supports the *motion for a new trial.* See Form 8.13.

---

The defendant, by [his/her] attorney, upon all of the files, records and proceedings in this case, and pursuant to Section _____, respectfully moves the court for the entry of an order setting aside the judgment of conviction entered against defendant and for a new trial.

AS GROUND, defendant asserts:

[Insert grounds for motion]

Dated _____, 20_____

[Closing]

---

**FORM 8.13**  Motion for new trial.

## § 8.5 SUMMARY

The primary categories of motions related to evidentiary issues were the chief focus of this chapter. From the initial coverage dealing with pretrial discovery and disclosure, to a request that the court evaluate the evidence in light of its potential prejudice, to the examination of suppression motions that might be filed in criminal practice, motion practice frequently covers the evidentiary dimension. Covered within were the various pleadings tactics and strategies involved in gaining access to evidence or in seeking its limitation at trial.

### *Notes*

1. CHARLES P. NEMETH, Litigation, Pleadings and Arbitration 324 (2d ed. 1997).
2. MARILYN J. BERGER, JOHN B. MITCHELL, & RONALD H. CLARK, Trial Advocacy: Planning, Analysis and Strategies 112–113 (1989).
3. BURGESS ELDRIDGE, Personal Injury Paralegal 14.3 (1987).
4. Fed. R. Civ. P. 35(a).
5. JOHN TARANTINO & DAVID OLIVIERA, Litigating Neck and Back Injuries 730 (1989).
6. Fed. R. Civ. P 34(a).
7. CHARLES P. NEMETH, Litigation, Pleadings and Arbitration 342 (1990).
8. Fed. R. Civ. P. 37(b)(2).
9. PATRICK J. DEVITT, Wisconsin Criminal Defense Manual A-125 (1981).
10. Fed. R. Civ. P. 34(a).
11. TARANTINO & OLIVIERA, *supra* note 5, at 730.
12. Robert G. Johnston & Thomas P. Higgins, *Motions in Limine: Use and Consequences in Illinois,* 26 J. Marshall L. Rev. 307, 308 (1993).
13. JOHN TARANTINO, in his work *Trial Evidence Foundations,* outlines the elements of a sound motion *in limine:*
    1. State your intentions to move *in Limine* to exclude the prejudicial evidence,
    2. Offer your reasons why you believe your opponent intends the offer of the evidence at trial,
    3. State the reasons why the evidence is inadmissible,
    4. Offer reasons why an advanced ruling is preferable to a trial objection,
    5. Cite to the judge specific legal arguments for case law support, to foster your opposition to the evidence.

JOHN TARANTINO, Trial Evidence Foundations 2-2 (1986).
14. Fed. R. Civ. P. 16(c).
15. MARK DOMBROFF, Dombroff on Unfair Tactics 486 (1988).
16. CHARLES P. NEMETH, Paralegal Resource Manual 698 (2d ed. 1995).
17. Fed. R. Evid. 403.
18. Model Code of Evidence Rule 303(e) (1942).
19. Fed. R. Evid. 403, advisory committee's notes.
20. JOHN A. TARANTINO, Strategic Use of Scientific Evidence 20 (1988).

21. Fed. R. Civ. P. 56. Illustrative of recent cases allowing for summary judgment in speculative toxic tort exposure cases is Christopherson v. Allied-Signal Corp., 939 F.2d 1106 (5th Cir. 1991). The Fifth Circuit, sitting en banc, affirmed the district court's summary judgment based upon exclusion of testimony of the plaintiff's expert, leaving the plaintiff without proof of causation. A summary judgment was upheld in Viterbo v. Dow Chemical Co., 826 F.2d 420 (5th Cir. 1987), a chemical exposure case, based upon refusal to accept the proffered opinion of an expert witness who admitted that his opinions were based upon the plaintiff's statements that (a) he experienced certain symptoms and (b) he thought the chemical was the only possible cause. The expert admitted the symptoms could have had numerous causes. The Fifth Circuit said the opinion simply lacked the foundation and reliability necessary to support expert testimony.

22. Fed. R. Evid. 403, advisory committee's notes.

23. CHARLES P. NEMETH, Paralegal Resource Manual 391 (1989).

24. 3 NORTH CAROLINA BAR ASSOCIATION FOUNDATION, INC., 1988 Practical Skills Course, Criminal and Juvenile Law 31 (1988).

25. *Id.* at 29.

26. BURTON R. LAUB & W. EDWARD SEEL, Pennsylvania Keystone, Lawyer's Desk Library of Practice 8–10 (1993).

# CHAPTER 9

# *Trial Evidence*

## § 9.1 INTRODUCTION: EVIDENCE AT TRIAL

Evidentiary preparation and concerns do not cease upon commencement of trial. Evidence activities accelerate as the tension, stress, and wide-ranging responsibilities of advocacy intensify. Learning how to package and use evidence at trial is this chapter's general focus. It is at trial that all the evidentiary knowledge thus far acquired is applied. It is at trial that the theoretical principles of evidence law come to practical fruition. It is at trial that the evidence collection process, the means of preservation, identification, and the foundational steps of authentication take on real life. Lawyers, investigators, legal specialists, and assistants see their hard pretrial work unfold. Evidentially, there is much to keep track of:

- coordinating the appearance of witnesses;
- assisting in the preparation of all files and documents;
- controlling the flow and handling of documents and exhibits during trial;
- assisting in the performance of legal research;
- compiling notes on the testimony of witnesses;
- insuring that all papers and documents have been filed properly;
- creating charts, diagrams, and other evidence tools; and,
- handling all demonstrative evidence.[1]

Litigation specialists need a "tool box" that facilitates the presentation of evidence. The most commonly used forms of presentation equipment are:

- Easels,
- Blackboards,

- Magnetic boards,
- Models,
- Aerial maps,
- Videotapes and VCRs,
- Television monitors,
- Overhead projectors with transparencies,
- Slide projectors and screens,
- 8mm movie projectors, and
- X-ray equipment.

In preparation for trial, those who are encumbered with these litigation responsibilities should rigorously stick to an evidence checklist that summarizes the multiplicity of evidence and advocacy functions. Nancy Schleifer's trial agenda checklist does just that. See Form 9.1.[2]

Police investigators and law enforcement support personnel are equally responsible for evidence organization at trial and should work closely and cooperatively with prosecutorial staff. The case team should tailor the trial agenda, plan, or outline

---

_____    Trial motions.

        _____    Motion in limine regarding evidence or testimony.

        _____    Motion to strike witnesses.

        _____    Motions for sanctions for failure to file or follow pretrial order.

        _____    Other motions _____

_____    Present all trial stipulations.

        _____    Stipulation that documents are authentic without the need for calling authentication witnesses.

        _____    Stipulation that copies will be acceptable as evidence without production of originals.

        _____    Stipulation that the following documents will be admitted without objection: _____

        _____    Other stipulations _____

_____    Jury selection. (Move for mistrial if error is claimed at this stage.)

_____    Opening statement.

---

**FORM 9.1**   Trial agenda checklist.

_____     Plaintiff's witnesses. (List witnesses in anticipated order.)

_____

_____

    _____     Proffer witness or testimony if not admitted.

    _____     Object if evidence or testimony is objectionable and judge has overruled the motion in limine.

_____     Move to admit additional plaintiff exhibits.

    _____     Identify and proffer exhibits that judge will not admit.

    _____     Request to have identified exhibits admitted.

_____     Plaintiff rests.

_____     Plaintiff to move to amend pleadings to accord with the proof if necessary.

_____     Defendant's motion for directed verdict.

_____     Defendant's witnesses. (List witnesses in anticipated order.)

_____

_____

    _____     Proffer witness or testimony if not admitted.

    _____     Object if evidence or testimony is objectionable and judge has overruled the motion in limine.

_____     Move to admit additional defendant exhibits.

    _____     Identify and proffer exhibits that judge will not admit.

    _____     Request to have identified exhibits admitted.

_____     Defendant rests.

_____     Defendant to move to amend pleadings to accord with the proof if necessary.

_____     Plaintiff moves for directed verdict; defendant renews motion for directed verdict.

_____     Jury instruction conference.

_____     Plaintiff's closing argument.

_____     Defendant's closing argument.

_____     Plaintiff's rebuttal.

**FORM 9.1**   *Continued*

to the particular case being litigated. Develop a case theme that expresses a clear-cut view of liability, innocence, guilt, or other legal result. Call it a story. Label it a theme plan of proof. For an example of a step-by-step evidentiary theme in an air negligence case, see Appendix D.

## § 9.2 EXHIBITS: RULES OF ADMISSIBILITY

Evidence, aside from its qualities of relevance and materiality, is referenced as an *exhibit*. Exhibits are packaged presentations of real, documentary, or demonstrative evidence. To be admitted, the exhibit's offeror follows various procedural steps to assure admission of the exhibit. A cursory review follows.

### Marking for Identification

The identification process varies according to local custom and procedure. Once the exhibit is ready for introduction, the proponent should state to the court respectfully, "Please mark this exhibit for identification." Court clerks, court stenographers, law clerks, and other personnel or other parties may be entrusted with this task. After the exhibit is noted and recorded, the advocate offering the exhibit must lay a foundation for purposes of admissibility.

### Laying the Foundation

Rules regarding evidentiary foundation, identification, and authentication have already been amply reviewed. Briefly stated, the proponent of the exhibit must deal with questions of relevancy; eliminate issues regarding prejudice, undue delay, waste, confusion, and cumulativeness; and provide an authoritative witness that can attest to the fairness and accuracy of the exhibit's representation. Foundational requirements have already been addressed in the context of FRE 901.

### Exhibit Examination by Opposing Counsel

As both a professional courtesy and a procedural requirement, the lawyer proposing the exhibit should hand it to the opposing counsel. In practice, this is pro forma, since pretrial inspection takes place during the discovery and disclosure phase.

### Offering the Exhibit into Evidence

After opposing counsel has had sufficient time to review the exhibit and without preliminary objection, counsel offers the exhibit into evidence by simply pronouncing, "Plaintiff's exhibit number P1 [or an identifier based on some other numerical system] is offered into evidence." In select jurisdictions, courtroom strategy may call for delay of an offer until the plaintiff's and defendant's cases are fully presented and all questions of evidentiary admissibility have been resolved.

## Judge's Inspection of the Exhibit

Procedural rules generally require that the exhibit be made personally available to the judge for inspection. Counsel should not forget the essential role the judiciary plays in the introduction, examination, and decision-making relative to evidentiary admissibility. The trial judge has enormous discretion in all matters of evidentiary judgment. The American Law Institute's Model Code of Evidence confirms the seminal role of the judges in evidentiary questions:

> The judge controls the conduct of the trial to the end that the evidence shall be presented honestly, expeditiously, and in such form as to readily understand . . .
>
> (j) whether a witness in communicating admissible evidence may use as a substitute for oral testimony or in addition to it a writing, model, design, or any other understandable means of communication, and whether a means so used may be admitted into evidence; . . .
>
> (m) whether or not an exhibit which has been received in evidence shall be available to the jury after its retirement to deliberate upon the verdict.[3]

## Opposing Counsel's Questioning of Authenticator

A witness who attests that an exhibit is a fair and accurate representation of a given subject matter is subject to foundational examination. See Figure 9.1, showing a projectile lodged in a wooden 2x4, inside of exterior siding. Who could authenticate?

Opposing counsel are reminded that the examination should extend only to foundational matters. Opposing counsel may wish to attempt to elicit testimony and information about the exhibit to present it in a negative and derogatory light. The scope of the examination may include, but is not limited to, the following types of issues:

1. the exhibit is not helpful;
2. the exhibit and the corresponding testimony do not aid the jury;
3. the exhibit is not relevant to the case at hand;
4. the exhibit has not been properly identified;
5. the proponent of the exhibit has failed to establish a proper foundation;
6. the exhibit is in a substantially different state than at the time of the issue currently being litigated;
7. the proponent failed to establish the chain of possession or custody.[4]

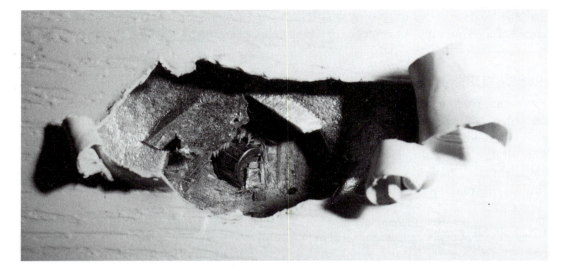

**FIGURE 9.1**   Who could authenticate?

## Ruling on Admissibility

At the completion of opposing counsel's examination of the authenticating witness, the court, after considering the foundational elements, content, and quality of the exhibit, will make a ruling on admissibility. If a court denies admissibility, the exhibit's proponent should demand an *offer of proof* to secure appellate rights. An offer of proof may be either oral or written.

## Testimony Relative to the Exhibit

Upon admission of the exhibit, testimony may be elicited by both counsel. The extent and duration of testimony largely depend on the exhibit's content and overall role in the litigation.

## Exhibit Goes to the Jury

Once testimonial examination has taken place, exhibits—whether documents, models, maps, charts, diagrams, or some other form—may be handed over to the jury for inspection. At the end of trial, exhibits that have been admitted into court will be made available to the jury during deliberations.

See Case Examples 9.1 and 9.2 for demonstrations of the preceding discussion.

| CASE EXAMPLE 9.1 | *Courtroom Formalities in Admission of Exhibits* |
|---|---|

**FACTS:** The prosecutor in an egregious assault case seeks to admit a broken beer mug that was used to crush the face of plaintiff. The attack caused multiple sinus fractures. The beer mug was found at the tavern location where the assault took place. Police Officer John Riley collected, packaged, and preserved the evidence with proper notations. Officer Riley is currently being called to the stand. The prosecutor requests that the exhibits be marked by the court's stenographer. The exhibit is shown to opposing counsel without objection, and the prosecutor asks the court's permission to approach the police officer. The court obliges.

Q. Officer Riley, I am going to present to you what has been marked and identified as *State's Exhibit 1* for identification purposes and ask you to review and examine it. Have you had sufficient time to examine this exhibit?

A. Yes.

Q. Can you please relate to the court and to the jury what this exhibit is?

A. This is a beer mug that I found lying on the tavern floor close to the location of the assault.

Q. How do you know this *State's Exhibit 1* is the same beer mug that you collected at the tavern location?

A. Aside from the evidence packaging label, which was immediately placed on the mug, I took a glass and metal inscriber and scratched in the first two initials of my name in the lower portion of the beer mug. Those two initials appear on the lower edge of the beer mug as I originally inscribed them.

Q. Is *State's Exhibit 1* substantially in the same condition as it was at the time you first saw it?

A. Yes, it is.

**QUESTION AND ISSUE:** Is the exhibit properly identified and authenticated?

**HOLDING:** Barring any unforeseen circumstances, admissibility is assured, since relevancy problems are small, disputes regarding the chain of custody are nonexistent, and the authenticating witness, namely, the police officer, has confirmed not only the integrity of the evidence, but also the substantially similar condition of the evidence to its condition on the day of its collection.

## CASE EXAMPLE 9.2 · *Photographic Evidence*

**FACTS:** Insurance investigator Mary C. Williams was called to an accident scene within minutes after its occurrence. Her supervisor asked her to provide a complete and comprehensive photographic exposition of an intersectional collision between a large tractor-trailer and a small Volkswagen Beetle. The Volkswagen Beetle was crushed under the tractor-trailer, and the victim in the Beetle was the insured, Robert Madden. Mr. Madden met his demise within seconds after this traumatic collision. The victim's insurance representative, Ms. Williams, produced an impressive array of photographic displays. Counsel for the insurance company wishes these photographs admitted in a defense to a wrongful death action. Initial formalities have been adhered to; namely, the exhibit has been properly marked, has been made available to opposing counsel, and is now ready to be identified and authenticated by Mary C. Williams.

> Q. Ms. Williams, I show you what has been marked as *Defense Exhibit C* for your review, asking that you examine it for purposes of identification. Have you had sufficient time to review and assess the quality and content of these photographs?
>
> A. Yes.
>
> Q. Please explain the content of *Defense's Exhibit C.*
>
> A. The picture shows the victim, Mr. Robert Madden, in a contorted position when in the crushed vehicle. Next to Mr. Madden is a bottle of Jack Daniels and a package of raw marijuana.
>
> Q. Is this picture a fair and accurate representation of the position of Mr. Madden on the day of this fatal accident?
>
> A. Yes, it is.

### QUESTIONS AND ISSUES:

1. Can it be argued that the photographic exposition is simultaneously relevant and biased?

2. Is it possible for the court to find that the picture will cause unwarranted prejudice during the jury's evaluation?

3. Is there any motivation on the part of the defending insurance company to highlight the illegal contraband and alcoholic beverage container found at this intersectional collision?

4. Could it be argued that the pictures as presented might be too gruesome?

5. Based on these lines of inquiry, should opposing counsel object strongly to the admission of the photographic exhibit?

**HOLDING:** Pictures denied admission.

## § 9.3 PRACTICE POINTERS ON TRIAL EVIDENCE

### Importance of a Trial Notebook

As evidence accumulates, its scope and magnitude often overwhelm the case team as the trial date nears. Individual and isolated pieces of evidence are not tough to decipher, but when applied to a complete trial, some pieces get lost in the shuffle. The most organized investigators and attorneys will forget or omit the evidence. An evidence-tracking system that organizes the many forms of evidence and correlates their respective functions is mandatory. *Trial notebooks* achieve this aim. "A trial notebook should be used for every major case. Its simplicity or sophistication depends on one's desires or needs."[5] The Georgia Institute of Continuing Legal Education suggests that the following topical concerns be divided or tabbed within a trial notebook:

- pre-trial notes
  - proof analysis
  - checklists
  - research procedures
  - stipulations
  - pre-trial orders
  - discovery digests
  - pre-trial motions
- jury selection
- opening statement
  - research/evidence
  - research/substantive
- plaintiff witnesses
- defendant witnesses
- exhibits list
- rebuttal charges
- final argument
- trial motions
- notes during trial[6]

Form 9.2[7] contains an alternative version of the trial notebook's content.

Trial notebooks organize exhibits according to theme, subject matter, and place of introduction in the litigation. Exhibits are further traced by their time of offering, reception or denial, and respective identification number.

Client Name & Matter: _____ File No.: _____

Responsible Attorney(s): _____ Date: _____

Check When Completed

_____ 1. Preparation Agenda

_____ 2. Analysis of the Issues

_____ 3. Outlines of Proof

_____ 4. Evaluation of Prospective Jurors, Voir Dire, and Notes

_____ 5. Case Summaries

_____ 6. List of Witnesses

_____ 7. Witness Files

_____ 8. Witness Sheets for Direct Examination

_____ 9. Notes for Opening Statement

_____ 10. Notes for Cross-Examination

_____ 11. Index of Discovery

_____ 12. Material to Be Used at Trial

_____ 13. Notes and Briefs on Law and Evidence, and Trial Motions

_____ 14. Requests for Charge

_____ 15. Notes for Final Argument

_____ 16. List of Exhibits and Exhibit File

_____ 17. Trial Agenda

_____ 18. "To Do" List

_____ 19. Medical Brief (if applicable)

_____ 20. Technical Notes

_____ 21. _____

_____ 22. _____

_____ 23. _____

_____ 24. _____

Notes: _____

_____

_____

_____

**FORM 9.2**   Trial notebook checklist.

## Preparing Exhibits for Trial

For an exhibit to be a successful evidentiary presentation, it must carve its own niche in the chronological order of litigation, display itself at the right time during the right argument, and be supported by a foundational witness.[8]

Trial exhibits, in both criminal and civil cases, can be intricate and voluminous. The character of an exhibit ranges from simple documentation to complex demonstrative models or visual presentations. See Figure 9.2.[9] In an age when visual imagery commands juror attention more than testimonial delivery—when seeing is believing—the seasoned practitioner knows that visual exhibits in the form of charts, graphs, photos, videotapes, and the like make or break a case.

Organizing exhibits for trial need not be a complicated operation. Experienced advocates classify or categorize exhibits according to their nature—that is, whether they are documents, expert findings or conclusions in the form of a report, transcribed or summarized depositions, or models, charts, diagrams, or other demonstrative items. Others develop a scheme of classification based on the time the exhibit will be introduced into the litigation. Some find it more convenient to typify exhibits depending upon the subject matter addressed.

As the trial draws near, the trial team will prepare a list of trial exhibits. On that list are columns for Motions in Limine, Exhibits Offered, Objections, and Exhibits Admitted. As the exhibits are offered, the information is entered on the computer so that a running list of offered and admitted exhibits is current. A current list is then distributed to all members of the trial team before the start of a new day.[10] At trial, a *master list* should be created for tracing the history of each exhibit. A *trial exhibit log* is reproduced at Form 9.3.[11]

Integrating the history of an exhibit within the trial notebook is an enviable strategy. See Form 9.4.[12] "Generally, the parties will exchange subsequent proposed exhibits before the trial starts, but under certain circumstances (e.g., oversight, stipulation that all deposition exhibit documents may be eligible as exhibits, different versions of the same document, rebuttal exhibits, etc.), exhibits may be added during the course of trial."[13]

Exhibit lists are largely a reflection of the case at hand. To illustrate, review the list of exhibits for a case alleging asbestos injury at Form 9.5.[14]

Other devices for tracking exhibits at trial are offered by various legal organizations, service providers, and stationery companies.[15]

## Copies and Reproductions

Most likely, the following individuals are permitted to review, inspect, or keep permanently a copy of the proposed exhibits:

- The judge,
- The trial clerk,

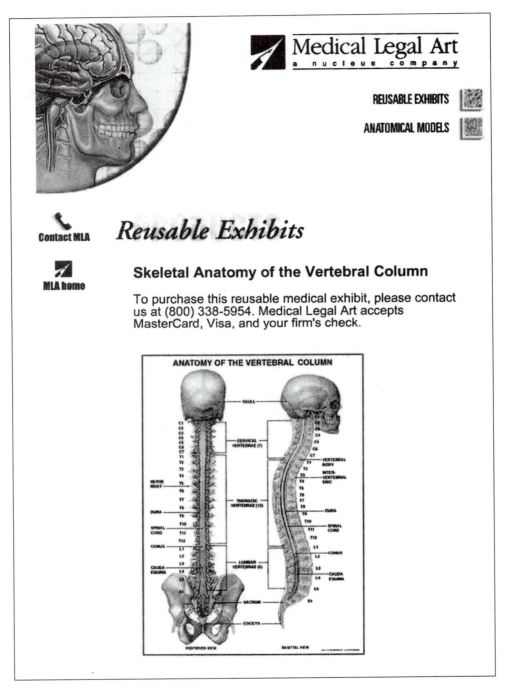

**Medical Legal Art**
a nucleus company

REUSABLE EXHIBITS

ANATOMICAL MODELS

Contact MLA

*Reusable Exhibits*

MLA home

## Skeletal Anatomy of the Vertebral Column

To purchase this reusable medical exhibit, please contact us at (800) 338-5954. Medical Legal Art accepts MasterCard, Visa, and your firm's check.

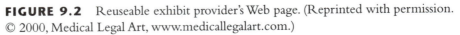

**FIGURE 9.2** Reuseable exhibit provider's Web page. (Reprinted with permission. © 2000, Medical Legal Art, www.medicallegalart.com.)

| Exhibit ID | Description | Offered | Admitted | Denied | Witness |
|------------|-------------|---------|----------|--------|---------|
|            |             |         |          |        |         |
|            |             |         |          |        |         |
|            |             |         |          |        |         |
|            |             |         |          |        |         |
|            |             |         |          |        |         |
|            |             |         |          |        |         |
|            |             |         |          |        |         |
|            |             |         |          |        |         |
|            |             |         |          |        |         |
|            |             |         |          |        |         |
|            |             |         |          |        |         |
|            |             |         |          |        |         |
|            |             |         |          |        |         |
|            |             |         |          |        |         |
|            |             |         |          |        |         |
|            |             |         |          |        |         |
|            |             |         |          |        |         |
|            |             |         |          |        |         |
|            |             |         |          |        |         |
|            |             |         |          |        |         |
|            |             |         |          |        |         |
|            |             |         |          |        |         |

**FORM 9.3**   Daily trial exhibit log.

- The witness testifying, and
- Opposing counsel.

## Labeling Exhibits

From the outset, a major admonition regarding the marking and labeling of exhibits is in order. Local rules and customs often dictate what marking method is acceptable. In fact, in some jurisdictions, trial exhibits will not be accepted under any circumstances unless fully outlined in an exhibit listing or other pretrial document. Pretrial conferences, under some state designs, require an exhibit listing. Consult local rules on the particulars of labeling, listing, and marking exhibits. Some general insights follow.

| # | Exhibits Added | Attorney's Set | Opposing Counsel's Set | Judge's Set | Witness's Set | Court Reporter's Set | Trial Paralegal's Set | Office Reference Set | | | | | | |
|---|---|---|---|---|---|---|---|---|---|---|---|---|---|---|
|  |  | 1. | 2. | 3. | 4. | 5. | 6. | 7. | 8. | 9. | 10. | 11. | 12. | 13. |
|  |  |  |  |  |  |  |  |  |  |  |  |  |  |  |
|  |  |  |  |  |  |  |  |  |  |  |  |  |  |  |
|  |  |  |  |  |  |  |  |  |  |  |  |  |  |  |
|  |  |  |  |  |  |  |  |  |  |  |  |  |  |  |
|  |  |  |  |  |  |  |  |  |  |  |  |  |  |  |
|  |  |  |  |  |  |  |  |  |  |  |  |  |  |  |
|  |  |  |  |  |  |  |  |  |  |  |  |  |  |  |
|  |  |  |  |  |  |  |  |  |  |  |  |  |  |  |
|  |  |  |  |  |  |  |  |  |  |  |  |  |  |  |
|  |  |  |  |  |  |  |  |  |  |  |  |  |  |  |
|  |  |  |  |  |  |  |  |  |  |  |  |  |  |  |
|  |  |  |  |  |  |  |  |  |  |  |  |  |  |  |
|  |  |  |  |  |  |  |  |  |  |  |  |  |  |  |
|  |  |  |  |  |  |  |  |  |  |  |  |  |  |  |
|  |  |  |  |  |  |  |  |  |  |  |  |  |  |  |
|  |  |  |  |  |  |  |  |  |  |  |  |  |  |  |

**FORM 9.4**   Exhibit trial history.

The Plaintiff's list of exhibits will include the following:

- All documentation relating to the buildings in question; these will consist of (without limitation)—
  - building specifications, plans, and blueprints
  - inspection reports
  - test results
  - photographs of building conditions
  - bills, invoices, and receipts for money spent in asbestos abatement and control
- All documents gathered from defendant's files and that plaintiff anticipates may be introduced as exhibits at trial on one or more of these issues
- All documents prepared by plaintiff's experts evaluating and/or summarizing plaintiff's claims, most notably those as to—
  - product identification (e.g., reports of constituent analysis, X-ray diffraction, transmission electron microscopy, phase contrast microscopy, and other expert protocols)
  - damage (e.g., all reviews and summaries of prospective costs determined by the expert)
- Specific depositions that might be read into evidence, particularly those from other cases
- Various medical and scientific publications that will be offered at trial as proof of the hazardousness of materials used, including—
  - published medical articles and key studies
  - heretofore secret documentation concerning tests and studies of hazards of asbestos by independent laboratories hired by various asbestos manufacturers
  - internal trade association documents
  - miscellaneous correspondence and communications by and between defendants and various trade associations, such as the National Insulation Manufacturers Association, the Thermal Insulation Manufacturers Association, the Magnesia Association, and the Asbestos Textile Institute
- Governmental and private industry monographs and documents touching on issues of the case, including—
  - various EPA guidance documents concerning asbestos in buildings
  - National Institute of Building Sciences Models Specifications for Asbestos Abatement
  - statutory and regulatory pronouncements governing asbestos control

**FORM 9.5**   Sample exhibit list. (Reprinted by permission of West Group.)

Defendants will want to include the following on its list of exhibits:

- All documents obtained from plaintiff that disclose early knowledge on plaintiff's part concerning deficiencies within its building and the failure of plaintiff to act on them

- All documents obtained from plaintiff that disclose acceptable conditions within plaintiff's building

- Architectural specifications that specify by trade name a product other than defendant's

- Documents that specify the manner in which defendant's product is alleged to have been used

- Reports of constituent analysis of alleged product samples

- Tests results, studies, publications, and other compilations that bolster defendant's hazard defense

**FORM 9.5**  *Continued*

Exhibit labeling is heavily influenced by local custom. Certain jurisdictions require that a color-coding system be used; that is, plaintiff and defendant exhibits might be labeled in contrasting colors—say, orange for defendant, green for plaintiff. Another format seen within the legal system is the consecutive numbering system. Defendant is assigned a certain set of numbers, serialized from 01 to 199, while plaintiff is supplied 200 to 399. These numbering systems, while logical, can often be confusing and cumbersome. Another predominate form of labeling and marking is the abbreviation model, with the abbreviation for plaintiff in the form of a "P" extended by numerals. This system translates into a P1–D1–P2–D2 sequence.

The majority of American jurisdictions prefer that exhibits be labeled by simple letters (Exhibit A, Exhibit B, Exhibit C) or by number (Exhibit 1, Exhibit 2, Exhibit 3). Legal suppliers have products available that correctly identify exhibits. For example, Suplee Envelope Company, Inc., produces exhibit labels. See Figure 9.3.[16]

Since there are so many unpredictable events during the litigation process, do not affix a label or other identifier to a specific exhibit until the court has admitted the exhibit. A good strategy is to prepare a tentative list of exhibits with identification numbers assigned and markers and labels filled out. If feasible, affix the exhibit sticker or other marking device in a uniform location, and be certain the point of fixture does not destroy the nature or content of the exhibit. Local custom may also dictate that the marking and labeling of exhibits is not a function of counsel. In some jurisdictions, the stenographer or court clerk is the only party who can mark the exhibits. Marking serves the purpose of confirming and cataloging the

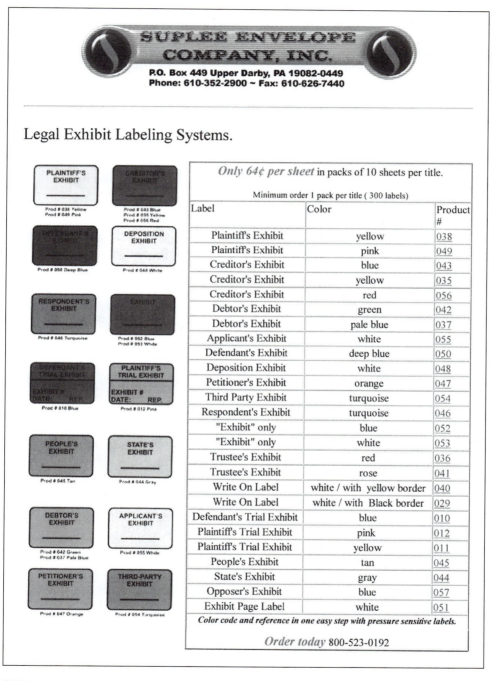

**Legal Exhibit Labeling Systems.**

| Label | Color | Product # |
|-------|-------|-----------|
| Plaintiff's Exhibit | yellow | 038 |
| Plaintiff's Exhibit | pink | 049 |
| Creditor's Exhibit | blue | 043 |
| Creditor's Exhibit | yellow | 035 |
| Creditor's Exhibit | red | 056 |
| Debtor's Exhibit | green | 042 |
| Debtor's Exhibit | pale blue | 037 |
| Applicant's Exhibit | white | 055 |
| Defendant's Exhibit | deep blue | 050 |
| Deposition Exhibit | white | 048 |
| Petitioner's Exhibit | orange | 047 |
| Third Party Exhibit | turquoise | 054 |
| Respondent's Exhibit | turquoise | 046 |
| "Exhibit" only | blue | 052 |
| "Exhibit" only | white | 053 |
| Trustee's Exhibit | red | 036 |
| Trustee's Exhibit | rose | 041 |
| Write On Label | white / with yellow border | 040 |
| Write On Label | white / with Black border | 029 |
| Defendant's Trial Exhibit | blue | 010 |
| Plaintiff's Trial Exhibit | pink | 012 |
| Plaintiff's Trial Exhibit | yellow | 011 |
| People's Exhibit | tan | 045 |
| State's Exhibit | gray | 044 |
| Opposer's Exhibit | blue | 057 |
| Exhibit Page Label | white | 051 |

*Only 64¢ per sheet* in packs of 10 sheets per title.

Minimum order 1 pack per title ( 300 labels)

*Color code and reference in one easy step with pressure sensitive labels.*

*Order today* 800-523-0192

**FIGURE 9.3**   Web page. (Reprinted with permission of Suplee Envelope Co. Inc.)

admission of an exhibit. "A piece of real evidence may be offered in evidence at any time after it is marked and after is it authenticated."[17]

Some final, practical thoughts relating to the packaging and presentation of exhibits are worth noting:

1. Where applicable, present exhibit materials in boxes, bags, envelopes, and other containers.
2. Depending on the size of the case, store documentary evidence in binders; all other evidence should be locked in a safe or steel cabinet.
3. Create exhibit backup sets in case of loss or destruction, and care for and maintain exhibits during the life of litigation.
4. Properly store packages and preserve exhibits with a biological or shelf life.
5. Have a file filled with extra exhibit labels and stickers.
6. Provide documentary evidence as a chain of custody.
7. Account for the best evidence rule by providing the original, if necessary.
8. Use self-authenticating documents, if possible.
9. Work cooperatively with opposing counsel to arrange stipulations.
10. Locate exhibits in the most favorable physical location in the courtroom.

## § 9.4 SUMMARY

Courtroom formalities of admissibility, labeling, exhibit production, and marking were a few of the topics covered in this chapter. Examples of trial evidence tracking systems were also provided. The role of a trial notebook in legal advocacy, as well as other insights on evidentiary controls during the trial phase, was offered. Aggressively, the proponent parlays the evidentiary theme that will set the course for the entire trial. Neither prosecution or defense should await the opposition to plan its trial strategy, but should formulate and execute its own.

### *Notes*

1. CHARLES P. NEMETH, Litigation, Pleadings and Arbitration 447 (1990).
2. NANCY SCHLEIFER, Litigation Forms and Checklists 12-7 (1991).
3. Model Code of Evidence Rule 105 (j), (m) (1942).
4. JAMES MCCARTHY, Making Trial Objections 4.2 (1986).
5. NEMETH, *supra* note 1, at 460.
6. INSTITUTE OF CONTINUING LEGAL EDUCATION IN GEORGIA, Georgia Lawyers Basic Practice Handbook 84 (1988).

7. GEORGE VETTER, Successful Civil Litigation: How to Win Your Case Before You Enter the Courtroom 72 (1977).

8. John Tarantino and David Oliviera stress this reasoned approach to the use of exhibits in light of jury evaluation. "[D]raw the jury's attention to those exhibits that you want them to focus on. Point out the salient portions of the exhibits that demonstrate the liability aspects or damage aspects of your case. Exhibits can be extremely potent towards an argument. The jury will focus on the exhibit, and look at it, while at the same time you are explaining the legal and factual significance of that exhibit for your case." JOHN TARANTINO & DAVID OLIVIERA, Litigating Neck and Back Injuries 8-45 (1989).

9. Medical Legal Art, 900 Circle 75 Parkway, Suite 720, Atlanta, GA 30339, <http://www.medical-legal.com/Reusables/reusables01.html>, visited January 19, 2000.

10. Anne P. Huffmann, *The Legal Assistant's Role in Automated Litigation Support,* 44 Am. Jur. Trials 79, 92–93 (1992).

11. BEVERLY HUTSON, Paralegal Trial Handbook 6-47 (1991).

12. *Id*. at 6-45.

13. *Id*.

14. John Klamann, *Cost Recovery Litigation Abatement of Asbestos Contamination,* 40 Am. Jur. Trials 317, 447–448 (1990).

15. KENT SINCLAIR, Trial Handbook app. G (2d ed. 1992).

16. Suplee Envelope Company, Inc., P.O. Box 49, Upper Darby, PA 19082-0499, 1-800-523-0192, Legal Exhibit Labeling Systems, <http://suplee.com/specialty/legaexlasys.html>, visited November 17, 1999.

17. 8 STANDARD PA. PRACTICE 2d §§ 52.1, 52.2.

# Evidence Supply Companies

**ACE Fingerprint Laboratories Inc.**
P.O. Box 288
Wake Forest, NC 27588-0288
Phone: (800) 426-7072 or
   (919) 556-9151
e-mail: acerel@mindspring.com

**AFP Supply**
432 West Main Street
P.O. Box A
Elizabethville, PA 17023-0076
Phone: (717) 362-2080
Fax: (717) 362-1066
Website: http://www.afpsupply.com

**Armor Holdings, Inc.**
13386 International Parkway
Jacksonville, FL 32218
Phone: (904) 741-5400
Fax: (904) 741-5407
Website:
   http://www.armorholdings.com

**Cellmark Diagnostics, Inc.**
20271 Goldenrod Lane, Suite 101
Germantown, MD 20876
Phone: (800) USA-LABS
Fax: (301) 428-4877
Website:
   http://www.cellmark-labs.com

**Crime Scene Products**
739 Brooks Mill Road
Union Hall, VA 24176
Phone: (800) 576-7606
Fax: (888) 384-3368
e-mail: evident@swva.net

**Evidence Collection & Protection, Inc.**
P.O. Box 3116
Kansas City, KS 66103
Phone: (800) 953-3274
Fax: (913) 342-2128
e-mail: ecpi@crime-scene.com

**The Evidence Store**
1761 Morris Avenue at Garden State
   Pkwy.
Union, NJ 07083
Toll-free: (800) 8-LAWPIX
Within N.J.: (908) 687-7205
Fax: (908) 686-7516
Pager: (800) 819-0076
e-mail: sales@evidencestore.com *or*
   Info@evidencestore.com

**Fesler's Inc.**
Website: http://www.feslers.com

**Forensic Technologies, Inc.**
1400 Energy Park Drive, Suite 20
St. Paul, MN 55108
Phone: (651) 659-0551
Fax: (651) 659-0651
e-mail: info@forensictech.com

**Gall's Inc.**
2492 Palumbo Drive
Lexington, KY 40509
Phone: (800) 477-7766
Fax: (800) 944-2557
e-mail: ID@galls.com

**Identicator Technology**
12300 Twinbrook Parkway, Suite 420
Rockville, MD 20852
Phone: (301) 468-2444
Fax: (301) 468-6455
e-mail: info@identicator.com

**Law Enforcement Equipment Company**
2520 Summit
Kansas City, MO 64108
Phone: (800) 821-3238
Fax: (800) 705-3326
e-mail: leeco-kc@worldnet.att.net

**Law Enforcement Supply Company**
1814 Beck Avenue
Panama City, FL 32405
Phone: (800) 637-6307
Fax: (850) 763-9031
Website: http://www.lawsupply.com

**Lightning Powder Company, Inc.**
1230 Hoyt Street SE
Salem, OR 97302-2121
Phone: (800) 852-0300
Fax: (800) 588-0399
Website:
   http://www.lightningpowder.com

**The Lynn Peavey Company**
Phone: (800) 255-6499
Website: http://www.peaveycorp.com

**Rehman Technology Services, Inc.**
18950 U.S. Highway 441, Suite 201
Mount Dora, FL 32757
Phone: (352) 357-0500
Fax: (352) 589-2855
e-mail: rtsi@surveil.com

**SIRCHIE Group Companies**
100 Hunter Place
Youngsville, NC 27596
Phone: (919) 554-2244 or
   (800) 356-7311
Fax: (919) 554-2266 or
   (800) 899-8181
e-mail: sirchie@mindspring.com

**Tri-Tech Inc.**
4019 Executive Park Boulevard, SE
West Southport, NC 28461
Phone: (910) 457-0094
Fax: (800) 438-7884

**The Visual Evidence Company**
The Caxton Building
812 Huron Road, Suite 201
Cleveland, OH 44115
Phone: (216) 241-3443
Fax: (216) 861-3762
e-mail: dcopfer@vevidence.com

# Trial Preparation Checklist for Medical Experts

Preliminaries:

1. Name
2. Professional address
3. Occupation
4. Educational background
   a. Schools attended (undergraduate; graduate; postgraduate)
   b. Specialty status (board qualified; certified; diplomate) explain
   c. Offices held—local; state; national
   d. Appointed positions
   e. Member of any boards
   f. Any published writings
   g. Any teaching duties
   h. Any lecturing before societies
   i. Special awards
   j. States licensed to practice in
   k. Licensed to practice in this state?

Examination:

1. Doctor, have you on occasion had the opportunity to see, take history from, examine, and treat [patient's name]?
2. On what date? Where?
3. Was a history taken at the time? If so, relate.
4. Was history obtained from other sources (previous reports)?
5. What were the patient's primary complaints at the time of the history?
6. Did the injuries appear to be compatible with the complaints and history taken, including history of trauma as described to you?
7. Did you take a past history? If so, explain (previous accidents; diseases; surgical; impairments).
8. Was an examination made at that time?
9. Where was the examination held?

10. Was the patient cooperative?

11. What observations were made at that time?

12. What examination procedures were used?

13. Did the patient appear to be in pain?

14. Was the patient taking anything for relief of pain?

15. If so, what was it (who prescribed it)?

16. Did the patient appear to be hurt?

17. Was the patient bleeding when first observed?

18. Describe lacerations (black and blue; etc.).

19. Was the patient in shock?

20. Did the patient complain of pain during the examination?

21. Were x-rays taken?

22. If so, were they taken under your supervision and control?

23. Did you interpret them?

24. What did the x-rays show (fractures; dislocations; malformations; subluxations; etc.)?

25. Point out areas indicating existence of abnormality.

26. How did the patient describe the area and location of pain?

27. Do you have an opinion that you can state within a reasonable degree of medical certainty as to whether the pain was real or simulated?

28. If so, state.

29. Doctor, describe the difference between objective and subjective findings?

30. Explain the meaning of objective symptoms.

31. Explain the meaning of subjective symptoms.

32. Was there anything in the examination to cause you to disbelieve complaints of the patient (malingering tests—explain)?

Diagnosis:

1. Did you arrive at a diagnosis?

2. State the diagnosis based on findings as a result of the examination.

3. Were the complaints of the patient in proportion to your findings?

4. Was your diagnosis based on your findings of the examination and history?

5. Was your diagnosis yours alone or in consultation with other doctors?

Treatment:

1. Did you undertake treatment?
2. If so, describe (be prepared to have daily records reviewed on a day-by-day basis).
3. Was the plaintiff hospitalized (prior to or after your treatment)?
4. How long was the patient hospitalized?
5. Do you anticipate further hospitalization?
6. Did the patient respond to the treatment?
7. Did the patient cooperate with treatment?
8. What future treatments do you anticipate?
9. Is the patient still under your care?
10. How long and with what frequency will such treatments continue?
11. Do you expect to treat the patient in the future? If so, how long?
12. What is your estimated cost of such treatment?
13. Did you prescribe vitamins, supplements, etc.?
14. Is the patient still taking this supplementation?
15. Did the patient undergo therapy?
16. If so, what type?
17. For how long was therapy rendered?
18. By whom?
19. Do you expect that it will be required in the future?
20. If so, what is the estimated cost?
21. Did treatment to the patient require any braces, casts, splints, collars, traction, or other devices?
22. If so, describe.
23. For how long a period?
24. Will it be required in the future?
25. If so, for how long?
26. Will there be any additional costs?
27. Was the patient in pain during the treatment?
28. Was the pain recurrent or constant?
29. Was the patient disabled during the treatment?

30. If so, to what extent?
31. When did you last examine the patient?
32. Describe his or her condition at that time.
33. Was the patient in pain at that time?
34. What were the character and severity of pain at the time?
35. Was the patient disabled at that time?
36. To what extent?

Future:

1. Doctor, in your expert opinion, can you state within a reasonable degree of medical probability whether the patient has reached maximum medical improvements?
2. Can you state within a reasonable degree of medical certainty whether the patient will suffer any permanent impairment in the future?
3. Can you state within a reasonable degree of medical probability the length of time treatment will have to continue in the future and the approximate necessary expenses of said treatment?
4. Do you have an opinion that you can express within a reasonable degree of medical certainty whether the patient will have to suffer pain in the future as a result of this injury?
5. Upon what factors do you base your opinion?
6. Doctor, what recommendations or limitations have you placed on this patient?
7. Have you done all you can for the patient?
8. In your opinion, within a reasonable degree of medical probability, can you state whether you feel that the injury sustained by the patient was a direct result of the accident of [date]?
9. Did you render a statement to the patient for your services?
10. In what amount?
11. Is this reasonable for like services in the community?

*Source:* MARK DOMBROFF, Dombroff on Unfair Tactics 446 (1988).

# Sample Plaintiffs' Request for Admissions

| | |
|---|---|
| DANIEL CELLUCCI | : COURT OF COMMON PLEAS |
| v. | : |
| GENERAL MOTORS CORPORATION | : JULY TERM, 1987 |
| and JOSEPH V. DeFALCO | : NO. 2803 |

### PLAINTIFFS' REQUEST FOR ADMISSIONS (SET I) ADDRESSED TO DEFENDANT GENERAL MOTORS CORPORATION

Plaintiff, by his attorneys, Eric D. Comfort, Esquire and WRIGHT, GARRETT, & JOHNSTON, hereby requests that the defendant make the following admissions within thirty (30) days after service for the purposes of this action only, and subject to all pertinent objections as to relevancy, which may be interposed at the time of the trial of this case.

### STATEMENT OF FACTS

1. Plaintiff Christopher Gardiner was a right front seat passenger in a 1990 Chevrolet Caprice at the time of the occurrence giving rise to this litigation.

2. At the time of the occurrence giving rise to this litigation, Christopher Gardiner was seated in the right front passenger seat of the 1990 Chevrolet Caprice.

3. At the time of the occurrence giving rise to this litigation, Scott Lee Baker was wearing the available three-point seat belt restraint system in the 1990 Chevrolet Caprice.

4. Defendant General Motors Corporation contends that in the accident occurrence Mr. Baker struck a portion of his head on the header of the 1990 Chevrolet Caprice.

5. The defendant General Motors Corporation contends that in the accident occurrence, Mr. Baker struck his knees on a portion of the instrument panel.

6. Defendant General Motors contends that in the accident occurrence, Christopher Gardiner did not strike the windshield with sufficient force or energy to cause damage to the windshield.

7. Defendant General Motors Corporation contends that in the accident occurrence Christopher Gardiner struck a portion of his head with a portion of the door of the glove box.

8. Defendant General Motors Corporation contends that in a full frontal barrier 25 mph crash of a "J" car, an unrestrained right front seat passenger, seated in an upright position, will make contacts within the vehicle with his or her head to structures that will limit the head injury criteria to less than one thousand.

9. Defendant General Motors Corporation contends that when a right front seat passenger is wearing the three-point restraint system available in the 1990 Chevrolet Caprice, then in a 30 mph full frontal barrier impact the restraint system will minimize or eliminate head contact to the windshield.

10. Defendant General Motors Corporation contends that Christopher Gardiner suffered head injuries because of an impact to the front of his head with an interior portion of the 1990 Chevrolet Caprice at the time of the occurrence.

11. Defendant General Motors Corporation contends that the Delta V of the accident vehicle (at its CG) that led to this litigation was no greater than 30 mph.

12. The right front passenger seat belt system includes the following physical evidence: routing loop transfer on webbing, bolt head imprint on routing loop, webbing strain, pulled stitching at its attachment to the scabbard, and outboard lap anchor.

13. Defendant General Motors contends that there is no evidence of upper torso contact by Mr. Baker with the instrument panel.

14. Defendant General Motors has found no evidence of upper torso contact with the instrument panel forward of the front seat passenger.

15. In every "J" car frontal barrier crash test conducted by General Motors at 30 mph, and involving an unrestrained front seat passenger, the passenger head struck and shattered the windshield.

16. In every General Motors frontal crash test of a "J" car at 30 mph, and involving an unrestrained front seat passenger dummy, that dummy caused damage to the upper instrument panel with its torso.

17. On June 28, 1984, General Motors released a statement to the media, and provided video film of crash test C6001B and C6001A, which involved a vehicle-to-vehicle front end impact of a 1984 "J" body car into a parked 1984 "J" car at a velocity of 81.6 KM/H (which is equivalent to approximately 50 mph and is comparable to a 25 mph frontal barrier crash test of one vehicle).

18. General Motors' press release of June 28, 1984 advises that the front seat dummy in the "J" car which struck the parked "J" car was unrestrained and that it initially contacted the car's interior at slightly below 25 mph.

19. The General Motors' press release of June 28, 1984 concerning the "J" car frontal crash test, using unrestrained dummies, stated that the dummies received low numbers for head injury criteria.

20. In the press release by General Motors on June 28, 1984, General Motors made the following statements concerning the crash test results of C6001B and C6001A:

> "Readings from the dummies indicated human passengers in a similar crash would have a low probability of serious injury, thanks to the crash worthiness of the vehicle designs themselves. GM is proposing its 'built-in' approach to safety as an alternative to other passive restraint systems. The auto maker says its approach offers significant protection for those who won't buckle-up and more protection to those who do."

21. General Motors Corporation has no physical evidence that the plaintiff Christopher Gardiner was not wearing his three-point seat belt restraint system at the time of the accident.

22. General Motors crash test no. C-5823 is the only frontal impact pole test conducted by General Motors involving a "J" car.

23. In crash test no. C-5823 there were two unbelted 50th percentile male dummies in the front seats of a 1983 "J" body car.

24. The front seat passenger in crash test C-5823 struck the windshield with his head causing damage to the windshield and made impact with the instrument panel with his upper torso and lower torso causing the damage depicted in the photographs and film of the test.

25. Daniel Cellucci was not driving the "J" car involved in this litigation.

26. There is no statute in Pennsylvania that makes it unlawful to ride in a motor vehicle as a passenger after having drunk alcoholic beverages.

27. In several of the "J" car frontal barrier crash tests produced by General Motors Corporation, in which a right front seat dummy is included and wearing the three point seat belt restraint system, the head of the dummy strikes the lower portion of the instrument panel in the area of the glove box.

28. Defendant General Motors Corporation agrees that in the vehicle in question, in the headliner there is an indentation which matches the configuration of a portion of the attachment of the rear view mirror assembly.

29. According to the deposition testimony of Janet Wyrick, when her husband came home on the evening of the accident he did not appear intoxicated.

30. Defendant General Motors Corporation has no scientific/toxicological test records to establish defendant Clyde Wyrick was intoxicated at the time of the accident.

31. General Motors Corporation does not have any medical records which indicate a blood alcohol test was done upon Clyde Wyrick.

32. General Motors Corporation has no evidence as to the seating position of Christopher Gardiner immediately before the accident.

33. Timothy Daniels was a volunteer of the Washington Volunteer Ambulance Service who was called to the scene of the accident involving the plaintiff.

34. When Mr. Daniels arrived at the scene, Christopher Gardiner was able to speak and move about on his own.

35. Defendant General Motors Corporation agrees that plaintiff suffered a closed head injury when he impacted the front portion of his head with an interior portion of the vehicle in which he was a passenger at the time of the occurrence giving rise to this litigation.

36. Christopher Gardiner suffered brain damage, which has made it impossible for him to accurately recall what he did on the evening of the accident.

*Source*: LARRY E. COBEN, Pennsylvania Products Liability Guide 269–273 (1992). Reprinted with permission of George T. Bisel Company.

# Plan of Proof —Air Negligence Case

1. Preflight check.

   a. inadequacy of instruction contained in owner's manual.
   b. wrong manual supplied.

2. Weight and balance limitations.

   a. failure to specify.
   b. inaccurate specification.

3. Airframe design generally.

   a. inadequacy to withstand lift pressures.
   b. inadequacy to withstand weight of aircraft.
   c. inadequacy to withstand thrust forces.
   d. inadequacy to withstand drag forces.
   e. inadequacy to withstand foreseeable loads imposed during maneuvers.
   f. inadequacy in rough air.

4. Structural element failure.

   a. inadequacy of materials to withstand foreseeable stresses and pressures.

5. Reciprocal engine failure.

   a. inadequacy of ignition system.
   b. failure to provide dual ignition system.
   c. specification of improper fuel.
   d. improper firing of fuel.
   e. inadequacy, or failure, of cooling system.
   f. failure to adequately specify known operating limitations.

6. Turbojet engine failure.

   a. creep failure of metal due to stress at high temperature.
   b. fatigue failure of metal due to cyclic stress, accentuated by high temperature.
   c. inadequacy of fuel-air mixture control, causing compressor stall.
   d. inadequacy of governing device, causing compressor stall.
   c. failure to adequately specify known operating limitations.

7. Turboprop engine failure.

   a. inadequacy of gears, propellers, or turbine to support stress imposed by speed of engine. (See elements under turbojet engines, supra)

8. Propeller failure.

   **a.** improper design for speed of engine.
   **b.** failure to provide adequate operating instructions and limitations.

9. Flight instruments.

   **a.** absence of necessary instruments.
   **b.** inadequacy of instruments.
   **c.** failure to provide adequate instructions on use.

10. Wing design failure.

    **a.** failure of wing or wing flaps to provide necessary lift.
    **b.** improper camber of wing for speed range of aircraft.
    **c.** improper design of high-lift device.
    **d.** failure to provide automatic adjustments to complement use of flaps.
    **e.** inadequacy of aircraft to provide lift for takeoff or climb in low air density.

11. Tail assembly design failure.

    **a.** failure to provide necessary stability.

12 Controls generally.

    **a.** inadequacy.
    **b.** super sensitivity.
    **c.** failure to provide adequate instructions on use.

13. Inadequacy of control wheel or aileron surfaces to produce or control "roll."

14. Inadequacy of control wheel or elevator surfaces to produce or control "pitch."

15. Inadequacy of rudder pedals and rudders to produce or control "yaw."

16. Inability of trim tabs to relieve pressure on controls.

17. Load factor.

    **a.** foreseeability of load factor imposed beyond structural limitations.
    **b.** failure to specify limit load factor.
    **c.** inaccurate specification of limit load factor.

18. Maneuvering speed.

    **a.** structural inadequacy to withstand severe gusts at maneuvering speed.
    **b.** failure to specify.
    **c.** inaccurate specification.

*Source:* 13 Am. Jur. Trials 153–154 (Supp. 1993). Reprinted by permission of West Group.

# Index

## A

Accuracy, of models, 95–96
Acknowledgment
  of instrument executed by attorney in
    fact, 129
  of instrument executed by individual,
    129
Actual belief, 34
Admissibility
  of expert evidence, 177–182
  lay opinion, 155–156
  relevant and material, yet inadmissible,
    9–11
  rules of, 121–131
    best evidence rule and exceptions,
      124–131
Admissions, 211–225
  answer to admissions (form), 224
  drafting requests for admissions,
    216–220
  drafting responsive pleadings to the
    request, 220–225
  pleading format (form), 218–219
  pretrial agreement on admissions
    (form), 55
  pretrial evidentiary requests, 211–212
  purpose and effect, 212–215
    procedural aspects of requests for
      admissions, 213–214
    responding to requests for
      admissions, 214–215
  requests for admissions, 211–212
    cover letter, 220
    drafting, 216–220

    form, 221
    procedural aspects, 213–214
    sample plaintiffs', 281–284
    timetable, 222
    to plaintiff, 217
    under Rule 36, 216
  response to admissions (form), 223,
    224
  sample plaintiffs' request for
    admissions, 281–284
Alteration of photographic evidence,
  83
Authentication
  of business/medical records,
    134–135
    elements necessary for admission,
      134–135
  by author, 133–134
    defined, 131–132
    of documents, 133–134
  by handwriting analysis, 135–140
    document expert questionnaire,
      138–139
    expert witnesses, 136–137
    lay witnesses, 135–136
    process of comparison,
      137–140
  models, 96
    anatomical dolls, 96
  opposing counsel's questioning of
    authenticator, 259
  photographic exhibit, 77–80
  of real evidence, 53–55
  self-authentication, 132–133
  silent witness theory, 88